21世纪英语专业系列教材

Chinese and Western

Cultures in the Context of Conflict, Collision and Convergence

冲突、碰撞与趋同下的
中西文化

祝吉芳 ◎编著

〔美〕Gladys Evertsen ◎审校

U0361992

北京大学出版社
PEKING UNIVERSITY PRESS

图书在版编目(CIP)数据

冲突、碰撞与趋同下的中西文化:英文/祝吉芳编著. —北京:北京大学出版社，2016.7

(21世纪英语专业系列教材)

ISBN 978-7-301-27271-8

Ⅰ.① 冲…　Ⅱ.① 祝…　Ⅲ.① 东西文化—比较文化—高等学校—教材—英文　Ⅳ.① G04

中国版本图书馆CIP数据核字(2016)第159065号

书　　　　名	冲突、碰撞与趋同下的中西文化
	CHONGTU、PENGZHUANG YU QUTONG XIA DE ZHONG-XI WENHUA
著作责任者	祝吉芳　编著
责 任 编 辑	李　娜
标 准 书 号	ISBN 978-7-301-27271-8
出 版 发 行	北京大学出版社
地　　　　址	北京市海淀区成府路205号　100871
网　　　　址	http://www.pup.cn　新浪微博:@北京大学出版社
电 子 信 箱	345014015@qq.com
电　　　　话	邮购部 62752015　发行部 62750672　编辑部 62754382
印 刷 者	北京虎彩文化传播有限公司
经 销 者	新华书店
	730毫米×980毫米　16开本　20.25印张　256千字
	2016年7月第1版　2022年8月第3次印刷
定　　　　价	58.00元

本书为 2015 年河海大学校级重点立项教材，是江苏省教育科学"十二五"规划课题（课题编号：D/2013/01/003）研究成果之一，受到"中央高校基本科研业务费专项资金资助"（supported by "the Fundamental Research Funds for the Central Universities"），资助项目编号为 2014B10814。

Foreword

    The reality of our relative backwardness compels us to import a lot from the Western countries. Today we learn English, read books about Warren Edward Buffett, wear nike shoes, drink Coca-Cola, listen to rap songs, drive Mercedes-Benz, and watch Hollywood movies. Our higher education tends to be Westernized, too— emphasizing analysis, criticism, logic, and formal approaches to problem-solving. What is tragic is that in spite of the seemingly prevalent westernization in China Westerners report they feel uncertain and uncomfortable in interacting with Chinese and there has been much coverage of communication breakdowns. I am convinced that much of this problem stems from the lack of mutual understanding of cultural background knowledge, for in reality the current westernization within China is superficial. It is due to this lack that some of our good intentions have been misinterpreted in the intercultural communication.

    In writing these pages, I have an ambitious goal. I hope I can display to the reader that most often the cultural differences are just differences of degree, and that acknowledging the cultural differences will lead one to re-examine his or her own culture. For this reason, this book is to focus on cultural comparison and contrast and tries to identify cultural differences as well as reasons behind the explicit or hidden discrepancies.

    Of course, we have in the past thirty years of reform and opening-up learnt a lot from the outside world. Likewise, the Western culture has changed a lot over the years through interactions with other cultures. Therefore, we should take a new look at different cultures and their recent changes, and get hold of the latest information about them. But given the limited space of this book and the great difficulty of comparing the ever-changing and dynamic cultural elements, I am to confine my attention to what are traditional and hence stable about Chinese and Western cultures.

The chapters of this book are arranged under five headings— East and West, Cultural Differences in Silent Languages, Cultural Differences in Thinking, Different Cultural Orientations, and Different Cultural Standards.

While this book was informed and enhanced by my international colleagues in Nanjing who have helped to make this a better book than it would otherwise have been, friends in SHSU and WCPC who have given me much food for thought, and academics who have studied and published their researches, there are two persons in particular to whom I owe a great deal of thanks: Dr. Tracy L. Steele and Mr. Fernando Mercier, who have offered invaluable help. I am also greatly indebted to my friend Gladys Evertsen and her husband Harry. This book has benefited enormously from their comments, suggestions, and corrections.

Nanjing
March 2016
Zhu Jifang, Ph.D

Contents

Part III　Cultural Differences in Thinking

Part I

East and West

"Oh, East is East, and West is West, and never the twain shall meet." This opening line of "The Ballad of East and West" by the famous English poet Rudyard Kipling(1865-1936) is often quoted to underline that two things are so different that they can never come together or agree. But, the fact is the "twain (two)" do meet.

In this part, the question about why we should compare Chinese and Western cultures is answered in Unit 1 after a brief introduction to the two civilizations and a review of cultural comparative studies in China. Traditional characteristics which may help to identify Chinese and Western cultures are then discussed in Unit 2. Unit 3 offers a reappraisal of the affinities or similarities that unite cultural traditions in the East and West.

Unit 1   Why Contrasting Chinese and Western Cultures?

Our most basic common link is that we all inhabit this planet. We all breathe the same air. We all cherish our children's future. And we are all mortal.

—J. F. Kennedy

Do you agree with former U.S. President J. F. Kennedy? If yes, why?

I do not want my house to be walled on all sides and my windows to be stuffed. I want the cultures of all lands to be blown about my house as freely as possible. But I refuse to be blown off my feet by any.

—Mahatma Gandhi

If you were having a face-to-face talk with the famous Indian politician, what would you say to him? Do you love meeting people from other cultures?

I   Ancient Civilizations and Cultures

To explain why we should compare Chinese and Western cultures, it might be better to start with the two major civilizations on earth—the Chinese inland civilization and the Western sea civilization.

1. Chinese Civilization and Culture

Surrounded by land on three sides, China with the Central Plains Region as the source of its civilization has long been isolated. This geographical isolation, together with its unique natural environment and ecology has endowed the nation with a unique cultural tradition and a distinctive social psychology. The self-reliant and self-supporting rural-based agrarian economy born out of this isolated land caused a greater isolation in dire need of the spirit of openness.

Encouraging people to stick to their homeland, be content with their simple life, follow the Way(*Dao* or *Tao*), happily labor at sunrise and rest at sunset, the orthodox Confucianism, a product of this civilization, has contributed much to the formation of the isolated and hence inward-bound Chinese culture. Its doctrine of "the integration of Heaven and man" pushed Chinese culture further down the road of the introversion or the inward seek(内求). The cardinal Confucian virtues of humanity and righteousness urged the ruler to "lovingly care for his people" and "regulate human relationships." Guided by the thought of "applying theory to reality(经世致用)" which emphasizes scholarship, ancient Chinese read not for knowledge or skills but for the Way by practicing "seriousness to straighten the internal life and righteousness to square the external life." They had little interest in pursuing "investigation of the things(格物致知)" into the realms of what we call natural or social sciences. The inward seek, so to speak, was what ancient Chinese pursued after.

As a consequence, in this inland civilization a culture of introversion or inward-orientation was gradually formed, and has nurtured many generations of Chinese marked by their home-orientation, non-action, tolerance, pacifism, lack of competing tradition, and absence of explicit time concept.

2. Western Civilization and Culture

Ancient Greece as the cradle of Western civilization is of a long irregular coastline with many fine harbors. The ecology of this place, consisting as it does mostly of mountains descending to the sea, favors occupations that require little cooperation with others such as hunting, herding, fishing, sea trade, sea transportation, and even piracy. With the exception of trade these economic activities do not strictly require living in the same community for a long time, which made people outward-bound.

It is the outward seek that ushered in the rise of natural sciences characterized by transcendence, conquer, and creation, which in turn inspired people to be more open and more outward-oriented. It is because of its outward-orientation that settled agriculture which requires cooperation and stability came to this civilization later than to inland civilizations, but quickly became commercial.

Gradually outward-bound Western culture was formed in this blue sea civilization surrounded by water on three sides.

II Cross-cultural Comparative Studies in China

Before the Sino-British Opium War(1840), Chinese and Western cultures developed like two streams running side by side on their own by following their own courses. But the Qing Dynasty's (1644—1911) defeat in the war (1838—1842) first opened the eyes and ears of Chinese to the rising Western world. And the Dynasty's subsequent defeat in the Sino-Japanese War of 1894—1895 turned their eyes and ears also to Japan which was assumed to be fast developing because people there had learned from the West.

1. During the Reform Movement of 1898

After the Opium War and shortly after the Sino-Japanese War, the Western powers began to occupy various ports of China by force, which badly upset Chinese people who had felt disappointed and disheartened. To bring a new hope to them, the leaders of the Reform Movement of 1898 such as Kang Youwei (1858—1927), Liang Qichao (1873—1929), and Tan Sitong (1865—1898) translated Western works to spread the Bourgeois ideology of Europe, and wrote articles to compare Chinese and Western cultures so as to found the theory of Constitutional Reform and Modernization. Although the Reform Movement didn't last long and failed in the end, it may be said to have made preparation for more systematic studies of Chinese and Western cultures during the 1919 May Fourth Movement.

2. During the May Fourth Movement of 1919

The aggressive invasion of Westerners and of Japanese against China had led Chinese intellectuals to assume that the humiliation and backwardness of China was due to the useless rigid obsolete Confucianism.

In May 1918 Lu Xun (1881—1936), hailed as "commander of China's cultural revolution" by the founding father of P. R. China Mao Zedong (1893—1976), used his pen name for the first time and published his first short story in vernacular *A Madman's Diary*, a scathing criticism of out-dated Chinese traditions and Confucian feudalism that were supposed to be "gnawing" at the Chinese. The impact of Lu Xun and other revolutionaries such as Cai Yuanpei and Hu Shih (1891—1962) was undeniably immense, given the fact that the whole young generation was transformed. During the tumultuous days of 1919, students in Beijing marched on the streets protesting the unequal treaty with Japan and blaming Confucianism for such an injustice. They angrily shouted "Down with Confucianism" and opened their arms and hearts for new ideas of science from the West. In short, the message sent by the Movement was clear: Up with Western scientism and down with Confucianism.

However, an objective voice could still be heard, for instance from Liang Qichao (1873—1929), a political activist and academician. Before he went to Europe, Liang Qichao's views were identical to those of the New Culture Movement which launched ruthless attack on Confucianism. After returning from Europe, he had acquired a new basis for critical reflection on modernity, and published *Journey to Europe*(《欧游心影录》), in which Liang refuted his previous views completely, advocating borrowing the spirit and methods of the Western science to reassess and reorganize the national cultural heritage in order to develop a new one.

Echoing Liang Qichao's theories in his *East and West: Their Civilizations and Philosophies*, Liang Shuming(梁漱溟) foretold that Western civilization would be doomed to eventual failure. Although he disfavored complete reform and adoption of Western institutions, Liang believed that reform in China was a necessity. Soon there appeared the debate between "Old Learning(Chinese)" and "New Learning(Western)." Although the contention lingered on in the following years, the latter had forced its way into prominence while the former gradually withdrew into obscurity.

Against this larger social background, Wang Guowei (1877—1927) advocated "going beyond the distinction between Chinese and Occidental Learning (学无中西)", while Lu Xun recommended his strategy of "looking for new voices in foreign cultures

(别求新声于异邦)." Those views turned out to be so prevailing that all sorts of Western theories and ideologies flooded into China through translated versions.

3. After the May Fourth Movement

Faced with "the Complete Westernization" as a trend of thought and the deteriorating economic situation, some professors in Shanghai jointly published a manifestation in 1935, openly advocating the necessity of constructing native Chinese culture.

With respect to "Westernization" or "construction of native culture," Zhang Dainian (张岱年) and other scholars came up with a proposition of "synthetic creation." This proposal emphasized that, in dealing with cultural issues, equal attention should be paid to what is the best both in Western culture and Chinese culture. Later on, Zhang introduced "cultural creationism" and uplifted the realistic significance of "synthetic creation" to the level of actualizing the rebirth of Chinese culture and national rejuvenation.

Similar proposals like those greatly encouraged and inspired Chinese scholars who attended to the construction of Chinese culture and consciously took up the responsibility for the future of the nation and its people.

4. After 1949

After 1949 when People's Republic of China was founded, Confucianism was officially condemned. Confucius-bashing reached a peak during the "Anti-Lin Biao and Anti-Confucius Campaign" when schools banned the Confucian classics and Red Guards blamed scholars for teaching the classical books that for centuries had served as a philosophical primer for China. Meanwhile, books on Marxism and Leninism were taught at school, read at workplaces and at home. Cultural studies of this period favored the two branches of Western thought and the traditional Chinese thought and culture were put aside.

5. In the 1980s

In 1988, much attention was cast on comparative and contrastive studies of

Chinese and Western cultures again. The television series "The Yellow River Elegy(河殇)" elaborated that compared to the sea civilization, the inland civilization had fallen. This epic television series initiated a whirlwind of discussion and debate when it was first broadcast nationwide. CCTV statistics claimed that over 200 million people watched it, making it one of the most popular series that year. Its scripts were published in the newspapers and in book form, which started a new wave of cultural comparative studies.

6. In the New Century

The first few years of the 21st century witnessed the decrease of traditional values and the appearance of some social ills—a result of the tragic collapse of Confucianism. More tragically, it seemed that no principle, no law, and no morality could offer help. People became confused. Then the Lecture Room of CCTV 10 initiated a sudden revival of Confucianism and other traditions in 2006. Confucian classics are no longer regarded as fossils, but as a value system that can help Chinese to find answers to many problems, since for more than 2,500 years the Confucian doctrines of humanity, righteousness, filial piety, etc. were the guiding principles of life and government in China.

With the revival of Confucianism, cultural comparative studies, particularly East-West studies, appear so important that many scholars have engaged in it and many colleges and universities have added relevant courses to their schools' curriculum.

III   Imperatives for Contrasting Chinese and Western Cultures

This book is a contrastive study of Chinese and Western cultures. As for why, eight reasons are to be presented.

1. The Harmonious Imperative

Though it has tried its utmost to build a harmonious and friendly relationship with the other countries since its reform and opening-up in 1979, China has to face disputes over some issues and cultural discomforts in international context. The reasons for this state of affairs are many and varied, some of them are beyond the control of anything China might do to try to correct them, but some are not. Take the very way we show our good intentions and politeness for instance. When presented a present, the polite way for us is to decline three times before accepting it and then putting it away without opening it or telling the giver how much I love the gift and how much I appreciate his kindness. This custom is incompatible with the so-called international practice, but it is something within our control and can be adjusted so that our good intentions can be better understood by foreigners.

It is not my argument that Chinese should be universally loved. Given the fact that communication breakdowns often occur in our interaction with others, we should try our best to learn more about differences between cultures in order to live more harmoniously with others in the global community.

2. The Peace Imperative

When different cultures encounter each other, there are often misunderstanding, bigotry, hostility, and even wars. The Japanese of 1543 called the Portuguese who landed on their shores "Southern Barbarians" since they arrived mostly from the south. We called the Japanese "Little Japs" before the normalization of Sino-Japanese relationship. It would be naive to assume that merely understanding different cultures would end wars, conflicts or misunderstanding, although peace problems do underscore the need for individuals to learn more about groups of which they are not members so that ultimately peoples, not countries, negotiate and sign peace treaties.

3. The Ethical Imperative

Intercultural communication presents challenging ethical issues. Ethics may be thought of as principles of conduct that help govern the behavior of individuals and groups. These principles often arise from communities' perspectives on what is good and bad. Some are stated very explicitly. For example, the concept of "filial piety" teaches that it is wrong not to honor one's parents. Many other principles may be less explicit—for example, every one, old or young, should be independent.

Ethical principles are often culture-bound, and intercultural conflicts arise from varying notions of what is ethical behavior. For instance, in terms of supporting the aged, some Chinese consider it unethical for Westerners to send their parents to retirement homes.

This contrastive study is expected to provide insights about ethical issues so that we can judge what is ethical and unethical according to variations in cultural priorities and identify guidelines for ethical behavior in intercultural contexts where ethics clash.

4. The Economic Imperative

On December 11, 2001, China formally joined the World Trade Organization (WTO). Since then both China and the rest of the world have had to run faster. This is because China's joining the WTO took China and the world to a new level of "offshoring" —with more companies (mostly Western ones) shifting production offshore and then integrating it into their global supply chains, for instance, a company takes one of its factories that it is operating in Iowa, America and moves the whole factory offshore to Ningbo, China. There, it produces the very same product in the very same way, only with cheaper labor, lower taxes, subsidized energy, and lower health-care costs. However, such companies are partly responsible for Chinese environmental pollution while bringing economic prosperity or employment opportunities. Therefore, we need to understand how business operates in other countries, especially in the West. We need to be able to negotiate deals that are advantageous to Chinese long-term development. We need to know Chinese and Western cultures in order to reduce economic losses for the benefit of both parties.

5. The Technological Imperative

Today we are connected via Internet, cell phones, e-mail, MSN, QQ, Skype, and Wechat to strangers. This change has affected the ways we form or maintain social relationships. In past centuries, social relationships were confined to the distance of an easy walk. Now we can be "accessed" in many ways and be involved simultaneously in many different relationships, even without real face-to-face contact. What does this have to do with cultural comparison?

Through high-tech communication tools we come in contact with people very different from us, often in ways we are not aware of. For instance, persons we talk to or students we teach on Wechat may speak languages different from our own, come from different countries, be of different ethnic backgrounds, and have quite different life experiences. As a consequence, miscommunication may arise from lack of mutual understanding, and increasing technology means, as it were, we cannot afford to be culturally illiterate in this shrinking interdependent world.

6. The Interactive Imperative

Interaction proves that big cultural differences can cause problems interpreting what the other person is doing. For example, a great majority of people in the United States and other Western cultures expect those with whom they are communicating to "look them in the eye," but direct eye contact is not a custom throughout the world. In some rural areas of China, children are taught not to look at another in the eye but at somewhere around the Adam's apple. To them too much eye contact is a sign of bad manners. For another example, when a good-mannered Chinese businessman tells his Norwegian client that he is uninterested in an offer by saying, " That will be very difficult", the Norwegian may eagerly ask how he can help. The Chinese may be mystified. To him, saying something is difficult is a polite way of saying indirectly "No way!" There are countless examples like these, which prove the complexity and difficulty of intercultural communication.

7. The Work Imperative

As is known to many, the rule of the market economy is that if somewhere has the richest human resources and the cheapest labor, the enterprises and businesses will naturally rush there and receive warm welcome there. Employment competition will be predictably worldwide and hence tougher. That's why the noted American economist Thomas L. Friedman reminds his daughters, "Girls, when I was growing up, my parents used to say to me, 'Tom, finish your dinner—people in China and India are starving.' My advice to you is: Girls, finish your homework—people in China and India are starving for your jobs." To get employed today, one really has to become more experienced at marketing himself in intercultural communication.

8. "Fortune Favors the Prepared Mind"

Those who find it impossible to work abroad may ask, "What's this got to do with me?" This point touches on the ultimate purpose of this book, which finds expression in the broad extent to which different cultures control our lives. In fact, culture is not an exotic notion studied by a select group of scholars. It is a mold in which we are all cast, and it controls our daily lives in many unsuspected ways. The best reason for the layman to spend time comparing Chinese and Western cultures is that he can learn something useful and enlightening about himself. This can be an interesting process, at times harrowing but ultimately rewarding. One of the most effective ways to learn about oneself is by taking seriously the culture of others. It forces you to pay attention to those details of life which differentiate them from you. "Fortune favors the prepared mind."(Louis Pasteur) If you want to be competitive and have a bright future, you have to be fully prepared.

IV Key Concepts

1. "Cultural Stereotypes"

Chinese wear white for mourning, whereas Westerners wear black; Chinese honor dragons as symbols of prosperity and auspiciousness while Westerners think of them as vicious monsters. Such stereotypes are right and may sharpen our cultural sensitivity.

Chinese throw female babies into the river; North Americans do not care about elderly people. Such stereotypes are insulting and can upset people.

It is necessary to note here that the terminology Chinese or Westerners use to indicate a people belonging to a particular cultural group—cultural stereotypes (i.e. ideas about people of other cultural groups based primarily on membership in that group), is unfit for all in a particular culture. Even if we make stereotypes of other cultures, we should inform ourselves about what is true and what is not because we can be wrong and offend other people. Each person is different, and this is what life is about.

2. "Keeping up with the Times"

China has undergone drastic changes over the years. Meanwhile, Western culture has changed a lot through communication with other cultures, too. We should keep up with the times in our cultural comparative studies. But given the great difficulty of comparing the rapidly changing cultural elements, this book is to pay special attention to what are traditional and thus stable about both cultures under discussion.

3. "Multiculturalism"

Western civilization is no doubt suitable for Westerners, but it will mean ruin for China if we try to copy it blindly. Such a view was held by German poet and novelist Hermann Hesse (1877—1962), too, as he said many years ago, "Every age, every culture, every custom and tradition has its own character, its own weakness and its own strength, its beauties and cruelties; it accepts certain sufferings as matters of course, and puts up patiently with certain evils. Human life is reduced to real suffering, to hell, only when two ages, two cultures and religions overlap." So it is important to advocate "multiculturalism" in a modern society and to let it known to the young generation exposed to both Chinese and Western influences that nobody else can protect our own culture. We are obliged to protect it ourselves.

Further Reading

1. Aldridge, O. (1993). *The Dragon and the Eagle*：*The Presence of China in the American Enlightenment.* US: the Wayne State University Press.

2. Friedman, T. L. (2005). *The World Is Flat: A Brief History of the Twenty-First Century.* New York: Farrar, Straus and Giroux.

3. Muller, G. E.(1976). *Philosophy of Literature.* Manchester, UK: Ayer Publishing.

4. Zhang, Y. (1998). *China in a Polycentric World: Essays in Chinese Comparative Literature.* Standford CA:Stanford University Press.

5. Anderson, W. T. (1990). *Reality Isn' t What it Used to Be.* New York: Harper& Row.

6. 董德福 (2003):《梁启超与胡适》,长春:吉林人民出版社。

7. 梁漱溟 (1999)：《东西文化及其哲学》，北京：商务印书馆。

8. 梁漱溟 (1987)：《中国文化要义》，上海：学林出版社。

9. 梁启超 (1999)：《梁启超全集》，北京：北京出版社。

10. 周宁　(2011)：《跨文化研究：以中国形象为方法》，北京：商务印书馆。

Unit 2   Traditional Characteristics of Chinese and Western Cultures

God gave every people a cup, cup of clay, and from this cup they drank life...
They all dipped in the water, but their cups were different.

—**Ruth Benedict**

For further study: Look for more hints that can help to account for cultural differences.

He is born differently; he is born for kowtowing and for quiet and peace, and not for football and the dog-collar and table napkins and efficiency. He sometimes thinks of himself as a pig, and the Westerner as a dog, and the dog worries the pig, but the pig only grunts, and it may even be a grunt of satisfaction. Why, he even wants to be a pig, a real pig, for it is really so very comfortable, and he does not envy the dog for his collar and his dog-efficiency and his bitch−goddess success. All he wants is that the dog leaves him alone.

—**Lin Yutang**

The images that people have of themselves are often quite different from the images people from other cultures have of them. Use Lin Yutang's description as a model and enumerate our self-portraits and our correspondent portrayal of Westerners. For each pair describe how much of the meaning is conveyed through words and how much is transferred through contrast. Rank the list from the most-frequently used to the least-used ones. Compare the rankings with those of your classmates.

I "There Are All Kinds of Birds When a Forest Gets Large"

The Chinese race is very big and the Western race is big, too. Undeniably Chinese are different from one another and Westerners are different from each other just as the saying goes, "There are all kinds of birds when a forest gets large(i.e. People come in all varieties)."

1. Different Chinese

The impact of material environment on the making of man is great. People nurtured in different parts of China, for example, differ in temperament, physique, and habits, which has been vividly depicted in *My Country and My People* by Lin Yutang (1895—1976), a world-famous literary translator, bilingual writer, and outstanding linguist. According to Lin, "...we have the northern Chinese, acclimatized to simple thinking and hard living, tall and stalwart, hale, hearty and humorous, onion-eating and fun-loving, children of Heaven, who are in every way more Mongolic and more conservative than the conglomeration of peoples near Shanghai and who suggest nothing of their loss of racial vigor. They are the Honan boxers, the Shantung (Shandong) bandits and the imperial brigands who have furnished China with all the native imperial dynasties, the raw material from which the characters of Chinese novels of wars and adventure are drawn.

"Down the southeast coast, south of the Yangtse(Yangtze), one meets a different type, inured to ease and culture and sophistication, mentally developed but physically retrograde, loving their poetry and their comforts, sleek undergrown men and slim neurasthenic women, fed on birds' nest soup and lotus seeds, shrewd in business, gifted in *belles-lettres*, and cowardly in war, ready to roll on the ground and cry for mamma before the lifted fist descends, offsprings of the cultured Chinese families who crossed the Yangtse with their books and paintings during the end of the Jin Dynasty, when China was overrun by barbaric invaders.

"South in Kwangtung (Guangdong), one meets again a different people, where racial vigor is again in evidence, where people eat like men and work like men, enterprising, carefree, spendthrift, pugnacious, adventurous, progressive and quick-tempered, where beneath the Chinese culture a snake-eating aborigines tradition persists, revealing a strong admixture of the blood of the ancient Yupeh(Yue) inhabitants of southern China. North and south of Hankow, in the middle of China, the loud-swearing and intrigue-loving Hupeh(Hubei) people exist, who are compared by the people of other provinces to 'nine-headed birds in heaven' because they never say die, and who think pepper not hot enough to eat until they have fried it in oil; while the Hunan people, noted for their soldiery and their dogged persistence, offer a pleasanter variety of these descendants of the ancient Ch'u(Chu) warriors."

Not all ethnically Chinese are the same, practicing strict or lenient child-rearing. Many Chinese sayings are in agreement with Lin Yutang's observance and meanwhile further prove the great impact of material environment on the making of man, e.g. *It takes all sorts to make a world* (一种米养百种人), *The material environment of a place nurtures a peculiar group of people* (一方水土养一方人), and *Every man has his taste* (萝卜白菜,各有所爱).

2. Different Westerners

Westerners (primarily Europeans, Americans and citizens of the British Commonwealth) differ from each other. Their differences are exhibited in what people jokingly say about Europeans:

"In an ideal world the policemen would be English, the car mechanics would be German, the cooks would be French, the innkeepers would be Swiss, and the lovers would be Italian. But in a living hell, the policemen would be German, the car mechanics would be French, the cooks would be English, the innkeepers would be Italian, and the lovers would be Swiss."

Jokes above may be regarded as stereotypes which can be misleading and upsetting sometimes, but may help us develop sensitivity to sub-cultural differences and individual discrepancy.

3. Notes on "Comparison"

Through comparison and careful examination, we can note that even persons from the same family are different in a variety of ways, including different ways of looking at things, different ways of dressing, different ways of expressing personality and goodness. So we hold this truth to be self-evident that comparison is very basic to human understanding; without comparison we cannot recognize anything.

II   Traditional Chinese Cultural Characteristics

However different the Beijing native is from the Nanjing local, the cultural integration of thousands of years exposes them to one culture with the following distinct characteristics.

1. Oneness (一统性)

a. One Territory, One Ideology, and One Politics

In 221 BC the state of Qin "swallowed up" the other feudal states and unified China. With this unification came measures for the standardization of weights, measures and writing script, the destruction of all feudal barriers between districts and the construction of better roads and communications. Great masses of people were forcibly moved to new areas for purposes of defense or resettlement, and labor gangs were sent to work constructing the Great Wall out of smaller defensive walls of the old feudal states. Never before had China been so unified in territory.

The vast land, held together by the terror of Qin's laws and the personal power of its first emperor, quickly disintegrated with the fall of the Dynasty. However, the Han Dynasty worked gradually to build it up again, unifying, organizing and standardizing the vast area brought under its control. This effort at standardization extended even to the realm of thought in which again the Han succeeded in accomplishing by gradual and peaceful means. Emperor Wu (156 BC—87 BC) of the Han made Confucianism the orthodox doctrine of the country while other schools of philosophy including the Taoist and Legalist schools were deemed heretical. From then on Confucianism had been the mainstream of Chinese philosophy for more than 2,000 years.

Accepting Confucianism as the statecraft in the Han Dynasty generated one ideology and one political system. In the later dynasties, Confucianism continued to unify ideology and political system largely through the imperial examination system—the only bridge to political success for young men.

b. One Tradition of Three Teachings

Many of us profess ourselves to be Taoists, Buddhists or even Christians, but seldom have we ceased at the same time to be Confucianists, for Confucianism since the time of its general acceptance has been more than a creed to be accepted; it has become an inseparable part of Chinese society and thought as well as of what it means to be a Chinese. Next to Confucianism the most important and influential native philosophy has undoubtedly been that of the Taoist school. In many ways the doctrines of Confucianism and Taoism complement each other, running side by side like two powerful streams through all later Chinese thought and literature, appealing simultaneously to the two sides of the Chinese character. There is an adage holding that every Chinese is a Confucianist when he is young, healthy, and successful, a Taoist when he is old, poor in health, and a failure, and a Buddhist when he needs spiritual comfort.

The introduction of Buddhism to China is an event with far-reaching results in the development of Chinese thought and culture. After a long and difficult period of localization, this new teaching managed to establish itself as a major system of thought, contributing greatly to the enrichment of Chinese philosophy, and as a major system of religious practice which has an enduring influence on Chinese popular religion. Indeed, it came to be spoken of along with the native traditions, Confucianism and Taoism, as one of the Three Teachings or Three Religions, thus achieving a status of equality with these beliefs.

Although the key difference between the three teachings lies in the fact that Confucianism is humanistic, Taoism naturalistic, and Buddhism spiritualistic, there are sayings such as *The three teachings are one. Three teachings return to one, The three teachings share one body. The three teachings merge into one* in China.

c. One Roof for the Fifty-six Ethnic Groups

The richness of Chinese culture finds expression in its diversity. China has always been a country of many ethnic groups. No matter which ethnic group is dominant, be it Hans, Mongols or Manchu, its people could live under the same roof, peacefully co-existing together and obeying the same ruler.

d. Education as the Only Bridge to Success

Confucius (551 BC—479 BC) has made great contributions to education in China. Before him, only the children of nobles had the opportunity to get formal education. It is Confucius who took the lead in Chinese history to bring education to all the people. For thousands of years getting education has been the only bridge to success, wealth, good life and family prosperity, especially for boys from poor families. No wonder Emperor Renzong (1010—1063) of the Song Dynasty wrote, "Study hard and you will become successful and be able to afford a big house. Study hard and you will become so successful that a beautiful woman wants to marry you(书中自有黄金屋,书中自有颜如玉)."

e. One Writing Script

The Chinese writing system was developed more than 4,000 years ago; the oldest extant examples of Chinese characters such as 日 and 月, which date back to the 14th or the 15th century BC when the Shang Dynasty flourished, are still used today. Chinese writing consists of an individual character for every syllable, each character representing a word or an idea rather than merely a sound; thus problems caused by homonyms in spoken Chinese are not a difficulty in written Chinese. The written language is a unifying factor culturally, for although the spoken languages and dialects may not be mutually comprehensible in many instances, the written form is universal. Those who invented the writing script were extremely clever. For instance, they drew three horizontal lines and connected them with a vertical line through the middle, calling the character 王 " **wang** (king)." The three horizontal lines refer to Heaven, earth and man, and that vertical line which passes through the middle joins the ways of all three, occupying the center of Heaven, earth and man, passing through and joining all three—if he is not a king, who else could he be?

f. Oneness of Heaven and Man

The Chinese view of integrating Heaven and man originates from the notion of the Way or Dao in the proposition that Dao consists of *yin* and *yang* in the *Book of Changes*. Lao Zi who lived about 500 years before Jesus Christ further illustrated the concept of Dao in Chapter 42 of his book *Dao De Jing or Laozi*, "Dao gives birth to One (chaos); one gives birth to Two (Heaven and earth); Two gives birth to Three (*yin*, *yang*, and harmony); three gives birth to the myriad things (道生一,一生二,二生三,三生万物)."

Two centuries after Lao Zi, Zhuang Zi (369 BC—286 BC) proposed that "the perfect man has no self for he has transcended the finite and identified himself with the universe (至人无己,天地与我并生,万物与我为一)." Gradually the theory that man is a part of the universe became rooted in the Chinese thought.

Dong Zhongshu (179 BC—104 BC), a Confucianist and politician of the Western Han Dynasty, further developed the worldview of oneness. He assumed that "the energy of Heaven and the energy of earth are unified, which consists of *yin* and *yang* and is manifested in four seasons and five agents." A number of Chinese sayings mirror the same idea of integrating man with Heaven rather than separating them, e.g. *Heaven affects human affairs and human behavior finds response in Heaven* (天人感应). *The law of Heaven and the feelings of humanity are in unison* (天理人情). *Heaven accords with human wishes* (天从人愿). *Heaven is angry and people are resentful* (天怒人怨). *Heaven's will brings about human affinity* (天依人愿), and *Heaven and humankind turn to one* (天与人归).

The Chinese character "天(*tian*)" is translated as "Heaven" in the above paragraph, although *tian* carries a wider sense than the English word "Heaven." *Tian* and *ren* (man) always react to and comply with each other. They can never be separated. Such a worldview of oneness is also reflected in the ancient Chinese axiom of living in an environment with a rockery, a pond, flowers, and a lawn.

2. Continuity

China is of the world's longest continuous civilization. It is true that there were times of division, but division was transient. There seem to be cycles of division and unification, but unification has outlived division. During its thousand years of development,

China has undergone various ordeals. On the one hand, it withstood a number of foreign intrusions such as the Huns' harassment in the Qin and the Han dynasties, the Mongolians and the Manchu rule in Yuan and Qing dynasties, and invasion of Western powers in the late 19th and early 20th century. On the other hand, it also suffered from domestic suppression by the autocracy such as the First Qin Emperor's burning books and burying Confucian scholars alive. Having experienced so much misery and ordeals, the traditional Chinese culture survives and becomes enriched and consolidated with time.

The major reason why traditional Chinese culture has so much vitality and continuity of life lies in its magnanimity and inclusiveness. As Oriental Studies Master Professor Ji Xianlin (1911—2009) said after he received a lifetime achievement award for translation, "The fact that our culture has been able to remain consistent and rich with 5,000 years of history owes much to translation. Translations from other cultures have helped to infuse new blood into this culture." And the principle of fidelity that all the Chinese translators are required to follow displays Chinese inclusiveness.

3. Inclusiveness

Traditional Chinese culture is a learning culture which has assimilated and incorporated various foreign cultures.

Initial Chinese culture originated mainly from Western Xia (西夏) and Eastern Yi (东夷) cultures. Yangshao (仰韶) culture was the representative of Western Xia culture; Longshan culture, that of the Eastern Yi's. The convergence of the eastern and western clan cultures laid a foundation for the Chinese culture, which was of multiple resources. In the Spring and Autumn period and the Warring States period, the culture of the states of Qin, Jin, Wu, Yue, Qi, Yan, Zhou and Lu was respectively blossoming in splendor and eventually grew into the culture of the Han nationality with Qilu culture as its core. In the later years Chinese culture continued to assimilate the cultures of ethnic minorities mainly from the west and the north, such as the Huns' (匈奴), the Qiang's (羌), Xianbei's (鲜卑), Rouran's (柔然), Gaoche's (高车), Tujue's (突厥), Huihe's (回纥), Qidan's (契丹), Nuzhen's (女真), Mongolia's, and Manchu's, and in the south, Baiyue (百越) and Bashu's (巴蜀) cultures; it has also assimilated Indian Buddhist culture, Arabian culture, Persian culture, and now Western culture. This extensive inclusiveness is very rare in the history of world culture. It typically reflects Chinese cultural spirit of magnanimity, self-confidence as well as inclusiveness.

Exhaling the old and inhaling the new, Chinese culture has been modified to be extensive and inclusive, eventually becoming more vigorous by learning, assimilating, and incorporating selectively.

4. Atheism

Basically China is a non-religious country. Common Chinese people care little about differences between religious and philosophical schools. They simply believe that deities personify justice and protect their interests. To them, there is no strict delineation between deities and human beings. Deities must come from somewhere and some of them are the sages of mankind. For instance, in his life on earth, Guan Yu was a great general and an upright man of the Three Kingdoms period. Upon his death he has been worshipped as the god of war.

5. Ethics as a Top Priority

Traditional Chinese culture cannot be evaluated by how many modern cities China has or how many modern inventions it has; its value expresses itself principally in its ethics.

The core value of traditional Chinese culture is to achieve moral excellence and improve one's spiritual state. The determination to be morally good is displayed in the aphorism *In the morning one hears the Way, so he may die in the evening without regret* (朝闻道，夕可死矣) (Confucius). To the virtuous ancient Chinese, human interests and desires were of less importance and hence not worth pursuing—*What a gentleman worries about is not poverty but whether there are right principles throughout the country* (君子忧道不忧贫) (Confucius). During the Song and Ming dynasties there arose Confucian arguments over whether human desires or heavenly principles should be chosen and slogans like *Survive on heavenly principles; root out human desires* (存天理，灭人欲) which emphasizes the supreme position of ethics in

Chinese society were put forward. The famous poem composed by notable Tang poet Liu Yuxi (772—842) explicitly displays the significance of ethics as a top priority. It goes:

陋室铭

山不在高,有仙则名;水不在深,有龙则灵;斯是陋室,惟吾德馨。

An Epigraph in Praise of My Humble House

A mountain needn't be high;

It is famous so long as there is a deity in it.

A lake needn't be deep;

It has supernatural power so long as there is a dragon in it.

My house is humble,

But it enjoys the fame of virtue so long as I live in it.

6. Introversion

Initially, Chinese assumed that there was a world or *tian xia* (literally, under Heaven) with an indefinite perimeter, and thereafter the cultures at the borders were absorbed inwardly by the powerful influence of Chinese culture. In contrast, Western culture tended to diffuse more outwards from a single center. The inward-looking Chinese culture mainly depended on internal forces for development while the expansion of Western culture relied on the forces of religion, colonization, and military might; Chinese culture allowed for the integration of all ethnic groups both within China and along its borders while Westerners engaged in numerous wars in order to gain commercial benefits. In short, a contrast of the historical development of China and the West reveals the inward-orientation of Chinese culture.

7. Peace-loving

Traditionally Chinese people are peace-loving and thus tolerant, accustomed to hardship and injustice for the sake of peace and order. Rarely do we give vent to our feelings in physical action, because an emphasis on peace and harmony is an essential feature of traditional Chinese culture. The search for moderation and the beauty of harmony has, since ancient times, always been at the core of traditional philosophical thinking. The thinkers, together with philosophers and educators of various dynasties, studied in depth and expounded the dimensions of peace and harmony, their significance and the pathways to their fulfillment, which has formed a comprehensive system of thought of moderation and harmony or *zhong he*, exerting a great influence on the morals, ethics and values of many generations of Chinese.

8. Fellow-townsmen Complex

No matter where the Chinese goes, his heart is linked by an invisible silk thread to his hometown. Even in the modern society, the phrase "seek roots" is not outdated, and looking for townsmen and establishing the association or the community of townsmen are still popular on the college campus and at workplaces(*dan wei*). Chinese community abroad is also overflowed with the sentiment of homeland. According to them, "we were, after all, members of the 'same family' 500 years ago and the same local accent represents a very good starting-point to develop friendship."

In "The Land of My Ancestors," the famous Chinese woman author Bing Xin (1900—1999) described this fellow townsmen complex(乡土情结) as generally warm and said, "I did not visit all the local attractions in Fuzhou. Everywhere we could find historical relics as well as villages and towns inhabited by relatives of overseas Chinese and returned overseas Chinese. Fujianese expatriates are found all over the world. They have mostly started from scratch by the sweat of their brow. When I met some of them on my visits to Asian, African, European and American countries, they all expressed warm feeling towards me while shaking my hands. As I ate Fuzhou food and sipped jasmine tea in their homes or shops, I felt that being a Fujianese, I could make myself at home wherever I travelled in the world."

III Traditional Western Cultural Characteristics

Western Christian heritage, scientific outlook, humanitarian elements, distinctive points of view in terms of the rights of the individual, etc., endow Western culture with the following characteristics.

1. Religiosity

Religion occupies an important position in ordinary Westerners' lives. Even political figures don't conceal their religious mentality in public speeches. In her exit speech made on June 7th, 2008 Hillary Clinton bluntly said, "So today I'm going to count my blessings and keep on going. I'm going to keep doing what I was doing long before the cameras ever showed up and what I'll be doing long after they're gone: Working to give every American the same opportunities I had and working to ensure that every child has the chance to grow up and achieve his or her God-given potential. Thank you all. And God bless you, and God bless America."

2. Pursuit of Science

The pursuit of science is closely associated with curiosity which characterized the ancient Greeks, predecessors of some of today's Westerners. Aristotle (384 BC—322 BC), one of "The Three Greek philosophers", held that curiosity was the uniquely defining property of human beings. When talking about the Athenians of a later era St. Luke, the famous evangelist, said: "They spend their time in nothing else but to tell or to hear some new things." The Greeks, far more than their contemporaries, speculated about the world they found themselves in and created models of it. They constructed these models by categorizing objects and events and generating rules about them that were sufficiently precise for systematic description and explanation. Therefore, they did very well in scientific fields like those of physics, astronomy, axiomatic geometry, formal logic, rational philosophy, natural history, and ethnography. This pursuit of science could be found in Copernicus, Bruno and Galileo, who suffered from the persecution by the Inquisition in the Middle Ages. The Westerner might not be the first in the world to take up science, but certainly was the first to put science in such a primary position of application to promote the development of human fundamental needs. Thus the West has been foremost in pioneering in the combination of theoretical research with practical applications. In a sense, it is the continuation of the practical spirit advocated by Greek thinkers like Aristotle, although such progress was checked by the Middle Ages. The rise of science and technology should also be ascribed partly to the European Renaissance and the Enlightenment Movement, which provided the necessary environment and encouragement to those great figures who ignored the authoritative religious forbiddance and freely and passionately pursued science.

3. Tolerance

Western culture, with the admission of Christianity to its ranks alongside Greek and Roman cultures, became integrated and established long ago. What's curious about this culture is that its three cultural sources were diverse, sometimes hostile. As is known to all, Romans tried to suppress Christianity and the Vatican was hostile towards Jewish migrants and their culture. One feels puzzled at the paradoxical events or phenomena arising out of the historical process of Western civilization in association with its three cultural sources. Tolerant attitudes as well as the practical spirit of Western culture, as in the conversion of Constantine the Great (c.274—337) to Christianity, are helpful guides to seeing the positive side of this religion. Tolerance is thus a virtue Western culture fostered in its early days, and has been passed on to the present day, for example, in the form of multiculturalism, a concept and phenomena which is becoming widespread among many Western countries.

4. Critical Spirit

The critical spirit, ushered in by the European Renaissance, is highly encouraged by today's Western education system.

As is known to many, the significance of the Renaissance lies in its confirmation and manifestation of humanist thinking and application. This movement supplies great inspirations to the Westerner in creative work and builds up his confidence in bringing about more achievements in art and literature. More important than the surface accomplishment is perhaps the critical spirit the European thinkers and practitioners fostered during the Renaissance. This critical spearhead was directed particularly against scholasticism as a core of theology at the time. Consequently, it paved the way for the development of science and secular culture. One example is the Reformation which largely changed the religious structure and content of Christianity, based on the whole on the revaluation and criticism of the Christian ideas represented by the Roman

Church and the Papacy.

5. Dichotomies

Greek philosophers such as Thales (625 BC—546 BC), Heraclitus (540 BC—475 BC), Plato (429 BC—347 BC) and Aristotle advocated dividing the world into two opposing parts: element and soul, reality and reason, matter and form. Their theories laid the foundation for the further development of the concept dichotomy or the dividing-one- into-two view adopted by Western culture. Apart from his physical skill, Archimedes (287 BC—212 BC) is remembered as saying more than two thousand years ago, "Give me but one firm spot on which to stand, and I will move the earth," applying the philosophical thought to scientific research. A dichotomy is also reflected in English proverbs such as **Heaven is conquered by obeying her**. Conquering or obeying, Westerners have no alternative but to make a choice.

6. Conflicts as a Cultural Standard (文化本位)

Given the fact that dichotomies are common in Western thought, it is not surprising to find that the conflict has become a Western cultural standard revealed in various aspects of the society such as presidential campaign speeches characterized by a warlike atmosphere in which the winning side has truth(like a trophy). In such speeches, the middle alternatives are virtually ignored. The presidential campaign, aggressive, original, challenging and ambitious, exemplifies the preference for conflicts. The formation of this cultural standard probably owes much to famous philosophers in Western history(see Unit 17).

7. Extroversion

Westerners used to live in a big space composed of many smaller ones. They were not isolated by geography, developing and unavoidably conflicting with one another. Therefore, they had a very strong sense of competition. Since their life style was open, they were disposed to be sociable, paying attention to their own individual roles and looking outward. This orientation has decided their focus—the world outside, which is displayed in their incessant outward expansion. An outward-looking or extroverted culture is thus developed.

The East-West dichotomy is a philosophical concept of ancient origin which claims that the two cultural hemispheres, East (represented by China) and West, developed diametrically opposed, one is more introversive while the other is more extroversive; the East is more intuitive while the West is more logical. Together, they form an equilibrium.

Further Reading

1. Clinton, H.(Saturday, June 7th 2008). "Hillary Clinton's exit speech".

2. Garreau, J. (1981). *The Nine Nations of North America*. MA: Houghton Mifflin.

3. Holcombe, C. B. (2013). *The Real Chinaman*. US: HardPress Publishing.

4. Russell, B.(1945). *History of Western Philosophy*. New York: Pocket Books.

5. Tannen, D. (998). *The Argument Culture: Moving from Dialogue to Debate*. New York: Harper, Collins.

6. 饶尚宽译注 (2006):《老子》,北京:中华书局。

7. 杨伯峻译注 (2006):《论语》,北京:中华书局。

8. 季羡林 (2007):《季羡林谈翻译》,北京:当代中国出版社。

9. 林语堂 (2000):《吾国吾民》,北京:外语教学与研究出版社。

10. 费孝通(2013):《全球化与文化自觉:费孝通晚年文选》,北京:外语教学与研究出版社。

Unit 3   Affinities Across Cultures

Some literary critics say that Chinese literati, especially poets, are mostly disposed to be decadent, which accounts for predominance of Chinese works singing the praises of autumn. Well, the same is true of foreign poets, isn't it? I haven't read much of foreign poetry and prose, nor do I want to enumerate autumn-related poems and essays in foreign literature. But if you browse through collected works of English, German, French or Italian poets, or various countries' anthologies of poetry or prose, you can always come across a great many literary pieces eulogizing or lamenting autumn. Long pastoral poems or songs about the four seasons by renowned poets are mostly distinguished by beautiful moving lines on autumn. All that goes to show that all live creatures and sensitive humans alike are prone to the feeling of depth, remoteness, severity and bleakness. Not only poets, even convicts in prison, I suppose, have deep sentiments in autumn in spite of themselves. Autumn treats all humans alike, regardless of nationality, race or class.

—Yu Dafu

Yu Dafu's arguments are very sound. For further thought: Give more examples to show affinities between Chinese and Western literature.

...since we are alike under the skin, what touches the human heart in one country touches all.

— Lin Yutang

For more affinities, read more across cultures.

I An Unexpected Affinity

In 2007 I happened to catch sight of American black woman writer Zora Neale Hurston's grave in the segregated cemetery Garden of Heavenly Rest in Ft. Pierce. I noticed a few pennies scattered on the vault. My friend Dr. Tammy Shadel smiled and explained, "That's a superstition, to throw coins on the gravesite, so the dead won't be broke." As I thought about Hurston's persistent money woes, Tammy added, "She died penniless in 1960, you know." By a remarkable coincidence, we use almost the same way to make sure our beloved ones enjoy a rich life after death, with the difference in that we burn notes which we make believe are issued by the so-called Hell Bank and stamped by the legendary Yama King. Thereupon we can see this custom of expressing good wishes for our beloved dead ones is both Western and Chinese. After all, we are human beings. Though exposed to different cultures we share some of the life experiences and feelings.

II Reading for More Cultural Affinities

Everyday we do lots of reading in English and Chinese. We read not only for improving our language level, but also for a good mastery of cultural differences as well as affinities. In this unit the latter is addressed.

1. Affinities in Textual Details

It is crucial that we should pay attention to concrete details in different texts, because differences as well as similarities become prominent on the level of concrete details. Most often we recognize the details and their distinctions in a text by comparing them.

Take, for instance, the official slogan of the 2008 Beijing Olympic Games "同一个世界, 同一个梦想". The Chinese catchphrase is believed to have conveyed the lofty ideal of Great Harmony(世界大同). Its English version "One World One Dream" denotes that there exists only one world where people share one dream—peace. In spite of the absence of the meaning of "tong (same)" which is repeated twice in the

Chinese slogan, the English message is as clear as its Chinese version: We wish to be part of the global community and civilization, create a bright future with others from other parts of the world, and contribute to the world peace, harmony, and prosperity.

2. Thematic Affinities

On the ground level of textual details, differences as well as affinities appear prominent, and on the level of total meaning of texts and literary traditions, thematic patterns also emerge to display affinities. Therefore, we never lose anything in comparison insofar as we do not pay attention to thematic patterns at the expense of textual details, or vice versa. Now consider thematic affinities in the creation myths of ancient China and ancient Greece—the cradle of the Western civilization.

a. The Earth Goddess and the Sky God

Most systems of myths have an explanation for the origin of the universe and its components. These myths are known as creation myths. In Chinese creation mythology, the sky is male and the earth is worshipped as the mother of all myriad beings.

According to the Greek creation myth, at the beginning of time there was only one being which they called Chaos, like the Chinese idea that the earth and the sky were mixed together. Out of Chaos then came the earth, a goddess called Gaia, who gave birth to Uranus, the sky god and the first ruler of the universe.

b. Childbirth Without Male Participation

Nuwa, a famous cultural figure, is supposed to have molded the first humans out of clay without male participation, hence it is suggested by some that Nuwa is the first Chinese deity.

In the ancient Greek myth, Gaia gave birth to the sky god without any help from any male.

c. Incest

Incest plays an important role in producing offspring in both Chinese and Greek myths. Tradition says that the god Fuxi is Nuwa's husband and brother. They are portrayed together with their tails intertwined, Nuwa with a compass(representing the earth) in her hand and Fu Xi with a set square(symbolizing Heaven) in his.

As the Greek creation myth goes, Uranus became his mother Gaia's husband, and together they had many offspring, including twelve of the Titans.

d. One Supreme God

Chinese gods form a large bureaucracy headed by the supreme emperor of Heaven, Jade Emperor. He rules over the government departments, mountains, rivers, etc. run by lesser gods. Jade Emperor's wife is Xi Wangmu, the queen mother of the west and the guardian of peaches and immortality. It is said that the Chinese emperor had a direct contact with Jade Emperor.

Zeus, King of the Gods, ruler of Mount Olympus, is the supreme deity in the Greek mythology. He is the god of the sky, like Jade Emperor. However, he seized power by overthrowing his father Cronus, the former sky god who had dethroned his father Uranus.

e. God of Love, God of Happiness, and God of Wealth

The Chinese lucky Ho-ho twins known as gods of love are often shown attending the god of wealth (*Cai Shen*). They bring prosperity as well as harmonious union between couples because the word "*ho*" means harmony. The twins are depicted with a lotus on their heads, standing on a bed of lotus flowers and carrying jars of lotus buds of purity and perfection. *Fu Shen* is the god of happiness.

In Greek mythology Eros is the mischievous Greek god of love. Some of his arrows have gold tips and cause people to fall in love. Others are tipped with lead and have the opposite effect. Aphrodite, the goddess of love and desire, was born from the foam of the sea. She devotes herself to pleasure and prides herself on never doing any work. Eros often assists her. Zeus' brother Hades is the god of wealth.

f. God of Death

Yan Luo(also know as Yanwang or Yama King), the god of death, is a terrifying ruler and judge of the dead in China. When people die, first their souls are weighed: The virtuous are light and the sinful are heavy. Then the souls must pass a number of tests and challenges. They are assaulted by demons, attacked by dogs, and then allowed one last glimpse of their home and families before being offered a drink of

Mengpo Tea, which wipes away all memories. Finally, each soul is reincarnated.

In the Greek mythology, Hades, the god of wealth, is also the king of the underworld and the god of death and the dead. He presides over funeral rites and defends the right of the dead to due burial.

g. War Gods

Guan Yu is the god of war in Chinese mythology. He was originally a humble seller of bean curd before he became a general, one of the three famous Brothers of the Peach Orchard, and in 1594 was elevated to the status of the god of war after he died.

The Greeks have two war gods. Ares is the god of fighting and Athena the goddess of strategy and wisdom. The more famous Athena sprang from the head of her father Zeus, fully armed and ready for battles.

3. Allegorical Interpretation of Canonical Works

In the ancient world physical love and sexuality were thought to be detrimental to moral cultivation and social stability. That is why love poems in canonical works have to be interpreted as about anything but physical love. Therefore, when we read about the seemingly passionate love in the *Song of Solomon* of the Bible, the Rabbis and Christian fathers would tell us that the text has nothing to do with love between a man and a woman, but the spiritual love between God and Israel, or between God and His Son, Jesus Christ. Verse 1 of the Song of Solomon goes:

This is the greatest song Solomon ever wrote.

A Shulamite woman says to King Solomon,

"I long for your lips to kiss me!

Your love makes me happier than wine does.

The lotion you have on pleases me. Your name is like perfume that is poured out.

No wonder the young women love you!

Take me away with you. Let us hurry!

King Solomon, bring me into your palace!"

The other women says,

"King Solomon, you fill us with joy. You make us happy.

We praise your love more than we praise wine."

The woman says to the king,

"It is right for them to love you!

Women of Jerusalem,

My skin is dark but lovely,

It is dark like the tents in Kedar.

It's like the curtains of Solomon's tent.

Don't stare at me because I'm dark.

The sun has made my skin look like this.

My brothers burned with anger against me.

They made me take care of the vineyards.

I haven't even taken care of my own vineyard.

King Solomon, I love you.

So tell me where you take care of your flock.

Tell me where you rest your sheep at noon.

Why should I have to act like a prostitute near the flocks of your friends?"

The other women say,

"You are the most beautiful woman of all.

Don't you know where to find the king?

Follow the tracks the sheep make.

Take care of your young goats near the tents of the shepherds."

King Solomon says to the Shulamite woman,

"You are my love.

You are like a mare that pulls one of Pharaoh's chariots.

Your earrings make your cheeks even more beautiful.

Your strings of jewels make your neck even more lovely."

...

The poetry is obviously about the love story of a man and a woman, but many Christian commentators interpret it as a picture of the Church as the Bride of Christ. God loves His only Son and has called out and prepared for him a beautiful virgin bride "without spot or blemish." If not, how could Solomon who had 700 wives and 300 concubines be the faithful and passionate lover this poem portrays?

When a text is canonized as all-important and providing guidance to truth and proper behavior, it is often necessary to interpret it allegorically to defend it against possible challenges to its canonical status. This is not only true of the *Song of Solomon* in the West, but also of the Confucian classics in China. Take, for instance, the first poem "Cooing and Wooing" in *Shi Jing* or the *Book of Poetry*, one of the five Confucian classics:

关关雎鸠,在河之洲。窈窕淑女,君子好逑。 参差荇菜,左右流之。窈窕淑女,寤寐求之。 求之不得,寤寐思服。悠哉悠哉,辗转反侧。 参差荇菜,左右采之。窈窕淑女,钟鼓乐之。

Its English version is:

By the riverside are cooing

A pair of turtledoves;

A good young man is wooing

A pretty maiden he loves.

Water flows left and right

Of cress long here, short there;

The youth yearns day and night

For the good maiden fair.

His yearning grows so strong,

He cannot fall asleep,

But tosses all night long,

So deep in love, so deep!

Now gather left and right

Cress long or short and tender!

O lute, play music bright

For the bride sweet and slender!

Feast friends at left and right
On cress cooked till tender!
O bells and drums, delight
The bride so sweet and slender!

（Tr. by Xu Yuanchong）

When we read "Cooing and Wooing" about the cry of a lovebird in the islet of a river and a young man wooing a pretty girl, Confucian scholars would tell us that the poem is not about love between a man and a woman, but about the virtue of a good queen whose only desire is to find people with virtue and talents and have all of them serve her king.

4. Similar Conceptual Metaphors

"The differences in environment, climate, cultural development, etc., among various communities may be extremely significant, but basically, human societies are linked by a common biological history. The objective reality in which they live is definitely not identical but it is by and large similar." (Chitoran) Influenced by shared non-cultural knowledge of human beings, both English and Chinese metaphorical concepts have three types: orientation metaphor, container metaphor, and structural metaphor.

a. Orientation Metaphors

For both Chinese and Westerners, an upright posture is associated with good mood and happiness, while a dropping posture is connected with bad mood and sadness, e.g. *My spirits rose* (我精神振作起来) and *I'm feeling down* (我情绪低落).

b. Container Metaphors

For both Chinese and Westerners, life is a container, e.g. *I've had a full life* (我的一生很充实) and *Life is empty for him* (他的生活空虚).

c. Structural Metaphors

Some structural metaphors are so common that we may not even notice that they are metaphors. Take the familiar metaphor of *life is a journey*, for example. Life is defined as a journey in many of the Chinese and Western works. For instance, in the essay "National Crisis vs. Heroic Nation" the famous Chinese revolutionary Li Dazhao says, "The historical course of man's life is just like a journey. A traveler on a long journey passes through now a broad, level plain, now a rugged, hazardous road. While a determined traveler cheerfully continues his journey up on reaching a safe and smooth place, he finds it still more fascinating to come to a rugged place, the enormously magnificent spectacle of which, he feels, is better, able to generate in him a wonderful sensation of adventure."

In *Metaphors We Live By*, George Lakoff and Mark Johnson extend "life is a journey" into other metaphors which can find equivalents in Chinese. The metaphors are:

The person leading a life is a traveler.

His purposes are destinations.

The means for achieving purposes are routes.

Difficulties in life are impediments to travel.

Counselors are guides.

Progress is the distance travelled.

Things you gauge your progress by are landmarks.

Choices in life are crossroads.

Material resources and talents are provisions.

Coincidently these metaphors are very popular with Chinese literati, as displayed in "National Crisis vs. Heroic Nation."

5. Depiction of Evil Characters in Literature

The approximately similar depiction of evil characters has been found in stories, for instance, about step-mothers who are given a negative connotation in both Chinese and Western literature. Contrasts in personality and physical traits between the biological daughter and the step-mother often appear to be an element in many Chinese and Western folktales like *Cinderella* where Cinderella is beautiful and soft-featured compared to the persnickety step-mother. The step-mother not only looks mean, but also has much sharper features. By and large, step-mothers are portrayed as evil and self-centered. They lack self-control, exhibiting hostility and acting on their passions without regard to anyone else's concern.

Step-mothers in Chinese and Western stories are also depicted as torturers of their step-children. Snow White's evil step-mother tried every means to kill her. Min Zi(闵子), one of Confucius' students was maltreated by his evil step-mother when he was little. In winter, the step-mother and her biological son were well-fed and clothed, but Min Zi had to go to bed on an empty stomach and had nothing to keep himself warm.

It is interesting that step-fathers in both Chinese and Western folktales possess an opposite character in contrast to the wicked step-mother. The kind step-father gracefully accepts his step-children and treats them as his own. With loving arms, he mercifully takes in his new wife, often an unwed-mother and her illegitimate children.

III   Key Concepts

1. "Affinities Across Cultures"

Far from simply calling for respect for our culture and other cultures, scholars have scrutinized texts in both Chinese and English and tried to forge links between the two cultures. This effort may first of all provides the reader with a new perspective to multicultural issues—with appreciation and understanding rather than tolerance and adaptation. Cultural commensurability provides a solid ground for the mutual respect of different cultures and unites cultural traditions in the East and West.

Secondly, the focus on affinities across Chinese and Western cultures may help the reader to appreciate the essence of human creativity and the richness of human imagination as well as expressions beyond the gaps of language, race, time, and space.

Thirdly, the comparison and contrast made with the intention to see the commonality between Chinese and Western cultures can serve as a springboard for the reader to study the cultural and textual encounters between China and the West. Similar efforts in the future will surely uncover many other unexpected affinities of concepts, expressions, themes and character depictions that are drowned in different texts.

2. "Uniqueness" "Differences" and "Similarities"

a. "Uniqueness"

The idea of uniqueness is very useful because uniqueness means being the only one of its kind, having no parallels or comparisons, but it is very difficult to find anything culturally significant that qualifies as something truly unique.

b. "Differences"

Difference is another matter, however, for it does not imply the only one in the universe, simply not exactly the same. In this sense, we do find many significant differences between the East and the West. Culinary art, for example, is obviously different. From ingredients and cooking methods to the way food is presented and served on the table there are remarkable differences. This is by no means a trivial case, because food is perhaps more culturally specific than anything else in our daily life. The fact that food is a basic necessity in our daily life, helps us realize that differences become prominent on the level of concrete details of things in reality rather than the conceptual level of ideas and themes. In China people often share the dishes at the table, but Westerners have their own plate individually. Not that there can be no sharing in the West, nor that individualism does not exist in China, but the way food is served may reflect on the different ways individualism and collectivism manifest themselves in China and the West. As long as we do not draw extreme conclusions from comparison, we may get some insight into different degrees of emphasis in different cultures.

c. "Differences and Similarities"

We can talk about differences only when we put things together in comparison, which means that differences and similarities are inseparable and always mutually implicated.

There are of course more differences on a more concrete level. For example, it is believed that classical Chinese literature does not have long epic poems and most dramas tend to have happy endings unlike many Western tragedies. In folk literature and oral traditions, however, long heroic poems do exist in some of China's minority cultures; it is too simplified to say that tragedy with unhappy endings is uniquely Western. For instance, Greek tragedies do not necessarily end in death or suffering. We can talk about the tragic in a broad sense, that is, the sense of being in a position to bring about suffering and death not totally of one's own doing, like a building driven away by a flood because of its height. If so, we may find many works in Chinese literature that give expression to precisely that sense of the tragic. For instance, the untimely death of Zhou Yu, the famous general of the State of Wu during the Three Kingdoms period, is a result of his narrow-mindedness.

We need to closely examine what seems to be, on the surface, very different between two cultures, look for thematic affinities and conceptual similarities under those differences, and then we will find some point of convergence as a point of departure in the intercultural communication.

d. "Differences and Frictions"

It is indisputable that there are huge differences between civilizations, which have occasionally engendered frictions. Nevertheless, it is misleading and dangerous to magnify such frictions into world political clashes and wars.

In a diversified world, it is only natural that different civilizations should co-exist. Chinese scholars have been stressing complementarities among different cultures, holding that it is necessary to draw on each other's strong points so as to make common progress. Just as the official Chinese document *Outline of Patriotism Education* states when it elaborates on patriotism, "Patriotism is not narrow nationalism. We need not only to inherit and develop the fine heritages of the Chinese people, but also to study and absorb the civilizations created by other nations, including capitalist nations. Only by so doing can the Chinese people make their due contributions to world peace and human progress along with other nations."

While acknowledging cultural differences makes it clear that "this is a difference of degree, not of kind," it should be emphasized that there is a common cultural ground on which people from the West and the East can stand, make meaningful comparisons and hence communicate effectively on an equal basis. As peace and development have become the mainstream of the world, all nations should show appreciation and respect for each other and develop together. Each of us must keep an open mind, listen to other parties, and be ready to accept what is true. This should be the case not only of interpersonal dialogue, but of intercultural communication as well.

Further Reading

1. Lakoff, G. & Mark Johnson. (1980). *Metaphors We Live By*. Chicago, IL: University of Chicago Press.

2. Goatly, A. (1997). *The Language of Metaphors*. London: Rutledge.

3. Anderson, W. T. (1990). *Reality Isn' t What It Used to Be*. New York: Harper & Row.

4. Zhang, L. (2007). *Unexpected Affinities: Reading Across Cultures*. Ontario, Canada: University of Toronto Press.

5. (1997):《圣经》,北京:中国基督教三自爱国运动委员会与中国基督教协会。

6. 许渊冲(2004):《中国古诗精品三百首》,北京:北京大学出版社。

7. 陈柏松(1997):《中西诗品》,河南:中州古籍出版社。

8. (1994年8月23日):《爱国主义教育实施纲要》,北京:中共中央印发。

9. 张隆溪(2014):《阐释学与跨文化研究》,上海:复旦大学出版社。

Part II

Cultural Differences in Silent Languages

Language is spoken verbally or non-verbally. The language which is spoken non-verbally through time, space, and the information sender's body movements like smiling, nodding, and even silence is known as silent language.

Silent language is subjective, so it is probably the hardest language to learn. You may assume it is easy to become part of the culture when you go to Germany if you are fluent in German. But even if you can speak perfect German, sometimes you find yourself unable to express yourself non-verbally in ways that the locals understand and carry on business and personal transactions. This causes communication breakdowns and misunderstandings in your interaction with locals because you speak a different silent language—although you speak perfect German like them.

How fluent can you be in a silent foreign language, then? The good news is: It is a learned art. The bad news is: There is no course that could help. As with all things, practice is the secret to getting better and becoming more sensitive to cultural differences in silent languages.

In this part, time which often talks silently but differently in different cultures will be explored in Unit 4; different cultural expressions in spatial language employed in social interaction and architecture will be discussed in Unit 5; body movements like smiles, nods and silence in different cultures will be investigated in Unit 6.

Unit 4   Time

Tomorrow never comes.

One cannot put back the clock.

—English proverbs

What does time mean to you? For further personal exploration and enlightenment: Look for Chinese proverbs that are at variance with the above two.

In October, big news rocked Stanford University, the Harvard of the West Coast. Zhu Diwen, a professor of Chinese descent in Stanford's Department of Physics, along with two other scientists, an American and a Frenchman, won the Nobel Physics prize in 1998 for their invention of a technique to cool atoms with a laser.

American born Zhu Diwen is of course a very "Americanized" scientist. He impresses others with his self-confident, humorous and witty conversation, while remaining refined and cultivated.

With his informal attire and satchel clasped behind his back, Zhu looks no different from other young men. His amiable and witty style of conversation has closed the gap between master and the students.

Throughout the past half month of media events, Zhu was seen dressed in Western-style clothes only when he met Jiang Zemin.

— From US News and World Report

Zhu Diwen, a Nobel-prize winner, has stricken us as informally dressed, but when meeting with important officials like former Chinese President Jiang Zemin he was dressed formally to show respect and of course wished to act, dress and be perceived as a professional. Suppose you are advising a friend who is going to spend some time in the States. Explain to him what changes he will need to make in his dressing when he interacts with different kinds of people and why.

I Time in China and the West

Time, though a silent language, often talks loudly but differently in different cultures.

1. Chinese Time and Western Time

Unlike the discrete and clearly-defined Western system of time, traditionally there are no very specific rules for time in China. Even if there were some in some cases, they would not be listened to very seriously.

a. Chinese Time

Traditional Chinese time springs from inside. It is an inside force that helps people to plan their life, which is revealed in the aphorism, "One who does not work hard in youth will grieve in vain in old age." It is widely believed that if all day is spent merely chatting idly, saying unreasonable things and showing off his cleverness, one will accomplish little and have a miserable life when old. In spite of that, time is seldom experienced as "wasted". Instead, the "wasted" time is usually regarded as taking a break, catching a breath, making preparation or accumulating energy so that one day when one's chance comes he will seize it and become successful and world-famous overnight, just as the idiom goes, "不飞则已,一飞冲天;不鸣则已,一鸣惊人(freely, an insignificant person who appears to be wasting his time will amaze the world by his successful maiden effort)."

In such a culture time is therefore not accurately calculated and carefully considered. Strictly speaking, there is no time concept at all at times. So after he has had a conversation with a person, an old Chinese scholar would comment, "Talking with you for one night is better than studying books for ten years." Chan(禅宗), practiced by many Chinese, aims to attune the Buddhist disciple's self inside himself to nature by suggesting "eating when hungry and sleeping when tired", not encouraging him to accurately plan his time. And the ideal life which has been aspired for thousands of years is to "labor at sunrise and rest at sunset".

Because of inexact calculation of time, promptness is not valued so highly in traditional China, which is reflected in imperatives like *Eat slowly* at dinner table, partings like *Walk slowly*, and comfortings like *Study slowly* and *Take your time* when comforting students who have been suffering academic setbacks. If their children are in a rush, traditional Chinese parents may scold them and say half-jokingly, "Are you rushing to reincarnation?" So to speak, promptness sometimes refers to immaturity, recklessness, and danger.

Preoccupied with leisurely life, traditional Chinese associate the past with the future, which explains a reason why Chinese time is treated very much like a mirror. One can observe himself in it and check up his outfit, hair and face to see if anything goes wrong. On the other hand, one can see his past in it and remind himself to avoid repeating mistakes in the future, just as Emperor Taizong (618—907) of the Tang Dynasty said, "Using history as a mirror allows one to see the future trends."

In a culture which pays so special attention to the past, forgetting one's past means negating one's past. Chinese are used to looking back. For many of us the past is the best teacher: What happened in the past is still relevant today. Since very ancient times, Chinese have possessed an unusual passion and respect for the past. According to historical records even the earliest dynasties appointed historian officials. The Chinese historian official was believed to be very trustworthy, because he was trained and required to be objective and he based what he wrote on government files of memorials, edicts, court decisions and other papers, and since he worked in an official capacity he had access to the dependable first-hand written material. If he wished to write down his own judgments, which he seldom did, he usually marked it so that the reader could readily recognize it. Like the royal houses, Confucianism encouraged and developed the sense of history and respect for the past. Two of the five Confucian classics, the *Book of History* and the *Spring and Autumn Annals*, supposedly compiled and edited by Confucius himself, are history works, transmitting information and giving moral lessons. Since ancient times, the study of history has always been a major part of Chinese education and citing historical examples has traditionally been among the principal techniques of Chinese argumentation.

Meanwhile, history is regarded as a cyclical succession of eras arranged in a fixed order by Chinese philosophy of history, which is also deeply influenced by Taoist theories. Not only eras, but also all of history experience changes, grow and decay in the form of a cyclical succession. This view is shared by many, just as famous Hong Kong entertainer Andy Lou(Liu Dehua) sings, "The flower has withered and died; it will blossom again next year as usual." In other words, time is handled as if it were part of a rotating circle, coming and going on a regular basis.

Also Chinese time is usually looked upon as a whole. Consequently we are mostly disposed to do more than one thing at a time.

b. Western Time

In the Western society time is imposed from outside. As an outside force, it helps people to organize their life, for instance, there are schedules to tell them what to do and when. In this culture, those who cannot schedule time are thought of as impractical.

For Westerners time is a line that has segments kept discrete for "one thing at a time", going ceaselessly forward. Therefore, Westerners tend to look ahead and are oriented almost entirely toward the future.

As late as even today, the ancient Greek sense of curiosity about the future is still very striking. Greeks liked new things and were preoccupied with change and future. They wanted to know how to overcome resistance to change and future so much so that scientific theories and even some pseudo-scientific ones were often given much attention. The desire for change needs to be satisfied by segmenting time and handling it like a single perishable material.

Since time is treated as if it were a perishable material, it can be earned, saved, spent, wasted, killed, run short or out of. Therefore, it should be accurately calculated and carefully considered and it is sort of immoral or rude to have two things going on at once on many occasions. In China the popularity of instant-boiled mutton, Sichuan spicy hotpot and Guangdong seafood hotpot owes much to "more than one thing at a time"—allowing or requiring eaters to cook while eating, talking and having fun. But for Western chefs cooking is their job. As for the eaters, sending food to their mouth is their part and it is bad manner to spit bones on the table. The mixture of cooking and eating at once in a Western restaurant is against their ethical rule, and thus almost impossible, but for Chinese a delicious blend of eating and cooking together is the best selling point for hotpots, especially in winter.

Promptness, though disfavored in traditional China, is highly valued in Western life. If people are not prompt or punctual, the unpunctuality or non-promptness is often taken either as an insult or as an indication that they are not quite responsible. Westerners feel so strongly about time that they have stressed this aspect of culture and developed it to a point unmatched anywhere in the world, especially in America, Switzerland and Germany. No wonder their handling of time is much criticized and many people attribute ulcers, diabetes, and hypertension to the pressure engendered by such a time system.

2. Two Views on Time

a. Circular View

Traditional Chinese look upon time as the rotation of a circle, going round and round ceaselessly. This circular outlook on time is revealed in classical literary writings. Qu Yuan, a noted patriotic poet of the Warring States period, wrote in his masterpiece *The Lament* (离骚), "The sun alternates with the moon; autumn returns after spring soon (日月忽其不淹兮,春与秋其代序)." For him time is not a one-way ticket, but a back-and-forth rotation like the endless cycle of the seasons. Many Chinese scholars lament that time really goes quickly, but meanwhile believe that it will come back soon as spring and autumn do. The circular view results in a sense of the abundance of time and accordingly doing things in an unhurried manner and making up for the lost time as time rotates is encouraged. Although we also sigh over "time waiting for no one (Tao Yuanming)" and feel "regret for the negligent loss of time (Han Yu)", yet we expect the favor of the time cycle and the shift from bad to good luck.

We hold the view of time as a cycle, and naturally cherish and revere the past. Hence we have been taught to keep diaries to record what has been done in the past even each day in order "to engage in introspection every day on three points"(Zengzi). So we tend to be constantly reflecting on our past behavior and trying to find out whether we have done anything offending or have shunned our responsibilities so that we could improve ourselves the next day.

On the whole, the circular view encourages respect for the past, an unhurried leisurely life style, and the practice of doing more than one thing at a time.

b. Linear View

Westerners tend to look upon time as a line moving towards the future and never returning, and therefore hold the future in high regard and carefully plan for it.

Just because they hold a linear view of time, Westerners have a strong sense of the shortage of time, and thus quicken their pace of life and habitually look ahead. That explains why Westerners are used to marking in their calendars what are to be done in the future and focusing much of their attention on planning for themselves. Future-oriented, they are inclined to defy authorities and enjoy working on something new instead of following the established routine.

On the whole, the linear view encourages respect for the future and the practice of doing one thing at a time.

II Two Time Modes

Based on his study, American anthropologist Edward T. Hall has termed doing more than one thing at a time "Polychronic" or "P-time." Inspired by his research, the author of the book groups Chinese time into the category of Polychronic time since Chinese system involves several things at once. Hall has termed doing one thing at a time "Monochronic" or "M-time." Since M-time emphasizes schedules, segmentation and promptness, North American time system is classified as a Monochronic one. The two time modes are logically and empirically quite distinct.

1. P-time

a. Polychronic Chinese

In China, there are some typical environments like the food stand on the street corner, where the stand owner is often seen trying to serve a group of people at once. There is no recognized order as to who is to be served next, no queue or sequence to indicate whose order has not been handled. For Westerners, it appears a riot is breaking out. However, it is normal in China that some people don't form lines. They form "huddles" around the stand owner, ticket booth, or bank clerks since Polychronic people are used to interacting with several persons at one time and are continually involved with each other whether at home or in the workplace. Tight scheduling or scheduling ahead of time is therefore difficult in some cases.

b. Cultural Features of the P-time Mode

This mode or "more than one thing at a time" system has affected the flow of information, the shape and form of the networks connecting people, and even helped to develop a host of important cultural phenomenon such as *one item with multiple functions, one organization with multiple obligations,* and *a jacket for different occasions*. For instance, a knife in the kitchen was used to sharpen a pencil, peel a potato, or cut melons, vegetables, bread, meat, cakes, sugar canes, firewood, etc. Today some people, though no longer poor and isolated from the outside world, are seen to be formally dressed in suits, ties and leather shoes when they do sports, go sightseeing or fishing. And many of us use the dishwasher as a dish rack and eat all meals in the kitchen.

The most striking feature of the P-time mode is the "killing-two-birds-with-one-arrow" mentality. For instance, we use jam jars as drinking glasses and we beat eggs with chopsticks. Take for another instance the age-old advice about cooking which says: "When you prepare a dish, you must keep three things in mind: It must be pleasing to the eye, the aroma must be appealing, and it must be appetizing." For this reason, you can expect that each Chinese dish, whether the most economical or the most elaborate, will always be colorful, have a delightful aroma or at least taste delicious. We sincerely believe in the old proverb "Good food brings happiness". What is implied is that food not only satisfies our hunger, but also serves as a reason for people to socialize together, an occasion for family members to communicate, an opportunity for a good chef to show off, etc.

The third characteristic that might have arisen out of the Polychronic "more than one thing at a time" is the practice of "a clever rabbit digs three holes for future use". For instance, we keep a thermos of hot water available at all times. Similar practice can guarantee at least one way out even if the most terrible thing should happen. No wonder Chinese are mostly disposed to be obedient and leisurely—unless we have no way out, just as the saying goes, "None will rise up in revolt unless there is no way out."

The fourth characteristic is that Polychronic individuals are oriented toward people, human relationships and family. In this culture, scheduling is not so valued since all the members have to be considered and what's more, anything might happen to any member at any moment. Caden is an American of Chinese descent. Six months ago he got a job in Nanjing. His relatives in Changzhou told him he was welcome to visit them at any time and the Intercity High-speed Rail Network (高铁) would make it convenient for him. He stayed with them for two weekends but did not enjoy himself. He found it hard to spend his time with his relatives because he never knew what was planned until he was hurried to go out to eat or visit some place. He did not like to be kept in the dark. Nurtured in Western culture, Caden failed to know that his relatives didn't tell him their plan because time cannot be considered carefully and thus things are so constantly changing in China that sometimes plans are found unable to be realized until the last second. In this sense, their silence about their weekend plan had nothing to do with their intention to keep him in the dark. Planning something early in China does not really mean that it is to happen since time is not handled so seriously that things are very likely to be out of our control. As a result, we Chinese are accustomed to planning late so that the plan can be realized.

2. M-time

a. Monochronic Westerners

"God has made man himself a creature of time." Time is so thoroughly integrated into Western society that it is treated as though it were the only natural and logical way of organizing life. For instance, people don't make an early morning call unless it is about a matter of utmost importance and extreme urgency; they don't make a phone call during sleeping hours unless the message involves a big secret or life and death.

Monochronism means doing one thing at a time. For most Westerners the ideal world is where they can center their attention first on one thing and then move on to the next. Scheduling makes it possible to concentrate on one thing at a time. Karl May is a German conducting business in Nanjing. When his meeting with a high-ranking official in the office was constantly interrupted, he felt upset and started wondering whether the official is as important as he was led to believe, and he even started to doubt how seriously his business was being taken. In his culture, such a meeting is usually uninterrupted for it is usually held in a closed office or a secluded place for privacy.

The "one thing at a time" system has deeply affected Western division of time. To make it easy to calculate and plan their time, Americans have divided their country into nine standard time zones covering all the states and its possessions. The time zone boundaries are under the authority of the Department of Transportation. Official and highly precise time keeping services are provided by two federal time agencies: a department of Commerce agency, the National Institute of Standards and Technology (NIST), and its military counterpart, the United States Naval Observatory(USNO). The clocks run by these services are kept highly synchronized with each other as well as with those of international time keeping organizations.

b. Cultural Features of the M-time Mode

The M-time mode has extended beyond the field of time. Take, for instance, the social world where people often have many friends at one time. Friendships in this mode are usually tied to specific circumstances or activities, so there have car-pool friends, leisure activity friends, neighborhood friends, etc. When they change circumstances and activities, they change friends.

The second feature that might have arisen out of the Monochronic "one thing at a time" mode is the existence of a "one-to-one" relationship. For example, in the Western kitchen a utensil is usually invented or bought for one purpose. Hence there is the fruit knife, the bread knife, the vegetable knife, the pizza knife, pencil sharpener, etc., quite contrary to traditional Chinese use of a knife for cutting, peeling or sharpening almost everything in sight.

The "one thing at a time" mode has found its way into such organizations as factories. The assembly line invented in America in the early twentieth century is still striking today. The assembly line in the factory refers to a manufacturing process in which parts (usually interchangeable parts) are added to a product in a sequential manner, greatly reducing labor costs and thus contributing a lot to the Western prosperity. Without the mode of M-time, Western societies might not be what they are today.

Another characteristic that might come out of the "one thing at a time" mode is people make appointments for almost everything, for instance, with their doctors for a session, professors for problems or even hairdressers for hair beauty. Suppose a Monochronic correspondent makes an appointment to see a Polychronic businessman at 1 pm. At 1 pm precisely she calls at his house and is surprised to find that several members of the businessman's family have called on him. In circumstances like this, the businessman will feel compelled to invite the reporter to join the party. As a result, the reporter who has scheduled her time very carefully is annoyed—she wants to conduct the interview straight away. The man has no alternative because if he does not entertain his family regardless of the schedule, the result might be endless criticism from his family. As a consequence, he will have to lose a good opportunity to promote his business.

The fourth characteristic is that time is handled as if it were an opportunity that might never come back again. Questions like *How often do you see Warren Buffett on the street* are asked when emphasizing the importance of opportunities. To seize the opportunity, people are taught how to make their case in 30 seconds or less because "the 30-second parameter is based on the typical attention span" (Milo O. Frank). That's a reason why the standard commercial or television "sound bite" in the West lasts 30 seconds.

3. Blending of P-time and M-time

Now all cultures with high technologies seem to incorporate both Polychronic and Monochronic functions. The point is each does it in its own way. Chinese remain Polychronic when looking and working inward—toward ourselves. But when dealing with Westerners, some Chinese are beginning to shift to the dominant Monochronic time mode which characterizes the Western society.

Some Westerners are both Monochronic and Polychronic, too. The French are Monochronic intellectually but Polychronic in behavior. On the surface American time is Monochronic, but in a deeper sense it is both Polychronic and Monochronic. M-time dominates the official worlds of business, government, entertainment, and sports. However, at home, particularly the more traditional home in which a woman is the core around which everything revolves, P-time takes over. How else can a woman raise several children, run a house, hold a job, and be a wife, mother, nurse, house maid, tutor, and chauffeur at once?

Of course, not all M-time and P-time are exactly the same. There are tight and loose versions of each. The banks and joint ventures in Polychronic China provide an excellent example of tight M-time. The pattern is not too different from schedules for office workers in the West. The difference is that in China the tightly scheduled Monochronic pattern is applied to foreigners who are not well integrated into the Chinese time mode, where emphasis is on developing a good working relationship and where safety is highly valued, for instance depositing and withdrawing money from the cashier, the bank counter or ATM.

4. Strengths and Weaknesses of P-time and M-time

Both M-time and P-time modes have strengths as well as weaknesses.

a. Strengths and Weaknesses of P-time

P-time culture is by its very nature people-oriented. Actually Polychronic Chinese are so deeply immersed in each other that we feel a need to keep in touch and have a good knowledge of each other, which makes our interactions very humane and warm, greatly reducing the sense of isolation, loneliness, and depression. As a matter of fact, our relationship with others is the very core of our existence, which has naturally formed a society of acquaintances where human warmth is easily accessible.

However, we depend on having gifted people at the top, and hence are slow and clumsy when dealing with something new or different. Without talented people at the top, a P-time bureaucracy would be a disaster sometimes. Because leaders deal simultaneously with many people, most of them stay informed about what is going on. So when considering setting up organizations, people exposed to P-time modes theoretically demand a much greater centralization of power, which may give officials more power than they need.

Many scholars believe that the principal weakness of P-time is the forming of bureaucracies. As functions increase, there is a proliferation of small bureaucracies not set up to handle the problems of outsiders. Actually the outsider traveling or residing in a place outside his own society of acquaintances sometimes find the bureaucracies cumbersome and unresponsive and assumes that one has to be an insider or have a friend or *guanxi* who can make things happen.

b. Strengths and Weaknesses of M-time

Monochronic Western culture is oriented to schedules, tasks, and procedures. Schedules can and frequently do cut things short just when they are beginning to go well. For example, investment funds run out just as the results are beginning to emerge. Orientation to tasks and procedures helps to make it likely for Monochronic organizations to become large and profitable, but the weakness is their blindness to the humanity of their members. "As anyone who has had experience with Western bureaucracies knows, tasks and procedures attach no importance to either logic or human needs, which is at least partially responsible for the reputation of American business being cut off from human beings and unwilling to recognize the importance of employee morale." (Edward T. Hall)

III Past-oriented Societies vs. Future-oriented Societies

Different views on time and different time modes help to build two kinds of societies: One is past-oriented and the other is future-oriented.

1. Past-oriented Societies

In past-oriented societies, the past is kept alive in language, TV theatres, films, dramas, stories, music and dance, religious practice and customs, which enables people to know their history. Tradition is therefore very important. With its rich cultural memory, China is past-oriented.

In China, we enjoy talking about historical events that took place a hundred or even a thousand years ago. We often look back to the Tang Dynasty when Chinese culture was at the height of its power and glory, and some of us like quoting honored philosophers and leaders from the past in debates or arguments. The policy-makers, when first introducing a new policy, may compare it to a historical event or support it with a quotation from a respected leader or philosopher of the past so as to give the policy more authority, because ordinary people may feel more secure when something new is defined as similar to something that occurred in the past.

The respect for the past in China was most obviously displayed in the cult of filial piety at Han court where it was a mark of respect for the emperor to his imperial ancestors and especially to the founder of the Dynasty that a ruler maintained intact the institutions inherited from them. Especially in later ages of the Han Dynasty this proved a strong deterrent to institutional reform. Innovators could not easily set aside such dynastic precedents. To do so was equal to a behavior of impiety toward the emperor's forebears.

To emphasize the importance of the past we often say, "One generation plants trees, against which another generation can lean and take a rest." The saying implies that one sows and another reaps. "Study the past and you will know the present" is also often quoted to explain why Chinese people react so strongly whenever Japanese rightists bring up the proposal of rewriting their country's history. In 2001, a woman published a picture of a famous film actress wearing a dress with a Japanese military flag on the cover of *Bazaar Magazine*. The Chinese public, sensitive over the war with Japan, responded furiously. The actress' relations with mainland audiences became strained. At a concert, she was attacked by a construction worker who said his grandparents had been killed during the war. Reflecting upon his actions, the worker told a Chinese magazine: "I know what I did wasn't right. But I believe my cause was just... As a famous Chinese person, she should have been aware of such an important event in Chinese history."

2. Future-oriented Societies

In future-oriented societies, people feel less need to rewrite or reinterpret their history, probably because they believe "No man is rich enough to buy back his past" (Oscar Wilde). In these societies conquering the limitations of the past or surpassing the accomplishments of the past are good reasons for them to take a new unbeaten trail. The Western society is such a future-oriented society.

In the West, the past is studied scientifically to find trends and patterns since the causes of present and future conditions can be found in the past, and therefore it is considered useful to investigate it in order to create a better future. With such an understanding, the Germans have been honest in their culpability: Students continue to take field trips to concentration camps. But people may have negative expectations for the future and their efforts may be directed at preparing for or preventing bad times ahead. This is revealed in predictions about future consequences if financial problems are not solved or the spread of panic of an epidemic is not prevented.

Westerners are good at planning for their future. They set goals and outline specific steps for reaching the goals. Children even as young as 10 years old are encouraged to plan their careers at school in their Career class, working people plan their summer vocations or even their retirement, and managers want to know the personal plans of their employees. Their attitude is that people act today because that action is a step toward the future they are preparing for. For many of them the past is of less use and the future is something to move them forward. Just as Hillary Clinton said in her exit speech in 2008, "Every moment wasted looking back keeps us from moving forward." Their attitude implies that the future can be controlled if the past is forgotten and some actions are taken today.

3. Yasukuni Shrine Visit

In future-oriented societies time is linear, which means that it moves only in one direction—from the past to the future. In past-oriented societies people are more likely to experience time as the rotation of a circle repeating itself. They may pay more attention to daily, seasonal, and historical cycles than people from future-oriented societies do. Different sense of time makes it hard for Westerners to understand the controversy over the Yasukuni shrine visit.

Yasukuni Shrine is the place where fourteen Class A war criminals are enshrined after World War II(WWII). The shrine is not run by the state and it is not a cemetery. There are no bones, ashes, graves, graveyard or headstones. Only the souls of the dead are "placed" there. In a book entitled *Talk of Ancestors* published in 1946 the author Kunio Yanagita states, "After death, the soul remains eternally upon this land. It is believed that the soul does not travel to a distant world. This faith has endured for centuries until the present day..." That can explain a reason why Japanese officials' visit to this place has been regarded to be hurting the feelings and dignity of the countries which fell victim to Japanese aggression during WWII. Our strong indignation also comes from the fact that the Japanese government and its leaders have never officially said sorry to us. Besides, some Japanese leaders have over and over again stirred up troubles on the history issue, which has made us very worried that period of history might be repeated.

Like Japan, Germany brought disasters to European people, but it said sorry officially and was forgiven and thus a new page was opened for the European history, although their historical perspective sometimes can influence perceptions: In Germany, one global delivery service found employees reluctant to wear the company's brown uniforms, because the Nazis wore brown uniforms, and "brown shirt" was a synonym for fascist.

IV Two Time Orientations

Different sense of time naturally leads to two different time orientations. One is long-term, the other short-term.

1. Long-term and Short-term Orientations

A culture with the long-term orientation is of characteristics such as adapting traditions to modern context, being sparing with resources, saving, accepting slow results, and respecting the demands of virtue. The long-term orientation emphasizes patience and long-term plan. People with long-term orientation believe that "worries will soon appear if one gives no thought to a long-term plan(人无远虑,必有近忧)" (Confucius), so they rear children for old age, and save food for crop failure.

A culture with the short-term orientation is of the following characteristics: respecting tradition, keeping up with the times, spending more and saving less, expecting quick results, seeking truth, etc. The short-term orientation emphasizes speed. People with short-term orientation believe in the proverb "Time is money".

2. Short-term vs. Long-term Orientations and Work Values

In China, the main work values include learning, honesty, adaptability, accountability and self-discipline; leisure time is not so important; profits five years from now are important, although we privately disagree on wide social and economic differences and deem these differences undesirable. Our investments in housing, guanxi(relationships, friendship) and education tend to be life-long; we are very saving. On the whole, we save for future use in case anything bad should happen to us. On the other hand, we remain very optimistic however hard life is for we believe what Zengzi said, "A scholar must be resolute and steadfast, for his burden is heavy and his road is long(士不可以不弘毅,任重而道远)." He means that virtuous talents with a strong sense of mission should have a long-term orientation, refusing to give in under tentative pressure.

In the West, main work values include freedom, rights, achievement, and thinking for oneself; leisure time is important; people emphasize the importance of this year's profits and agree that reward by abilities is a good system; personal loyalties vary with business needs; many persons are not so saving. What's more, people spend future's money today.

3. Different Expectations of Friendship

Gabriel Lindman and Bao Gang first met in their history class at an American university. Bao Gang, a freshman from China, was excited to get to know an American friend. He hoped that he and Gabriel would become good friends.

At first, Gabriel was very friendly. He greeted Bao Gang warmly before class. Sometimes he offered to study with Bao Gang. He even invited Bao Gang to have lunch with him. But after the semester, Gabriel seemed distant. The two former classmates didn't see each other a lot on the campus. One day Bao Gang decided to call Gabriel. Gabriel didn't seem interested in talking to him. Bao Gang felt hurt. "Gabriel said we were friends. And I said friends were friends forever." In his letter to friends at home he wrote, "Americans are fickle."

Bao Gang feels upset because he doesn't understand the way Americans view friendship. Chinese expect friendship to stay the same over a long period of time, maybe for a lifetime. In China a true friendship is a relationship that endures through changes. In the West a person is likely to change even "best friends" several times over the years. Even the relationship in which people feel close emotionally and tell each other their secrets and personal problems may not survive life changes such as graduation from a university or a big change in economic circumstances. Friendship, like many other relationships including marriage, depends on frequent interactions. If the people involved do not see each other and interact regularly, the relationship is apt to wither or even die like a tree which has been uncared for and forgotten.

Further Reading

1. Hall, E. T. (1959). *The Silent Language*. New York: Doubleday & Company.
2. Hall, E. T. (1976). *Beyond Culture*. New York: Doubleday & Company.
3. Levine, R. V. (1997). *A Geography of Time: The Temporal Misadventures of a Social Psychologist.* New York: Basic Books/Harper Collins.
4. Levine, R. (2008). *Journeys in Social Psychology: Looking Back to Inspire the Future*. New York: Psychology Press.
5. Frank, M. O. (1990). *How to Get Your Point Across in 30 Seconds or Less.* New

York: Pocket Books.

6. Hofstede, G. (2005). *Cultures and Organizations: Software of the Mind.* New York: McGraw-Hill.

7. Smith, A. H. (2003). *Chinese Characteristics*. New York: Eastbridge.

8. 杨伯峻译注 (2006):《论语》,北京:中华书局。

9. 胡文仲,(2000):《跨文化交际学概论》,北京:外语教学与研究出版社。

Unit 5   Space

18 July 2006: At last week's G–8 summit in St. Petersburg, United States President George W. Bush stepped behind German Chancellor Angela Merkel, reached for her shoulders, gave her a brief massage and then kept walking. Visibly startled and uncomfortable, Angela Merkel threw up her arms. A moment to be remembered, it seems within hours, links to photographs and video footage of the surprise neck grab were already racing across the Internet—from YouTube to Technorati. "Bush: Love–Attack on Merkel!" read the headline in the German tabloid Bild. Several websites denounced commander in chief Bush as the "Groper in Chief". Though the neck rub happened nearly one week ago, Bush is still feeling the rub today. A vocal debate is brewing in several US newspapers and blogs about whether the president has simply made a minor faux pas or whether he may even have sexually harassed his colleague. "You could use this video for sexual harassment training," Democratic Party activist Martha Whetsone told the San Francisco Chronicle newspaper. "It's something you'd show and say, 'No one in a boss' position should be doing that.'"

—A news report

What do you think of the massage? Was it a harmless bit of fun between two equally powerful leaders? Or was it a deeply unacceptable example of workplace sexual harassment?

We shape our buildings and then they shape us.

—Winston Churchill

Churchill said this during the debate on the form that Parliament should have when it was rebuilt following the bombing of London during World War II. It is only recently, however, that space has begun to be recognized as influencing the direction as well as the outcome of behavior. For discussion: Give some examples related to the conception and use of space in Chinese life.

I Spatial Language

We often hear people say things like *He's my bosom buddy. Xiao Hong is a distant relative. She kept him at arm's length during their first meeting. The old man kept his distance from the visitor. Nobody is nearer his heart than his daughter. He was once regarded as one of Mr. May's closest advisers.*

Obviously, to define their interpersonal relationships or set a limit we use space which usually refers to body distance and body touch in social interactions.

1. Don't Cross the Line—the Social Distance

No matter how close you are with your friends or family, there are invisible boundaries that you cannot afford to cross and invisible or visible space you cannot get in without invitation in all cultures. In other words, there should be some physical distance. For instance, it's improper to walk with your Western friend hand-in-hand or arm-in-arm. It is rude to touch her or him sometimes. On the other hand, it's improper to kiss your Chinese friends. Your kiss will embarrass them. And there should be speech boundaries, too. There are no friends with whom you can talk about everything or you needn't be careful in your choice of words when you talk. As language users, we know how powerful words are. They are comforting, soothing, but sometimes hurting and killing. So don't cross the line.

2. Body Distance

Some people misjudge how close they should sit or stand when they are talking to strangers or acquaintances, and they may end up making a poor impression on others either because they get too close, or stay too far away. Ji Wen, a young man of eighteen, likes to be with people, especially native English speakers so that he can practice his language skills. But he finds some of them turn away from him or step back when he is near them. Although they don't cover their nose or mouth, he doubts whether he makes people feel sick because of his bad breath, unaware of the fact that if you find that other people keep moving further back when you stand close to them, it does not necessarily mean they don't like you because of your bad breath. It might mean that you are invading the territory they consider as their personal space. About the only time people willingly allow a stranger into their personal space is when they need medical treatment, or when they can't prevent it, such as when on a crowded bus or elevator. Of course people get very close to each other when they feel a very strong attraction.

Based on his in-depth observation, American Anthropologist Edward T. Hall established four distances for American culture in 1959:

1) Intimate distance: 1-18 inches. It is reserved for intimates.

2) Personal distance: 1.5-4 feet. It is a transitional distance between 1) and 3).

3) Social distance: 4-12 feet. It is reserved for business.

4) Public distance: 12-25 feet. It is observed on formal occasions.

China is a country of propriety. The *Book of Rites*, the fourth one of the Five Confucian Classics before the Qin Dynasty covers the most minute rules for the conduct of everyday life. But there are no written rules for what distance is proper for what kind of relationship so that we are still intuitively adjusting body distances in our daily social life.

Body space or personal space is one of the cultural differences that we first notice when dealing with people from other cultures. In general, North Americans prefer more distance than we do. Some Western Europeans, such as Scandinavians and Germans, like even more space. Differences in how close to stand are a source of misunderstanding. Philip Lung, a New Yorker who teaches Oral English in Hohai University, told me about his discomfort caused by some Chinese behaviors. The other day he waited in line for his train ticket at Xikang Road train ticket office. He noticed that people were impatiently standing very close to each other. He wanted to make people aware of his discomfort by keeping a distance from the person in front of him. However, the people behind him pushed him to move forward, which greatly upset him.

To this behavior, my explanation is that traditionally we have had the concept of shared space, particularly in public places; the concept of privacy or personal space is fairly new in China where in some traditional big families it is impolite and unacceptable to shut your bedroom doors in daytime.

3. Body Touch

In all cultures, the closest body distance denotes body touch. But in terms of body touch, different cultures have different customs. Take hugging for instance. Hugging is a touch which has very obvious sexual connotation on most occasions in China. Only lovers or husband and wife hug—usually in private. In the West, hugging, whether at a time of meeting a friend or at the parting, usually has no sexual connotation. It is warmer, more enthusiastic, and less formal than a handshake and does not necessarily convey a romantic message. Women tend to hug each other more than men hug women, but both are common. Despite the growing Western influence in Chinese life, women and men who are friends still do not hug or kiss each other in public. Such actions would be considered something very unusual between a man and a woman if they were not lovers.

The other day I happened to log on to a Jason's Blog and found a paragraph very eye-opening. It says:

In China, a common complaint of Western mothers is that Chinese often fondle their babies and very small children. Such behavior—whether touching, patting, hugging or kissing—can be quite embarrassing and awkward for the mothers. They know that no harm is meant, and that such gestures are merely signs of friendliness or affection, therefore they cannot openly show their displeasure. On the other hand, such actions in their own culture would be considered rude, intrusive and offensive and could arouse a strong dislike and even repugnance. So the mothers often stand by and watch in awkward silence, with mixed emotions, even when the fondling is by Chinese friends or acquaintances.

II   Spatial Language and Culture

In *The Silent Language* (1959), Hall elaborates on how people from different cultures orient themselves in space and classifies some cultures as high contact and others as low contact.

1. High Contact Cultures

"In high contact cultures what people sense when they are close to a person or object is most important."(Hall) Chinese culture can be classified as high contact—at least in comparison with Western culture and its closer spatial language brings people much human warmth. On a typical Chinese campus, students of the same gender putting their arms around each other, walking arm-in-arm or even holding hands can be seen almost everywhere. Boy students often huddle around newspaper displays in a fashion of close contact and some of them don't mind squeezing twenty pals into one room for three on festive occasions. In the park, people of the same gender are seen holding hands, walking shoulder to shoulder, or touching each other a lot.

However, some close contact or touching takes place not because of friendship or kindness, but because time presses or there isn't much room. For instance, when crossing the street, we sometimes brush others but keep moving on as if nothing had happened since it is so crowded and everybody is in a hurry, but if two people collide, a brief apology might be offered, and then they continue with their business. When we get on a bus, if the person behind you touches or pushes you, you will not be angry and should consider it normal, otherwise you will be regarded to be out of your mind, since it is unavoidable to brush each other when you are rushed to get on the bus by the driver. To be honest, nobody likes this kind of unintentional touch.

It's dangerous to generalize that Chinese culture is high touching. You can give some examples to refute my argument. For instance, a typical Chinese does not put his arm around his wife's waist when having a walk in the park. You can also use scene of greeting and good-bye at any airport or train station as an evidence to prove that we are not physically affectionate even to our families. There typical Chinese are seen with all the feelings expressed in the eyes and in the practical things loved ones do for one another, which has been vividly described by the famous Chinese essayist Zhu Ziqing (1898—1848). In "The Sight of Father's Back" Zhu wrote, "I said, 'Dad, you might leave now.' But he looked out of the window and said, 'I'm going to buy you some tangerines. You just stay here. Don't move around.' I caught sight of several vendors waiting for customers outside the railings beyond a platform. But to reach that platform would require crossing the railway track and doing some climbing up and down. That would be a strenuous job for father, who was fat. I wanted to do all that myself, but he stopped me, so I could do nothing but let him go. I watched him hobble towards the railway track in his black skullcap, black cloth mandarin jacket and dark blue cotton-padded cloth long gown. He had little trouble climbing down the railway track, but it was a lot more difficult for him to climb up that platform after crossing the railway track. His hands held onto the upper part of the platform, his legs huddled up and his corpulent body tipped slightly towards the left, obviously making an enormous exertion. While I was watching him from behind, tears gushed from my eyes. I quickly wiped them away lest he or others should catch me crying... When he came near the train, I hurried out to help him by the hand. After boarding the train with me, he laid all the tangerines on my overcoat, and patting the dirt off his clothes, he looked somewhat relieved and said after a while, 'I must be going now. Don't forget to write me from Beijing!' I gazed after his back retreating out of the carriage. After a few steps, he looked back at me and said, 'Go back to your seat. Don't leave your things alone.' I, however, did not go back to my seat until his figure was lost among crowds of people hurrying to and fro and no longer visible. My eyes were again wet with tears." Indeed it is unlikely that typical Chinese will put their arms around the returning or departing dear one and squeeze him or her. And it is more unlikely for them to kiss their mom or dad.

Today there have appeared in China many so-called "empty-nest" families with only aged parents at home and their children living abroad or in another city. Probably that's why more and more pets such as dogs and cats are seen in my community. They might be kept to satisfy the need for touch, I assume.

Thus we can see Chinese do not use touching on every occasion, although we use it relatively more than Westerners.

2. Low Contact Cultures

In America, some children don't know who their biological father is. Some women don't know who fathered their children. There is a very famous daily TV show known as "Maury Show" which helps people with these problems they need to work on. In this show, there are women who slept with different men, men who slept with different women and the children they have produced. The interactions among the host, audience members and the show stars are usually very unexpected, dramatic and exciting. Here is a question: Does the popularity of the show mean that Americans are not sensitive to physical contact?

No, Americans are very sensitive to physical contact. They say "excuse me" whenever they feel they might touch somebody. "I'm sorry" is usually the answer when they find themselves in others' way, especially when they touch somebody unintentionally, even among family members and best friends. Western culture, especially American culture, is low-contact, today even lower than anytime in American history. Why?

America is a complex country. There are people of different races, different cultures, different personality, different backgrounds, and different incomes. America is also widely known in China as a very free country. Many Chinese assume Americans can enjoy complete freedom of speech, press, publication and sex. This assumption is by and large misleading. As a matter of fact, the freedom is based on many preconditions, especially in terms of freedom of sexuality. In America mass media is powerful. It has a great impact on the trend of American culture. Sex is a topic favored by mass media. There is a good coverage of sexual harassment cases, missing cases, or murder cases, especially when the cases are about pretty young attractive women, the mass media covers it all day long and in great details. Over the years, there have been several sensational sexual harassment cases that have caught much attention. In Nov. 2007, a junior high female student of 13 years was seen hugging both her girl friend and her girl friend's boyfriend in the hallway. This school in southern America decided to put her in the detention room as a punishment. In 2004, Mr. Li was sued by his male colleague who declared that Li harassed him sexually in a public bathroom. Li, a new immigrant from China, felt wronged, explaining that he assumed he and this colleague of his got along well and a pat on the shoulder is a greeting and a gesture of friendship in China. What made Li more confused is that two of his colleagues said they witnessed how Li harassed his colleague sexually. Li ended up in 3 years of house arrest. Americans are learning people. From these cases they learn that if they want to live in peace, they have to develop a habit of avoiding physical contact with others. The middle schools are giving students such lessons. It was true in the past that relatively high status people (e.g. *supervisors, adults, men*) could touch lower status people(e.g. *workers, children, women*), but the rules about this are changing. Now there is much concern about sexual harassment in the workplace and about the possibility of sexual abuse of children by caregivers such as teachers and activity leaders. This concern has resulted in further restrictions on touching in the Western society. Touching of lower status people by higher status people has become suspect as it could indicate a sexual intention.

On the whole, Western culture is comparatively low-contact. That explains a reason why the gesture of affection George W. Bush gave Angela Merkel stirred up a heated debate in the United States and Germany. To us, it is natural for close friends to massage neck or back for each other. Aren't Bush and Merkel close friends? The point is that the touch took place between two Westerners. In the West, among strangers, acquaintances, and great friends, people are sensitive to body touch. Uninvited touch is regarded to be rude and offensive, a violation of personal rights. The correct way for Bush might be to ask Merkel first for permission, "Could I give you a massage?" or "Do you mind if I give you a massage?" If Merkel agreed, she would say, "Yes, I would love to have a massage." or "Sure. Why not? It is free, isn't it?"

Indeed there are too many sexual harassment cases, which make the alleged offenders lose their dignity, jobs, families, and money. Indeed there is too much sex-related body contact in Western films and TV drama, which unavoidably remind people of sexual harassment. But films and TV dramas are not about real life. The real life can only be found in real life and courtrooms. So don't touch Westerners without asking for permission.

Here comes the problem: People need touch, need human warmth, and need to be part of another person's life. How do Westerners satisfy this basic human need?

Don't feel sorry for them. They have their own ways to satisfy their need for human touch. They watch people hug, kiss, touch, push, punch, strike, beat, or trample people on TV or in films, which can explain a little bit why mass media is full of sex and violence. There is a hidden large market for topics about sex and violence.

Secondly, they keep pets. An American woman writer joked about herself at an interview this way, "What can you write about me? A middle-aged woman and her four dogs?" Most of the pets they keep are warm-blooded animals because these animals can pass warmth. My neighbor Kitty Green lost her husband Peter 20 years ago. Her only son doesn't live with her and she doesn't want to live with him (American independence). She bought a dog and named it Peter. Peter's smile, tremble, tears, jumps, and noise are her favorite topics. When she watches TV, Peter sits in her arms; when she sleeps, Peter sleeps beside her and it is fun to listen to him snort. Peter keeps her busy all day long. She washes him, feeds him, combs him, takes him to see his vet, dresses and undresses him, walks him, trains him, educates him to be polite, helps him to make dog friends...

Thirdly, people try their utmost to refresh their love by giving each other gifts on important occasions, praising each other, thanking each other, kissing each other, hugging each other, talking to each other... When their marriage unfortunately ends up in divorce, they are not afraid of seeking new love and throwing themselves into another love affair. By new love, I mean remarriage or cohabitation. Cohabitation is popular in America. A man and a woman live together not as husband and wife but as boyfriend and girlfriend. There are many reasons behind cohabitation; keeping love fresh and alive is one of the main reasons.

Fourthly, they go to church on a regular basis. Some people don't believe in God, but often go to church. Why? The Ten Commandments given to Moses by God commands his children to be kind, nice, polite, and friendly to others. Mary Jefferson, my 23-year–old neighbor, likes being hugged, which is the only reason for her to go to church every Sunday. Usually there are two services in the church on Sunday morning. One is traditional for old and middle-aged people, the other contemporary for young people. Mary chooses traditional service, because hugs from older people are warmer and more comfortable for her.

Fifthly, they like making new friends, entertaining friends at home and holding parties for friends and family members. Hugging is acceptable on these occasions.

Anyway Westerners are still talking a lot about touching and especially honor the hug as expressing emotional warmth, affection and care. For instance, when we watch a game on TV we often see Western players hugging their teammates. In this case we see the role of touching in creating bonds among the members of a group. So the point is not that Westerners use very little touching, but that they are relatively low touching and sensitive to body touch.

3. Misinterpreted Contact Language

Different spatial languages may lead people into very embarrassing situations.

When Dorothy received an invitation to attend her Chinese neighbor's birthday party, she was thrilled. She has always admired the Chen family. She is very fond of Will, the about-to-be-married son, and feels extremely close to Mrs. Chen, his widowed mother. After the beautiful party, Dorothy and Mrs. Chen soon became great friends. One day, Dorothy gave Mrs. Chen a very beautiful necklace. Mrs. Chen loved it so much that she felt she should give Dorothy something in return. So she gave Dorothy a purple clay teapot. Dorothy was very pleased. One week later, Dorothy invited Mrs. Chen to her home. They wrapped *jiaozi* together and enjoyed the meal a lot. Then they walked upstairs to watch TV—hand in hand. Then Dorothy sat beside Mrs. Chen and gently grasped her hand. Mrs. Chen lightly squeezed her hand in return while watching an interesting TV drama, feeling very happy that she could make so great a friend in the U.S. Suddenly Dorothy tried to kiss Mrs. Chen, who was shocked and cried at the top of her voice, "No! I'm not a lesbian!" Obviously Dorothy was hurt. She asked accusingly, "Why didn't you tell me earlier, then?"

In China it is natural for a woman to develop a close relationship with another woman. The physical intimacy between women like walking arm in arm, holding hands, sitting close to one another and even sharing one bed is standard, whereas kissing is abnormal. But in America women would hold hands only if they were lesbians or bi-sexual.

III   Spatial Language and Life

Space finds expressions in many aspects of life.

1. Housing

Regarding architecture, Chinese distinguish between what is public and what is private, what is male and what is female, what is outside and what is inside. In this inside-outside pattern, the inside is female and private while the outside is male and public. The traditional Chinese architecture features high walls and heavy gates. Walls and gates as well as gate men are more common in China than elsewhere. The front of a house that presents to the outside is plain, unwelcoming, even forbidding, and the walls are thick to protect what is inside.

If you think about this inside-outside pattern in relation to Chinese life, you may have noticed that people from other countries are commonly called *laowai* (foreigners) rather than Englishmen or Indians. The inside-outside pattern also operates within Chinese society as can be seen in the phenomenon of "localism" in business and the Chinese characters *wai* (outside) and *nei* (inside).

Western architecture lays great stress on fences. American poet Robert Frost once said, "Good fences make good neighbors." The statement implies that Western life puts weight on privacy protection. Take the traditional Western concept of housing for instance. The typical Western home requires an area of privacy, which is often formal and regimented. Physical features like doors, hedges, and fences reflect an emphasis on privacy, which is pervasive throughout Western life. By the way, taboos about age, wage, religion, marital status, or even white hair are also regarded as a protection of one's privacy.

2. Classrooms

Most Chinese classrooms have large raised podiums with students sitting in rows below and in front. This design reinforces the authority of the teacher and encourages a teacher-centered style of learning. Moreover, the classroom usually has an open front door and an open back door as well as two big bright windows on both walls so that everything is seen clearly from outside. The design is an indication of much care for the students from the teaching faculty.

Most American classrooms have movable tables and chairs that would make it easier to arrange the students into work groups so that teachers would easily move among the groups monitoring their work and offering advice as needed, because most American teachers prefer the role of a facilitator, a person who defines tasks and goals and arranges activities to achieve them. They see themselves as a coach, resource person and motivator instead of the main source of knowledge for the students. Most elementary and middle school classrooms are closed, with only one door but no window, so they have electric lights on and air-conditioners to control the temperature, which is a display of respecting privacy and personal development.

3. Office Buildings

In any culture, the location of one's office in a company or a governmental department has something to do with the person's position or status.

In China, the department manager's desk or office is often placed in the last row behind his subordinates'. In that location, he can have better leadership, seeing how his subordinates are working and keeping in close contact with them at the same time.

In America, those who are of higher positions usually have their offices higher in the building, with beautiful scenery outside and a quiet environment, and above all far from visitors. Those with lower ranks usually have an office lower in the building, with easy access to visitors and not so pleasant scenery to enjoy.

In Germany, people habitually close their offices so as to obtain a closed space to ensure the independence and privacy of their activity.

4. Different Interpretations of a Door Unshut

Max Krueger, a young German engineer, is Wang Ling's new next-door neighbor. After a few interactions, they become friends. One day he asked her to talk for a while in his room. Wang Ling agreed happily. She followed Max into his apartment room and deliberately left the door ajar. When Max found the door not shut, he went to close it. Wang Ling felt so uncomfortable with the tightly closed door that she appeared very absent-minded and distracted, which made Max really uncomfortable.

In China, tradition has it that it is inappropriate for a man and a woman to be alone together, especially in a closed space, and therefore we are taught to leave the door ajar when alone with someone of the opposite sex so that others would know you are not doing anything inappropriate, because the open door links the confined space to the outside and hence offers a shared space with others. However, leaving the door unshut so that people would not be skeptical about your chastity is absurd for Germans. Even if the relationship between Max and Wang Ling did involve physical intimacy, a German like Max would believe that is no one else's business, not to mention that it is not safe to leave the door unclosed in a building occupied by so many people.

IV   Changes We Cannot Afford

Today Chinese spatial language, especially in architecture, has been greatly influenced by Western spatial language, which the authority cannot afford to take for granted. Former British Prime Minister Winston Churchill said many years ago, "We shape our buildings and then they shape us." Now there is a great concern about the fact that the high-rise apartment buildings in China are making us drift further away from the harmonious society we enjoyed before. Fourteen years ago I lived in a traditional Chinese building with a big courtyard which was like a big sitting-room for all the occupants of the building. The 58 families in that building were very close. We used to talk, help, and support each other like a big family. Since we moved to Longjiang—a new Western-style neighborhood in Nanjing, things have changed. My present neighbors avoid eye contact with me when we wait for the elevator together, not to mention smiling, talking, or even helping one another. My present home is in a really big, modern and compartmental building, but the human warmth we enjoyed before has been replaced by suspicion, distance, and coldness.

Takeo Matsuda, a successful housing "tycoon" who helped to bring affordable American-style houses to Japan, is now afraid that those houses may have contributed to the rising violence in Japanese families and schools. According to her, "Japanese families were very tight. We all studied together and slept together." The American home compartmentalizes the family, so children grow up leading "separate lives" and, as a consequence lack training in having consideration for others. Matsuda states that now "we have everything", but "we don't help each other."

These changes, to be frank, might not be what we can afford.

Further Reading

1. Hall, E. T. (1959). *The Silent Language.* New York: Doubleday & Company.

2. Hall, E. T. (1966). *The Hidden Dimension.* New York: Doubleday & Company.

3. Furnham, A. & S. Bochner (1986). *Culture Shock: Psychological Reactions to Unfamiliar Environments*. London: Methuen.

4. Mackerras, C. P. (2013). *China in My Eyes: Western Images of China Since 1949.* Beijing: China Renmin University Press.

5. Samovar, L. & R. Porter. (1994). *Intercultural Communication: A Reader.* Belmont, CA: Wadsworth.

6. 胡文仲 (2000):《跨文化交际面面观》,北京:外语教学与研究出版社。

7. 黄时鉴主编 (2001).《东西交流论谭》,上海:上海文艺出版社。

8. 许力生 (2004):《跨文化交流跨文化交际英语教程》,上海:上海外语教育出版社。

9. 周宁(2006):《天朝遥远:西方的中国形象研究》,北京:北京大学出版社。

Unit 6　Smiles, Nods and Silence

There is language in her eyes, her cheek, her lip, Nay, her foot speaks.

—Shakespeare

How do you understand the remark made by the noted English playwright William Shakespeare?

A smile is a curve that sets everything straight.

—Phyllis Diller

What do you say to this definition?

Man is a speaking animal, but the bulk of information in face-to-face communication is sent or received through silent language channels such as smiles, nods, and silence.

I　Smiles

In physiology, a smile is a facial expression formed by flexing those muscles near both ends of the mouth. It can also be found around the eyes. As a silent language, a smile talks a lot, from which we can get much information in the intercultural communication.

1. Smiles in the Intercultural Communication

a. Classification of Smiles

There are many kinds of smiles. Three of them are arranged under different headings as follows:

1) A Put-on Smile

The put-on or fake smile is a performance smile intended to hide true feelings or mislead others. For example, when we meet someone who we think is the "one", we may deliberately attempt to manipulate the person into thinking we are relaxed, happy, and enjoying ourselves. We change the shape of our mouth, even bare our teeth but the smile doesn't properly reach our eyes or spread across our face because we merely wear a smiling mask.

2) A Genuine Smile

A genuine or felt smile transmits delight or enjoyment and draws the other person emotionally closer because the smiler appears to be saying, "I like me, I like you and I like life. I want to share this good feeling with you." In most people you'll notice a twinkle or what looks like a feeling of "amusement" or somewhat "mischievous" expression in their eyes. A genuine smile is a natural and effective way to connect with people emotionally.

While a forced or put-on smile can be switched on and off at lightning speed, a genuine smile is hard to produce on demand because it depends on and is controlled by real-time emotions.

3) Others

People smile for all sorts of reasons. There are the happy smile, the contempt smile, the dampened smile, the miserable smile and a number of others. Smiles have a powerful effect on humans. But not all smiles are equivalent and not all smiles enhance the smiler's likeability. For instance, when some young men in China are asked if they have a girlfriend they usually look away with a smile, which strikes non-Chinese as rude and inscrutable.

b. Chinese Smiles

A smile in China is not only a silent language of pleasure, happiness, amusement, appreciation or understanding, but also means that the smiler is polite, interested, understanding, friendly, sorry, sad, embarrassed, confused, uncomfortable, helpless, at a loss as to what to say, sympathetic, or even judging, and hence there are some smiles in China that will cause negative reactions by Westerners. To illustrate, here are selections from a letter by an American to his friends back in the United States on

Chinese smiles that often cause cross-cultural misunderstandings:

In a classroom, a Chinese girl was asked to answer a question. She stood up and smiled, without making any sound. The American teacher looked at himself and didn't see anything funny. So he asked her the question again. The girl just smiled but said nothing. (Note: The teacher was angry. He didn't know that the girl smiled to cover her embarrassment because she wasn't able to answer the question.)

In a dining room, an American dropped a plate quite by accident and felt bad. The Chinese who had seen this began to laugh, compounding his discomfort and causing anger and bad feeling. (Note: In fact, the Chinese laughed not at the American or his bad luck—whether he is a foreigner or a Chinese. The laughter has several meanings: Don't take it seriously; laugh it off, it's nothing; such things can happen to any of us, etc.)

When an American was parking her bicycle, a Chinese boy accidentally bumped into her. She fell and was quite awkward and angered when the boy said with a smile on his face, "Sorry. Terribly sorry." (Note: A Chinese smiles when he / she apologizes and feels sorry. The tragedy is that an American smiles only when he/she is happy. So the American felt very humiliated.)

As a typical Chinese, I hate to see some people laugh at, for instance, a speaker who has poor pronunciation, a person who has made a seemingly stupid mistake, a guy who improperly gets himself dressed, or the disabled. I feel upset about this judging smile, believing nobody is in the position to judge others. Unfortunately judging smiles are often seen here and there, which is neither encouraged nor criticized because it is assumed that "smile is better than cry". It is believed by many that smiles represent a positive attitude toward life or at least a response to life, and what's more, it represents a philosophy with profound connotations.

c. Western Smiles

According to Westerners, a smile often denotes pleasure, happiness, amusement, kindness or acknowledging the presence of someone. Their smiles confuse Chinese on some occasions, too. One Chinese student in America told his friend, "On my way to school, a girl whom I don't know smiled at me several times. I was a little surprised."

His friend said: "When I was walking on the campus the first day, many people smiled at me, which made me quite ashamed. I hurried to the bathroom to see if anything was wrong with my clothes. Now I'm used to all smiles." It is not unusual for Americans to exchange smiles with complete strangers. They smile at people on the street, at the airport, in restaurants, shopping malls and so on. They consider it a friendly gesture. However, generally speaking, Chinese people do not smile at strangers. Of course, Westerners do not always go around smiling at strangers in a corridor, elevator, or other confined space, although it is not uncommon to see this happen. Acknowledging the presence of someone else is more common when there are few or no other people around. Thus, a Westerner will walk down a crowded street in a big city and not make eye contact with anyone. However, if that person goes into an office building and gets on an elevator with one other person already in the elevator, they are likely to exchange a brief smile or nod, or maybe even a quiet "Good morning" or other greetings. People usually do not want to intrude on a stranger's privacy, but pretending they are not there by avoiding eye contact or other acknowledgement is seen as rude.

2. Misinterpreted Smiles

There are many books that say the smile is universal. Yes, it's a universal movement but it is not interpreted in the same way. For example, traditional Chinese believe that the smile is a sign of frivolity. If something is important and serious, you don't smile too much. That's not so for many of us because now we have learnt that we have to smile in order to convey the right feeling.

During my stay in America, I smiled to everybody around me and to my happiness, this effort paid off. One day, Eve Steine, a sweet lady from Sweden told me that her purse was stolen. I was very sympathetic and asked her with a smile on my face, "What is in your purse?" I think I had a smile, but I am sure I sounded sympathetic. "A debit card, 200 bucks, a checkbook, a bunch of keys... and my green card!" "Oh, I'm so sorry to hear that!" I said and felt really sorry for her. But I did not know what to say to comfort her, so I chuckled to hide my embarrassment—in spite of myself. "What's funny?" Recognizing the change in her voice, I realized I had failed to transmit the correct information to her. I lost no time to explain, "Sorry, Eve. In China, we laugh or smile when we feel sympathetic. Very often, the person caught in a helpless situation would also laugh or make a joke to ease the embarrassment." Eve's response was, "Thank you for explaining the difference to me." I know it is hard for a Westerner to accept such a smile in such a context. She would interpret a laugh or a smile in such a setting as a sign of either insensitivity or worse—pleasure that the victim had lost her purse because she was disliked. Later I was told that a typical Western response on this occasion would have been to look at her sympathetically without any smile at all and listen to her.

As is mentioned above, a smile can be misinterpreted, especially when it involves people from different cultures. One day Will Smith went into a Chinese restaurant in New York. "A roast meat wanton soup, please. Will it be long?" asked Will. Li Xiao, a waiter, answered with a smile on his face, "No. It will take only two or three minutes, sir." Will sat down and looked around him. It was a very clean restaurant and there were already many diners.

Three minutes passed, then five minutes. Will got impatient. Noticing Will's impatience, Li Xiao promised him smilingly, "It won't be long. It won't be long." Will waited for another five minutes. When Li Xiao finally put the soup on the table, Will was already very hungry. Li Xiao was very sorry about what had happened and smiled before he spoke, "I'm really sorry to keep you waiting for so long, sir. And I want you to know it will never happen again." As he said, he looked at Will with the smile he had been wearing since Will stepped into the restaurant.

Will stared at Li Xiao and said, "Are you sure you are sorry? You don't look sorry at all!"

Li Xiao's smile was frozen on his face: He never expected Will to take his apology so negatively! He became desperate and tried harder to make himself understood. "Sir," he managed to smile again, "Trust me. I really feel terribly sorry about it."

Will unhappily said, "If you're really terribly sorry, how can you smile?"

To Li Xiao, the smile is an important part of the apology since it indicates respect and embarrassment in China. However, it is very hard for Will Smith to believe that smiles can be used as a sign of respect and apology. A Westerner might be expected to look at his listener in the eye and definitely not to smile when apologizing. In this case, different perspectives to a smile made things worse.

3. Smiling—a Good Policy

Though different perspectives to a smile may cause misunderstandings and communication breakdowns, people are encouraged to smile more in all cultures. As the saying goes, "None will hit a smiler in the face." All the courtroom judges, Chinese and Western, are equally likely to find smilers and non-smilers guilty, but they give smilers lighter penalties, a phenomenon called the "smile-leniency effect". And scientists have found that smiling, real or false, can trick the body into feeling better.

Smiling—is it a good policy? Of course it is. Smile more, then. Smile to the world and it will smile back.

II Nods

Different cultures assign different meanings to the silent body language—nodding.

1. Nods in the Intercultural Communication

a. Western Nodding

In the Western concept, a nod of the head is a gesture used to indicate agreement, acceptance or acknowledgment.

"Nod" or "nodding" can also be used as a slang term to describe the physiological side effect related to consuming heroin or other opiates.

b. Chinese Nodding

In China, nodding doesn't necessarily mean agreement, acceptance or acknowledgment. Of course it doesn't really mean disagreement. Sometimes it is an indication of listening, attention, politeness, or nothing but a "habitual movement" (Yi Zhongtian). Therefore, sometimes Chinese nodding is very difficult for foreigners to interpret.

2. Nodding Is Not Universal

Nodding, as a silent language, means agreement, acceptance and recognition in both Chinese and Western culture. However, nodding in China, does not always carry the same meaning as Westerners assume. For instance, sometimes Chinese nodding simply suggests that the listener is listening. Polite Chinese people (except close friends or lovers) seldom have eye contacts when talking to each other. Therefore, to keep the conversation going, nodding serves as an indicator that "I'm listening". This difference has caused many misunderstandings. Here is a selection from one of my students' journal:

Our international teacher Will Block has been in China for at least seven years. We felt he is more Chinese than some of the natives until one day last year. Before class that day, he came with two friends from the States and asked whether some of us could take them to a bar not far from the campus after class. Silence. Then, some of us nodded. Happily, Will started the class, thinking some of us would surely do this since we nodded. To his great disappointment, he watched us leave the classroom one by one after class as usual, leaving two guests waiting there. Nobody went up. Even nobody said sorry or goodbye. We just left, as if we hadn't heard Will's request in the first place. This was a real embarrassment for him. He didn't know how to explain to his friends, who were warmly welcomed by his students a moment ago. How could this ever happen? Who was to blame?

And here is another story:

One day, a Swede went to China on business. He hired a car and a Chinese driver. When he told his driver to take him to his hotel, the Chinese nodded at once. The Swede was very happy that he was understood so soon. So he closed his eyes and waited for the car to move. But to his surprise the car didn't move. He opened his eyes, asked why before giving more detailed directions and got many other nods from his driver. This time he was confused because the driver seemed have no intension to drive. He became angry and shouted: "Why do you nod to me and refuse to drive me to my hotel at once?" The driver nodded and answered, "Yes, yes, sir! But where are you going?" The Swede was too surprised to say a word.

Because of lack of enough knowledge about nodding or because of inadequate preparation for the differences, some Westerners find nodding doesn't always talk to them explicitly when they are in China.

III Silence

Silence refers to the absence of speech, but it is widely believed that a silence not only screams but also kills sometimes.

1. Silence in the Intercultural Communication

Silence can be used in different situations.

a. Silence in Physiology

Physiologically, silence means hesitation, stutters, self-correction or the deliberate slowing of speech for the purpose of clarification or processing of ideas. These silences are short.

b. Silence in Debate

Silence in debate is the rhetorical practice of saying nothing when an opponent would expect something to be said. Poorly executed, it can be very offensive, like refusing to answer a direct question. However, well-timed silence can completely throw an opponent and give the debater the upper hand.

c. Silence in a Family Conflict

Silence can mean anger, hostility, disinterest, or any number of other emotions.

The scene is a small bathroom and the time is early morning before going to work. The husband is shaving and the wife enters to blow dry her hair.

Wife: Am I disturbing you?

Husband: (silence)

Wife: (silence, walks out)

A family conflict is taking place. Driven by the principle of politeness, the husband uses silence which is self-evident to his wife, and the wife's silence not only strengthens the message sent by her husband through silence and adds another piece of information, "Ok, I'll come back when you're done."

d. Silence in Law

The right to silence is a legal protection enjoyed by people undergoing police interrogation or trial in certain countries. The law is either explicit or recognized in many legal systems.

e. Silence in Spirituality

A silent mind, freed from the onslaught of thoughts and thought patterns, is both a goal and an important step in spiritual development. Inner silence is understood to bring one in contact with the divine, the natural, and the ultimate reality of this moment. All religious traditions imply the importance of being quiet and still in mind and spirit for transformative and integral spiritual growth to occur. In Christianity, there is the silence of contemplative prayer such as centering prayer and Christian meditation. In Buddhism, allowing the mind to become silent is implied as a feature of enlightenment.

f. Commemorative Silence

A common way to remember a tragic accident and the victims or casualties of such an event is a commemorative silence. This usually means one or more minutes of silence, in which one is supposed not to speak, but remember and reflect on the event instead. A commemorative silence may be held at a workplace, a school or similar institutions. Sometimes a government will advertise a commemorative silence for a specific period at a specific time, which everybody is encouraged(but not forced) to honor. For instance, the Chinese government announced three minutes of silence in respect of the victims of the Yushu Earthquake on April 14, 2010.

g. Silence in Collective Decision-making

As is known to us, silence is employed to create suspense in public speaking and story-telling. But few have noticed the use of silence in collective decision-making. And the chairperson tends to assume that silence as "yes" and happily fall into the "assumed yes" trap. Actually silence on this occasion might mean(especially in China): *I'm still thinking about it. / I may agree but am not sure yet. / Yes, I agree. / No, I don't agree but I'm not going to say it out loud here. / No, I don't agree but I'll never admit to it.*

2. Differences Between Chinese and Western Silence

a. Western Silence

People from Western culture will feel uneasy when one party falls silent and usually try their best to fill up the silence with small talk. According to cultural norms, silence can be interpreted as positive or negative. For example, in a Christian Methodist faith organization silence and reflection during the sermons might be appreciated by the congregation while in a Southern Baptist church, silence might mean disagreement with what is being taught or perhaps disconnectedness from the congregated community. Therefore, sometimes it is difficult to interpret the message being sent by a person who is silent (i.e. not speaking). It could mean negative emotions.

Besides, famous Western scholars such as Sigmund Freud (1856—1939) interpreted silence as a resistance. Consequently, silence in an argument is sometimes regarded as "passive aggression"— making the other person look bad by pretending to be mild-mannered or even not interested.

"Silence gives consent", so runs an ancient maxim of common law. From this maxim flows a widely applied legal principle: the rule of tacit admission. Based on the theory that an innocent man would loudly deny a serious charge, the rule holds that a suspect silent in the face of an accusation has tacitly admitted the crime. And such silence can later be introduced at his trial as an indicator of guilt. So Westerners (especially North Americans) cannot stand silence. As soon as silence falls in, they will try to break it up, thus appearing to be very noisy and aggressive to some Chinese.

b. Chinese Silence

On the contrary, Chinese choose to be silent on many occasions such as when a sensitive subject is broached, when we feel embarrassed, when we know we are wrong, when the other party is very angry, when we don't know what to say and how to say, and when somebody is speaking. Reasons for silence are summarized as follows:

First, we choose to be silent in an argument so that we will maintain face and avoid losing it. Once both parties become more reasonable, face that can be translated to mean "dignity, prestige or reputation" can be saved. On the other hand, we hope our silence can shut up the other party. When trying to talk those involved out of an argument, Chinese pacifiers are used to quoting the saying, "If each of you says one thing less, there's nothing to argue about."

Besides, Chinese regard silence as a respect for the speaker, which is revealed in Confucius' comment on his disciple Yan Hui's silence, "I can talk with Hui for a whole day without him making any comment on anything I said—as if he were stupid. When he retires, I examine his conduct, and find him able to illustrate my teachings. Hui is not stupid."(Book 2: 9)

Thirdly, silence is a means of learning, which is highly valued by parents and teachers.

Fourthly, silence is a symbol of good cultivation and wisdom. In China people believe what Lao Zi says, "He who knows does not speak; he who speaks does not know(知者不言,言者不知)."

3. Misunderstood Silence

a. Misunderstood Silence in a Family Conflict

Michael White, a British businessman, and Li Meimei, a retired woman worker, have been married for very nearly three and a half years. For the first two years, they were very happy and it is only this last 18 months that there have been problems. This is when Jenny (Meimei's only daughter who works and lives in Shanghai) began to mention about Mama and Dad looking after her baby when she had one. Michael made it known that he would not live in a house with a baby. He had done that with Jennifer (his first wife) for 40 years with their four children back in England, enjoyed every minute of that time, but would not repeat it again. Meimei agreed with him and they gave Jenny some money to employ a babysitter. But since Jenny finally had a baby boy in March, Meimei has been spending most of her time babysitting in Shanghai. One day Michael couldn't help rushing to Shanghai and reminded Meimei of their agreement. Meimei said she would not go back until the baby is able to toddle around. However, Michael urged Meimei to go back with him to Nanjing leaving

Jenny some money as they had agreed, but Meimei insisted she should spend another year babysitting before going back when the baby is older and stronger.

The argument soon became tense, and Meimei fell silent. She simply refused to respond to Michael's angry words. The silence made Michael more and more upset—so much so that he shouted at the top of his voice at Meimei and finally banged the door closed and left for the railway station in great anger.

You may wonder why Michael didn't shut up in spite of the fact that Meimei voluntarily gave in by saying no more in the argument. For Chinese, Meimei stopped saying anything in the argument, which means she knew she was wrong. Usually, when a Chinese person chooses to be silent in an argument, it would mean the person feels guilty or the person wants to stop the argument by not talking any more out of good intention, or both. The latter often means tolerance as one intends to keep a harmonious relationship with the other. Meimei shut up, hoping that her silence could stop Michael, for she knows (according to her experience in China) if she says one thing less, there's nothing to argue about. In this sense, Meimei was actually taking the initiative to yield.

However, Michael assumed according to his experience in England that Meimei's silence was "passive aggression"— not yielding at all! As a result, they are talking about divorce now.

b. Misunderstood Silence in Class

"Raise your hands if you agree!" Dr. William N. Brown begs his Chinese graduate students.

No response.

"Then raise your hands if you disagree!"

Still nothing.

"How about raising your hands if you're awake?"

Some glance about awkwardly, but none dare raise their hands, or break the silent vigil they've kept since primary school (*The World of English*, 1996,10:44).

Dr. William N. Brown is uncomfortable. In his culture, silence can be puzzling. If people disagree with what you are saying, many of them will remain quiet. Silence may not suggest agreement; often it only means that they consider it impolite to argue further. On the contrary, Chinese choose to be silent on many occasions like when we want to show respect to the speaker and when we are having a class. Unfortunately, Dr. Brown doesn't understand his Chinese students and goes on to make further requests, which could only make himself more and more upset and his students more and more awkward.

Further Reading

1. Bull, P. (1983). *Body Movement and Interpersonal Communication.* New York: Wiley.

2. Hall, E. T. (1959). *The Silent Language.* New York: Doubleday & Company.

3. Hall, E. T. (1966). *The Hidden Dimension.* New York: Doubleday & Company.

4. Hall, E. T. (1976). *Beyond Culture.* New York: Doubleday & Company.

5. (2004). *Face-to-face Communications for Clarity and Impact.* Boston, MA: Harvard Business School Press.

6. 胡文仲 (2000):《跨文化交际学概论》,北京:外语教学与研究出版社。

7. 饶尚宽译注 (2006):《老子》,北京:中华书局。

8. 杨伯峻译注 (2006):《论语》,北京:中华书局。

9. 易中天(2006):《闲话中国人》,上海:上海文艺出版社。

Part III

Cultural Differences in Thinking

"We are thinking animals." (American Heritage Dictionary) Thinking is a mental form and process, which allows us to model the world and deal with it according to our objectives, plans, ends, and desires. It proceeds in various forms and structures—concepts, statements, categories, inferences, hypotheses, theories, etc., which record and generalize the socio-historical experience of mankind.

Instruments of thinking are language and other sign systems such as the abstract symbols of Mathematics or the concrete images of art. The elements of these systems support such basic operations of thinking as abstraction, generalization and mediation. Abstraction enables us to ignore an object's inessential properties and relations and concentrate on those that are relevant to the intellectual task in question. Generalization enables us to classify large numbers of phenomena according to certain essential attributes. Meditation enables us to reach a good outcome, which is within our control.

As thinking animals, our reasoning, visions of the world, categorizing and attitude towards life are subject to thinking. Here five dimensions of thinking are to be elaborated on in this part. They are:

- *Intuitive vs. logical thinking*
- *Dialectical vs. analytical reasoning*
- *Holistic vs. atomistic visions*
- *Categorizing objects by relationships vs. by attributes*
- *Non-controllers vs. controllers*

Unit 7   Intuitive vs. Logical Thinking

According to some Anglo-American observers, the Germans even drank and danced on Sundays. The Germans, however, would have it no other way, Sunday or any day of the week. "Now I began to feel rather proud of my success and my achievement," wrote Max Krueger, "and it was my intuition to attempt to transplant German cordiality and sociality in this foreign land. To this end I built a dance pavilion and bowling alley. The beer necessary for such occasions was imported from St. Louis." Later Sundays became days of relaxation in parks and beer gardens.

—Glen E. Lich

For discussion: Make a brief comment on Max Krueger's "intuition" by incorporating your own experience.

The Chinese hate the phrase "logical necessity" because there is no logical necessity in human affairs.

—Lin Yutang

How do we Chinese arrange human affairs, if not in a logical way?

Problem solving without creative thinking is a garden without seeds.

—Anonymous

What does creative thinking mean to you?

I   Definitions of Intuitive and Logical Thinking

Thinking is a way of reasoning or judgment, and it has a particular form, variety, or manner, known as thinking mode. Two thinking modes are to be discussed in this unit: One is intuitive and the other logical.

Intuitive thinking is considered to be creative and constructive right-brain thinking, whereas logical thinking is believed to be analytical and objective left-brain thinking.

Normally intuitive thinking is unfocused and nonlinear. It sees many things at once and views the big picture. Usually intuition comes into its own in conditions like time pressure, dynamic conditions, and unclear differentiation between the observer and the observed. It works best where the observer has experience in a particular situation. It is difficult to teach intuition in the classroom.

In contrast, logical thinking is focused, linear, and dealing with one thing at a time. It contains time, and tends to the abstract. This thinking mode is efficient in conditions like adequate time, relatively static conditions, and a clear differentiation between the observer and the observed. It is best suited for dealing with complexities, and works best where there are established criteria for analysis. Logical thinking is necessary when an explanation is required. It can be taught in the classroom.

The traditional Chinese is oriented to think intuitively, whereas the Westerner is inclined to think logically.

II Philosophy and Thinking

It is widely believed that traditional Chinese society is intuition-based in its way of thinking while Western society is logic-based. The difference is believed by many to be attributed to philosophy which comes from human life and in turn guides human life.

1. Traditional Chinese Philosophy and Intuitive Thinking

It should be noted here that logic did exist in traditional Chinese philosophy, for instance the Logician (名家) and Moist (墨家) doctrines of the pre-Qin period, but priority has been given to intuitive thinking.

a. Mencius' Theory on Intuition

Mencius, as one of the most frequently quoted philosophers in China, has a bearing on Chinese intuitive thinking. It is known to many that Mencius is very emphatic on the nature of right and wrong. For him, the nature is self-evident, which characterizes his intuitive thinking, as revealed in the paragraph below:

"I like fish and I also like bear's paws. If I cannot have the two together, I will let the fish go, and take the bear's paws. So, I like life and I also like righteousness. If I cannot keep the two together, I will let life go and choose righteousness (鱼，我所欲也，熊掌，亦我所欲也；二者不可得兼，舍鱼而取熊掌者也。生，亦我所欲也，义，亦我所欲也；二者不可得兼，舍生而取义者也)."

In this sense righteousness or morality is self-evident to man, and man should take care not to lose it. Then Mencius gives an example to prove that a man cannot but intuitively choose what is right:

"Here are a small basket of rice and a bowl of soup, and the case is one in which the getting of them will preserve life and the want of them will bring death; if they are offered with an insulting voice, even a tramp will not receive them, or, if you first tread upon them, even a beggar will not stoop to them (一箪食，一豆羹，得之则生，弗得则死，呼尔而与之，行道之人弗受；蹴尔而与之，乞人不屑也)."

Mencius' intuitive theory is based on several factors: human dispositions, common approval, and decisions made during the course of one's life. This intuition, therefore, is not identical with immediate insight, though the latter is clearly a part of the whole process. Meanwhile Mencius' theory of intuition tells us that the ability possessed by men without having been acquired by learning is intuitive ability, and the knowledge possessed by them without the exercise of thought is intuitive knowledge.

Many years after Mencius' death, the Neo-Confucian school in the Song and Ming dynasties put forward the theory of "intuition as substrate and wisdom as function (直觉为体，理智为用)" to reflect a sense of intuitively emphasizing life, nature, and experience.

b. Buddhist Emphasis on Intuition

Buddhism attaches an exclusive importance to meditation, a means of transforming the mind. Patriarchal Meditation (祖师禅), as taught by the Patriarch Bodhidharma (菩提达摩祖师), requires no intellectual effort, but direct intuition of the Buddha-mind. The result of this meditation is enlightenment which may come suddenly or gradually. In other words, this major tradition has been "sudden enlightenment preceding gradual cultivation". No any other school of Buddhism, like Chan (禅宗), put aside scriptural studies or philosophical discussion in favor of a purely intuitive approach to enlightenment. It is because of this distaste for book-learning, Chan is known as the doctrine "not founded on words or scriptures (不立文字)." Therefore, its teaching is "transmitted from mind to mind (以心传心)," that is, directly from one master to his disciple on a one-to-one basis, without the intervention of rational and logical argumentation.

c. Limitations of Intuitive Thinking

Intuition, as a type of thinking mode, has its limitations. It can only be applied to human affairs and actions; it cannot be applied to the solution of the riddles of the universe; nor can it be employed to make a discovery systematic, scientific and thus widely promoted. For example, most people believe that the circulation of the blood in the body was discovered by the English physician William Harvey (1578—1657) and hold that it is he who first brought the idea to the attention of the world when he published his discovery in 1628. Harvey was, however, not the first one to recognize the concept, and ancient Chinese had made the discovery 2000 years before. But why is Harvey remembered as the first to discover the circulation of the blood? Because ancient Chinese with the intuitive thinking mode took many things granted, believing it is unnecessary to explain a discovery or invention in steps since it is self-evident and everyone knows it by intuition.

2. Western Philosophy and Logical Thinking

It should be noted that intuition does exist in Western philosophy, but logical thinking has been given priority by Western philosophers.

a. Aristotle's Logic

Aristotle's logic has had an unparalleled influence on the history of Western thought, especially his theory of the "Barbara" syllogism:

If A is predicated of all B, and B is predicated of all C, then A is predicated of all C.

By predicated, Aristotle means A belongs to B, or all B's are A's. We can substitute subjects and predicates in this syllogism to get:

If all mammals (B's) are warm-blooded animals (A), and all rabbits (C's) are mammals (B's), then all rabbits (C's) are warm-blooded animals (A).

b. Francis Bacon's Inductive Method

Francis Bacon (1561—1626), an English philosopher, statesman and essayist, is best known as a philosophical advocate and defender of the scientific revolution. His works established and popularized an inductive methodology for scientific inquiry. The so-called inductive method is a process of using observations to develop general principles about a specific subject. A group of similar specimens, events or subjects are first observed and studied; findings from the observation are then used to make broad statements about the subjects under examination. These statements may then become laws of nature or theories frequently used in the logical thinking process.

c. John Stuart Mill

The British philosopher John S. Mill (1806—1873) was committed to the idea that the best methods of explaining the world are those employed by the natural sciences. He focused on four different methods of experimental inquiry that attempt to single out from the circumstances that precede or follow a phenomenon the ones that are linked to the phenomenon by an invariable law. The four methods of induction—the methods of agreement, of difference, of residues, and of concomitant variation(契合法、差异法、剩余法和共变法)—provide answers to questions by showing what we need to demonstrate in order to claim that a causal law holds, and therefore makes it useful in scientific discovery and invention. In this way John S. Mill further promoted the application of logical thinking.

III Application of Two Thinking Modes

1. Intuitive Thinking in China

a. Popularity of Intuitive Aphoristic Sayings

In a number of countries such as China and UK, the ability to spontaneously produce aphoristic sayings at the right moment is a key determinant of social status. Many societies have traditional sages or respected heroes to whom aphorisms are commonly attributed, such as Confucius, the Seven Sages of Greece, or King Solomon. The biggest difference between Chinese and Western aphorisms is that images are more often used in Chinese aphoristic sayings because we are used to thinking intuitively in terms of pictures. For instance, many years ago Confucius lamented the decaying morality by eulogizing the pines and cypresses, gentlemen among trees, and said, "Only when it gets cold can we see that the leaves of pines and cypresses are the last to wither and fall(岁寒,然后知松柏之后凋也)." This intuitive way used to clarify his position can also be found in his famous remark, "Tyrannical rule is more ferocious than a tiger(苛政猛于虎)", which vividly explains why it is necessary to set up a humane government.

Emperor Taizong of the Tang Dynasty greatly missed Wei Zheng, his faithful adviser, after the latter died. He stated, "Using copper as a mirror allows one to keep his clothes neat. Using history as a mirror allows one to see the future trends. Using a person as a mirror allows one to see what is right and what is wrong. When Wei Zheng died, I lost a mirror." The emperor explicitly illustrated the importance of Wei Zheng by using the image of a mirror.

Highly intuitive aphorisms are often quoted by ordinary Chinese people, educated or uneducated, because they correspond to our thinking habit and are easily accessible. For instance, to sing in praise of the collective power, we quote, "One swallow does not make a spring (一只燕子不是春)." To explain how we form a holistic view of something we say, "One fallen leaf shows it is autumn (一叶知秋)." These sayings reflect an intuitive perspective very different from the Western one which is mainly logical, e.g. *You cannot step twice into the same river because the man is different and the river is different, He is a fool who cannot be angry, but he is really a wise man who will not.* Of course, we can also find some Western sayings very intuitive like *If you see the teeth of the lion, do not think that the lion is smiling at you.*

b. Faith in the Power of Intuition

Having a faith in the power of their "intuition", ancient Chinese men of letters went about explaining the mysteries of the human body and the universe. The whole science of Chinese medicine and physiology was based on the intuitive Taoist philosophy of the Five Agents or Elements (*wu xing*)—metal, wood, water, fire and earth. For them the human body is in itself a symbol of the universe in its composition. The kidneys represent the water, the stomach represents the earth, the liver represents the fire, the lungs represent the metal, and the heart represents the wood. A man suffering from high blood pressure is considered to have too warm a "liver fire", while a man suffering from indigestion may be referred to as having too much earth.

The faith in their intuition led Chinese literary critics to have summarized efficient methods of writing such as *detachment of style* (超脱的艺术风格), *lightness of touch* (轻松的笔触), and *bring out the salient point* (重点突出). Meanwhile these methods also have their respective equivalent expressions which are rather intuitive, easy to remember and thus more popular with Chinese exposed to the intuitive thinking committed to images, e.g. *the method of watching a fire across the river* (隔岸观火), *the method of dragonflies skimming across the water surface* (蜻蜓点水), and *the method of painting a dragon and dotting its eyes* (画龙点睛).

Unchecked by scientific imagination, intuition has a lot of free room and often borders on a naive imagination according to Lin Yutang. Some kinds of traditional Chinese medicine popular among ordinary people are based on some fantastic association. The toad that has a wrinkled skin is used in the cure of human skin trouble, and there is a popular belief that a schoolboy should not eat chicken's claws lest he should develop the habit of scratching his book, walls, and desks.

c. Intuition and Chinese Verbs

It is believed that logical thinking is denoted by nouns and intuition, on the other hand, intuitive thinking mainly involves verbs. There are more verbs in a Chinese sentence. Verbs tend to come either at the beginning, in the middle or at the end of sentences, and all are in more salient locations than in English where verbs are more commonly buried in the middle, e.g. *My work, my family and my friends are more than enough to fill in my time.* Its Chinese version is 我必须工作,料理家务,结交朋友,忙得不可开交. In the original there is only one verb, but in its Chinese version there are three. More nouns in English and more verbs in Chinese influence our way to relate to the world.

d. Intuitive Belief in the Power of Words

Our belief in the power of words is surprisingly great. This intuitive belief may be traced down in all aspects of life. For instance, motives for traditional Chinese artistic works such as the bat and the deer are popular because the word "bat(*fu*)" is a homophone for "luck" or "happiness" and the word "deer(*lu*)" is a homophone for "official power". Other words are evidently taken quite seriously, too. A couple will look troubled when presented with a clock (*zhong*) which suggests the end of the marriage since "clock" is a homophone for "end (*zhong*)". They won't like books as presents because "giving books (*song shu*)" sounds like "delivering defeat" in Chinese. And good-mannered people will not give their friends an umbrella because doing so implies that the family of the gift receiver is going to be dispersed. Many of us do not quite know whether it is true or not, but "people say", and we are not interested in conducting a survey to verify it or use the logic to think about it.

e. Traditional Education

"The aim of the Chinese classical education has always been the cultivation of the reasonable man as the model of culture. An educated man should, above all, be a reasonable being, who is always characterized by his common sense, his love of moderation and restraint, and his hatred of abstract theories and logical extremes."(Lin Yutang) This explains why studying by memorizing as many facts, concepts and ideas as possible is considered more important at school than studying by analyzing, debating, and discussing. Scholars exposed to traditional education, without focusing their attention on logic and analysis, are more likely to live on intuition, which to some extent hinders the development of Chinese science and technology. Consider the paragraph quoted from the *Torrent Trilogy* by famous writer Ba Jin (1904—2005): "Some say that there is at first no road at all and that a road is created simply by the treading of passers-by. Others say that there is at first already a road available before more and more people come to walk on it. I don't want to judge who are right or who are wrong. I am still young. I want to live on. I want to conquer life. I know the torrent of life will never stop. Let's see where it is going to carry me!" This paragraph displays how Ba Jin allowed himself to be driven by the torrent of life, intuitively maintaining that the torrent was equal to the power of positive thinking.

2. Logic Thinking in the West

a. English Grammar and Logical Thinking

To native English speakers, whatever your goals are, a grasp of English grammar—a description of logic and logical thinking process, is necessary if you want to improve your speaking and writing skills. Grammar courses can help you gain confidence in your ability to produce work of clarity and logic. Since English grammar has clearly defined rules, studying grammar encourages logical thinking.

But for Chinese speakers, grammar is less important, so contextual and pragmatic cues can be the only kinds of cues the hearer or reader has to depend on. Chinese sentences thus do not stress the form, clarity or tense. They can be incomplete, and parts of speech are flexibly used, and their meaning can be solely expressed by words without caring about the logic or grammar, for example, 头发掉了一些 (literally, hair lost some; freely, you have lost some hairs) and 白菜买了一大包 (literally, cabbages bought a big bag; freely, I have bought a big bag of cabbages) have no actors; 中国队大胜日本队(literally, the Chinese team greatly won the Japanese team) and 中国队大败日本队(literally, the Chinese team greatly defeated the Japanese team)have actually the same meaning—the Chinese team was the winner. In the absence of a restrictive linguistic logic, the Chinese writer or speaker feels free to express himself or herself.

b. Popularity of Logic

"Logic" is one of the Westerner's favorite singular words, e.g. *Still don't get the logic of "she's pretty but not beautiful", You need a lot of work on your logic, and I don't see any logic in this.*

The popularity of the detective stories also reveals Western love of logic. Take for instance Sherlock Holmes, the famous fictional detective of the late nineteenth and early twentieth centuries. As a brilliant London-based consulting detective, Holmes is famous for his intellectual prowess and is renowned for his skillful use of "logical reasoning". As a matter of fact he was so loved by readers that when his creator, Sir Arthur Conan Doyle, planned to let him die, the poor Scottish author and physician received threatening letters from his readers and was compelled to give up that decision.

Apart from detective stories, games involving logical thinking skills such as brain teasers, math stumpers and puzzles are also popular in the West.

IV   Impact of Thinking Modes on Writings

1. Impact of Intuitive Thinking on Chinese Writings

When we write we are apt to save the best for the last, intuitively starting from big to small, from far to near, from whole to part, from causes to effect—a way of climax. So to speak, we tend to give the background, then reasons to get the readers' or listeners' sympathy, understanding, and attention (i.e. cause-effect sequence). Usually Chinese textual structures are: *Because A, and because B, and because C, thereforeso.../If..., then.../Although..., but....* For instance, the introduction of a bilingual book begins this way: "老人家走的路多, 吃的饭多, 看的书多, 经的事多, 享的福多, 受的罪多, 可谓见多识广, 有丰富的经验, 老人家说的话多是经验之谈, 后生小子不可不听也." Obviously the structure is in the sequence of cause-effect. Its English translation below retains the original writing sequence:

"Old men, who walk more roads, eat more rice, read more books, have more experiences, enjoy more happiness, and endure more sufferings, are experienced and knowledgeable, with rich life experience. Thus, what they say is mostly wise counsel, and young people should listen to them."

Some of my American students reported they felt a little bit confused when they read the beginning lines of the above English version. They didn't understand what it is about until they came to the end of the introduction—because the thinking thread runs counter to their thinking mode which is usually anticlimax in the sequence of effect-cause.

2. Impact of the Two Thinking Modes on Western Writings

a. Impact of Logic Thinking

Westerners usually start straight with the main point by putting the most important at the beginning to get the readers' or listeners' attention and consideration—a way of anticlimax, which means you are supposed to say what you want to say, then say why. They tend to put effect at the beginning, then reasons (i.e. effect-cause sequence). In a paragraph they usually start with a topic sentence, and then continue to handle the topic views. Here is an example of an English paragraph that displays the impact of logic thinking:

"Frame your position so that it appeals strongly to the people you want to persuade. You can do this by knowing what they are thinking and what their concerns are. This requires not being so intent on getting your own message out that you fail to listen to what is being said."(Betty A. Marton)

Some Chinese readers who know nothing about Western thinking would feel confused when they read the beginning line that the author is intentionally creating an eye-catching effect and thus is in need of sincerity.

b. Impact of Intuitive Thinking

Intuitive thinking, though less used by Westerners, is more often employed in their literary works. Now let us make a comparison of the following English original and its two Chinese versions:

Vast lawns that extend like sheets of vivid green, with here and there clumps of gigantic trees, heaping up with rich piles of foliage.

Version 1: 草地宽阔, 好像地上铺了鲜艳的绿绒似的毡毯, 巨大树株, 聚成一簇, 绿叶浓密, 一眼望去, 草地上东一簇, 西一簇, 这类的大树可不少。

Version 2: 宽阔的草坪宛如翠绿的地毯, 成片的参天大树点缀其间, 绿叶浓密,层层叠叠。

The English original begins intuitively from far to near, from big to small, from whole to part and hence paints a well-organized beautiful word painting. But in Version 1, neither of the two creative thinking— the intuitive thinking and the logical thinking are harnessed, which explains why this version appears disorderly and confusing, just as the saying goes, "Problem solving without creative thinking is a garden without seeds." In Version 2, the translator keeps the intuitive thinking mode of the original by creatively rendering the original into Chinese and allows the Chinese reader to move his eyes comfortably from far to near and from whole to part.

V Logic in China and Intuition in the West

"The most striking difference between the traditions at the two ends of the civilized world is in the destiny of logic. For the West, logic has been central and the thread of transmission has never snapped..."(Angus Graham) But logic has a different destiny in China.

1. Destiny of Logic in Ancient China and Greece

a. Early Death of Logic in Ancient China

In China there are only two short-lived movements of little influence that share the spirit of logical inquiry that has always been common in the West. They were started by the Logicians and the Moists. The Logicians in fact made little progress toward a formal logic, though they were interested in knowledge for its own sake. The Moist tradition embraced several logical concerns, chief among them the ideas of necessary and sufficient conditions and the principle of non-contradiction. Their evangelistic approach and readiness to discuss or debate with anyone may explain why the Moist canon the *Mozi* is so much concerned with logic and dialectics. In the portions believed to represent Mo Zi's teaching there is a laborious, almost painful attention to step-by-step argumentation, but Mo Zi never formalized his system and logic died an early death in China. Except for that brief interlude, traditional China lacked logic.

b. Popularity of Debate and Rise of Logic in Ancient Greece

The best explanation for the Greeks' concern with logic is that they saw its usefulness in argumentation or debate. The Greek had a tradition of debate. A commoner could challenge even a king and not only live to tell the tale, but occasionally sway an audience to his side. Debates occurred in the marketplace, the political assembly, or even in military settings. Homer made it clear that a man is defined almost as much by his ability to debate as by his bravery as a warrior.

2. Logic and Intuition Today

a. "The Age of Intuition" in Modern Western Countries

Nowadays Western executives no longer scoff at intuitive thinking. Many freely admit that intuition is a key element in the mental processes that lead to conclusions and decisions. In fact, the higher a person rises in an organization, the more intuition he needs for long-range planning. Typically, creative intuitive thinking is strongest at the top and at the bottom.

Today when people are undecided, they are often advised by experts, "Think not, your intuition is better." Toffler, the famous American futurist, even went so far as to coin a term "the Age of Intuition" in his book *The Third Wave*. By that he means the world has entered into a time of using intuition a lot in solving their problems.

b. A Blend of Logic and Intuition in Modern China

Today many scholars may refute the argument that there is a great distinction between the intuitive East and the logical West. Seeing is believing. Western visitors to China will find nowadays' China is blending different cultures from various epochs and nation-states. Modern buildings and ancient shrines are usual neighbors in China. The Western products of logic thinking such as high-rises and electrical appliances are co-existing with those of the intuitive thinking such as calligraphy and traditional Chinese paintings. Meanwhile, it has been widely known in China that intuition is limited where the task is complex and uncertain, where the observer lacks experience, or the observation is distorted by biases. This weakness means a tendency to produce a fixed mindset that ignores new data. Therefore, we are encouraged to use our logical thinking ability a lot. When logical and intuitive abilities are combined, the result is naturally "holistic".

3. A Confusing Public Sign

Culture, capable of exerting influence upon the content and structure of writing, engages in an interactive relationship with language.

A few years ago in a certain big department store dedicated to providing its customers top quality service, some American visitors noticed a sign in both Chinese and English that reads, "残障顾客专用电梯 (Disabled customers must use the elevator)." They were confused about whether that sign means kindness or discrimination.

For us Chinese, of course it means kindness and the sign is a kind reminder to the disabled who prefer the privilege of being able to use the spacious elevator only for the disabled (because the other elevators are often packed with people since China has a big population). To show our hospitality and politeness, concern and warmth, we tend to give seemingly high-handed advice by using sentence patterns like "You must..." e.g. 你一定得尝尝这道菜(literally, you must taste this dish), 感冒了一定要多喝水 (literally, you have a cold so you must drink more water), and 你一定得乘这个电梯试试 (literally, you must use the lift). However, sentences like these appear very aggressive to the Westerner. In Chinese the intuitive implication of hospitality easily dissolves the logical relationship between people and turns the relationship into that of family members or close friends since Chinese culture is family-centered and people-oriented. Therefore, commandments like these imply that *I do care about you. I feel close to you. We are like family,* and *I wish I could be of great help*. And it has been taken for granted that everyone on earth can get the message intuitively, never expecting that Westerners receive and process information in a very different way.

Westerners remind and give advice, too, but they seldom use the word "must" by keeping a logical distance away from the target, for "must" in English is usually used to give commands to which there is no alternative. The use of "must" makes Westerners uncomfortable since they believe in equality and independence. Often, in Western formal or legal documents, the word "shall" is substituted for "must" as it has a less demanding connotation, but implies no alternative.

Further Reading

1. Lich, Glen E. (1996). *The German Texans.* San Antonio, TX: University of Texas at San Antonio Institute of Texan Cultures.

2. Wechsler, Howard J. (1974). *Mirror to the Son of Heaven.* New Haven: Yale University Press.

3. Brislin, Richard W. (1990). *Applied Cross-Cultural Psychology.* London: Sage Publications.

4. Aristotle (1976). *Ethics* (trans By J.A.K. Thomson). London: Penguin Books.

5. Marton, B. A. (2004). "Mastering the Art of Persuasion", *Face-to-face Communications for Clarity and Impact.* Boston, MA: Harvard Business school Press.

6. Toffler, A. (1980, *The Third Wave.* New York: Bantam Books.

7. 刘毅 (2001):《英文谚语辞典》,北京:中国青年出版社。

8. 周云之主编 (2004):《中国逻辑史》,山西:山西教育出版社。

9. 马玉珂主编 (1985):《西方逻辑史》,北京:中国人民大学出版社。

10. 杨伯峻 (2006):《论语译注》,北京:中华书局。

11. 张忠利、宗文举 (2002):《中西文化概论》,天津:天津大学出版社。

13. 蔡希勤 (2005):《老子说》,北京:华语教学出版社。

14. 张培基 (2006):《英译中国现代散文选》,上海:上海外语教育出版社。

Unit 8   Dialectical vs. Analytical Reasoning

Medicine in the West retains the analytical, object–oriented, and interventionist approaches that were common thousands of years ago: Find the offending part or tumor and remove or alter it. Medicine in the East is far more dialectical and has never until modern times been in the least inclined toward surgery or other heroic interventions. Health is the result of a balance of favorable forces in the body; illness is due to a complex interaction of forces that must be met by equally complex, usually natural, mostly herbalist remedies and preventives.

—Anonymous

What reasoning modes are separately used in Traditional Chinese Medicine and Western medicine?

Two tigers sharing one mountain?
Unless one is male, the other female (一山难容二虎,除非一公一母).

—Anonymous

The short message was very popular with Chinese cell phone users during the three-day New Year holiday of 2015. Can this message draw the same attention in the West?

I   Proverb Preferences Across Cultures

Here are two sets of proverbs that appeal to many readers:

1) Sow nothing, reap nothing.

The squeaky wheel gets the grease.

The wealth of the mind is the only true wealth.

2) Haste makes waste.

    Words cut more than swords.

    Your strong points are your weak ones.

Proverbs of group 2 are apparently contradictory: Haste is not equivalent to waste, words cannot cut, and strong points are not equal to weak points. Proverbs of group 1 appear pithy, but none expresses contradiction. Actually proverbs in group 2 are more common in a Chinese compendium of proverbs than in a Western collection, and we Chinese prefer the proverbs with contradictions and Westerners are inclined to like the proverbs without them better. Many scholars ascribe differences in proverb preferences solely to cultural differences in reasoning.

II   Dialectical Reasoning

In Western thought analytical reasoning gains the upper hand while there is a mode of reasoning in Chinese thought, traceable to the ancient times, which has been called dialectical reasoning or synthetic reasoning.

1. Definition of Dialectical Reasoning

Dialectical reasoning means moving back and forth between contrary lines of reasoning, using each to cross-examine the other. This is what juries usually do in arriving at a verdict: Consider arguments and evidence for and against a case, points and counterpoints. It is a process in which opposing facts and ideas are weighed and compared for the purposes of determining the best solution, resolving differences, and coming to the most reasonable conclusion on the basis of the evidence.

Dialectical reasoning focuses on contradictions as well as how to resolve or transcend them, or find the truth in both. It is best applied in resolving controversial issues and assessing opposing positions. Often there are several possible ways of resolving questions and understanding issues rather than one single right answer. This reasoning mode can be used in situations where information is incomplete, where many approaches may compete, and a person has to decide which one is the most reasonable based on what is known even though there is no clear-cut solution.

2. Three Principles of Dialectical Reasoning

a. Principle of Change

Ancient Chinese philosophers emphasized the constantly changing nature of everything. According to them, the world is not static but dynamic and changeable. "Constant reversal is the movement of the Tao (Dao or Way), and being weak is the function of the Tao. All things under Heaven come into being from visible concrete beings, and all beings come into being from the invisible Tao(反者道之动。弱者道之用。天下万物生于有,有生于无)."(Lao Zi) Since everything is in constant flux the concepts are fluid and subjective rather than being fixed and objective. So it is believed that "When the people of the world all know beauty as beauty, there arises the recognition of ugliness; when they all know the good as good, there arises the recognition of evil. And so, being and non-being produce each other(天下皆知美之为美,斯恶已;皆知善之为善,斯不善已。有无相生)."(Lao Zi)

Like our predecessors, we have the same faith in the principle of change and assume that things are constantly changing, and movement in a particular direction may be a sign that events are about to reverse direction, for instance, poverty is regarded as a sign that one is to enjoy a happy life in the future, as the idiom goes, "苦尽甘来(literally, bitterness means sweetness is around the corner; freely, happy life is the result of hard work)."

b. Principle of Contradiction

Because the world is in constant change, oppositions, paradoxes, and anomalies are continuously being created. Therefore, new and old, strong and weak, good and bad, exist in everything; opposites complete each other; the two sides of any apparent contradiction exist in an active harmony, opposed but connected and mutually controlling.

Take *xu* and *shi* for instance. *Xu* and *shi* are two concepts commonly used in Chinese philosophy and everyday life. *Shi* roughly corresponds with *solid, complete, tangible,* and *exact*, whereas *xu* is roughly equivalent to *illusory, sketchy, intangible,* and *obscure*. *Xu* and *shi* are contradictory and complementary elements which form a dialectical unity. The organization of Chinese sentences is mostly a blend of *xu* and *shi* since Chinese grammar lays stress on meaning perception, which makes it possible and essential to use as few words as possible in sentence construction, e.g. (literally, she has a cousin; [he] lives in Nanjing; [we] have called him, and [he] will be here in an hour). Although this sentence has *xu* instead of *shi* subjects, the meaning is clear. If we put those *xu* subjects back into the sentence (她有个表兄，他住在南京，我们已经打过电话了，他一小时后到达), then the sentence with all its *shi* subjects and predicates will look and sound very clumsy, because it does not correspond with the habitual way of expression. The emphasis on the combination of *xu* and *shi* is not only a characteristic of the Chinese language, but also shown in the traditional painting, architecture, opera, etc. The principle employed in these activities is known as the principle of contradiction.

c. Principle of Relationship

Chinese reasoning is also based on the principle of relationship. The strong belief in change and oppositions has led us to view the world in a holistic way: We see a great deal of background events; we are good at observing relationships between events; we regard the world as complex and highly changeable and its components as interrelated; we see events as moving in cycles between extremes; we feel that control over events requires coordination with others. In one word, we see the big environment as well as objects in relation to their environments so much so that it is difficult for us to visually isolate objects from their environments, and the principle we follow is that of relationship.

d. Relationship Between the Three Principles

The three principles of dialectical reasoning are interrelated. Change produces contradiction and contradiction causes change; constant change and contradiction imply that it is meaningless to discuss the individual part without considering its relationship with other parts and its past states. The principles also imply another important tenet of Chinese thought, which is the insistence on finding the Middle Way between extreme propositions. In China there is a strong presumption that contradictions are apparent and that "A is wrong and B is not right either." This stance is explicitly revealed in the Chan Buddhist dictum that "the opposite of a great truth is also true."

3. Impact of Dialectical Reasoning on Writings

How does dialectical reasoning influence Chinese writings? For further exploration, it is necessary to consider typical steps to write an article in Chinese. Let's take for instance an essay written by famous Chinese author Yu Dafu.

Step 1: Introduction

We are supposed to begin the essay with one of the three options: Make an introduction to the purpose or context for the article; elaborate upon why the subject is worthwhile; define or explain key ideas, concepts, situations, controversies, etc. For example:

A Chat about Marriage

By Yu Dafu

The other day, Mr. Lin Yutang said something to the effect that women's only career lies in matrimony.

Step 2: Thesis

Go on with one of the two options: Clearly state the thesis before presenting arguments for the thesis; describe and evaluate the reasons and supporting evidence for the thesis. For instance:

Now, an eminent French writer declared at a press interview after arriving in Shanghai that men should stay bachelors if they want to achieve success in life.

Step 3: Antithesis

Impartially present the antithesis before describing how it is contrary to the thesis or describe and evaluate the supporting arguments and evidence. For instance:

Washington Irving was a confirmed bachelor, but in his Sketch Book there is an article extolling the wife as a graceful and lovely life-long partner. Charles Lamb, also a single man, in A Bachelor's Complaint of the Behavior of Married People, one of his essays signed "Elia", speaks mockingly of married people with their inevitable postnuptial fruits—the Children.

Marriage or no marriage, which is more desirable? That sounds like the chicken-and-egg question, which, though often discussed, remains a perpetual puzzle. Generally speaking, one who has no family dependants is not supposed to rent a house, one who has no petticoat influence in the government should refrain from becoming an official, an unmarried male writer is in no position to write about "my wife". All these seem to hit at the advantages of marriage. But, to get married, you need to have five prerequisites, namely, money, leisure, employment, good looks and potentness, of which all are not always available. What is more, after your marriage, your offspring will come to this world of themselves. And in a world with overpopulation, economic crisis, educational bankruptcy and deteriorating public morals, they may, just as Charles Lamb says, through their own acts of indiscretion, be sent to the gallows. With such a terrible misfortune befalling your family, how could you still have wedded bliss to speak of?

Step 4: Conclusion

Conclude the article with one of the three options below:

Adopt the original thesis while rejecting the antithesis; adopt and advance the antithesis while giving up the original thesis; conclude by synthesizing the best aspects of the thesis and antithesis, and find a Middle Way. The conclusion needs to summarize, weigh and compare the ideas, point out the significant strengths and weaknesses, advantages and disadvantages of the two positions, and explain how and why the conclusion has been reached. For instance:

Thinking the matter over and over again, I cannot but come to the conclusion that neither matrimony nor bachelorship has anything to recommend itself.

III   Analytical Reasoning

There is a dialectical tradition that has occupied a place in Western thought since the time of Immanuel Kant and Friedrich Hegel, but the Hegelian or Marxist dialectic has been held to be more "aggressive" because the effort is toward obliterating contradictions. What gains the upper hand in Western thought is still analytical reasoning.

1. Definition of Analytical Reasoning

In the philosophy of German philosopher Immanuel Kant (1724—1804), analytical reasoning represents judgments made upon statements that are based on the virtue of the statement's own content. No particular experience, beyond an understanding of the meanings of words used, is necessary for analytical reasoning. For example, "John is an orphan" is a given true statement. Through analytical reasoning, one can make the judgment that John's parents died or dumped him when he was little. One knows this to be true since the state of being without parents is implied in the word orphan; no particular experience of John is necessary to make this judgment. To suggest that John lives with his mother or father—given that he is an orphan—would be self-contradictory.

2. Three Principles of Analytical Reasoning

Westerners are not aware of how committed they are to analytical principles that conflict directly with the spirit of Chinese dialecticism. The analytical principles used in their reasoning process are the principle of identity, the principle of non-contradiction and the principle of stability.

a. Principle of Identity

The principle of identity holds that an object is itself and not some other objects. In the Hollywood film *Who-am-I* Jackie Chan, a secret agent, fell from a crashing helicopter. Waking up in a village of local natives, Chan had no memory of who he was, thus being addressed as "Who-am-I". With no identity, Chan was thirsty for the answer because loss of identity implies loss of life in the Western thought. Luckily toward the end of the film, he gradually realized who he was through analytical reasoning and acting from the principle of identity. It happens that a Chinese folk song "For Whom" is also about identity, but we have no idea about who the praised person is even after we finish the song probably because individual identity is interwoven with group identity and the context, or personal identity is decided by one's relationship with others. The lyrics of the song are as follows:

泥巴裹满裤腿，汗水湿透衣背，我不知道你是谁，我却知道你为了谁。为了谁，为了秋的收获，为了春回大雁归，满腔热血唱出青春无悔，望穿天涯不知战友何时回。你是谁？为了谁？我的战友你何时回？你是谁？为了谁？我的兄弟姐

妹不流泪 。谁最美? 谁最累? 我的乡亲,我的战友,我的兄弟姐妹。

b. Principle of Non-contradiction

The principle of non-contradiction holds that a position can't be both true and false: A and not-A are impossible.

Modern Chinese are of course well aware of the same analytical principles that Westerners hold dear and make use of analysis in some contexts. But in our view, the principle of non-contradiction applies only to the realm of concepts and abstractions. The differences in the two stances toward contradiction have some interesting consequences. For instance, Chinese worship many gods (e.g. *Tian*, the supreme god, *the river god, the moon god, the sun god*, etc.) while Western Christians only believe the power of God, regarding God as the only true God; abortion is not good for Chinese, but acceptable and necessary while Westerners equate abortion to feticide, the killing and murder of a human fetus; for Chinese the opposite of a great truth is also true, but Westerners believe that the opposite of a great truth is false and a lie.

c. Principle of Stability

Ancient Greek philosophers are inclined to believe that things don't change much or if they are really changing, future change will continue in the same direction and at the same rate. And the same is true of ordinary modern Westerners who, like the ancient Greeks, see the world in a stable state; they see objects as discrete and separate from their environments; they see events as moving in linear fashion when they move at all. Therefore, they have developed a sense of controllability. On the contrary, Chinese believe in the uncontrollability since anything unexpected can happen in this constantly changing world.

3. Western Emphasis on Analytical Reasoning Ability

Analytical reasoning is very influential in every department of Western societies. That explains why analytical reasoning ability has been so highly emphasized by Western educational system that it has been included in many kinds of level examinations. Take, for instance, the GRE or the Graduate Record Examination—a standardized test that measures the aptitude of promising graduate students.

Administered by the Educational Testing Service(ETS) of the USA, the GRE takes three basic forms: the General Test, Subject Tests, and the Writing Assessment. The General Test, most often referred to as the GRE, measures verbal, quantitative, and analytical reasoning skills. The Subject Tests measure achievement in eight disciplines. The Writing Assessment consists of two analytical writing tasks.

Undoubtedly analytical reasoning is encouraged by people in authority and the whole society, which explains why people spend so much time improving their analytical reasoning ability. When they are little, Westerners are encouraged to play games that involve analytical reasoning skills. Here is a famous problem: Four men (A, B, C, D) and four women(W, X, Y, Z) are going rafting in two rafts. Each raft holds exactly four people, and the groups of people in the two rafts follow these conditions:

1) There are exactly two men and two women in each raft.

2) Either A or B, but not both, must be in the first raft.

3) If W is in the first raft, then C must also be in the first raft.

4) If Y is in the first raft, then B cannot be in the first raft.

If B is in the first raft, which of the following can be the other three people in the first raft?

(A) A, X, Z

(B) C, D, W

(C) C, W, X

(D) C, X, Y

(E) D, W, Z

Obviously to solve the problem, analytical reasoning should be used. Through practice like this, people become good at this kind of test and what's more important, people have improved their ability in analytical reasoning through repeated efforts.

> **IV   More About Two Reasoning Modes**

1. Weaknesses of Two Modes

The strengths and weaknesses of the two reasoning modes are self-evident. Here the focus will be on their weaknesses.

a. Weaknesses of Analytical Reasoning

As is known to many, life is not easy in China. Yet owing to the dialectical reasoning which can stop us from feeling extremely bad about ourselves, we seem to be happier, less anxious and less depressed than Westerners. Let us take as an example different ways of dealing with some contradictory information stemming from conflicts between a mother-in-law and her daughter-in-law. In such a sensitive relationship, we are inclined to find fault on both sides and look for solutions that will move both sides to the middle because they are family. But Westerners, accustomed to analytical reasoning, are in terrible need to figure out who is right in an argument or conflict, disregarding the fact that however bad the mother-in-law and her daughter-in-law are in relationship they are family. At the interpersonal level which involves conflicts including those among family members, you really don't need to find the truth and then blame one side for the causes of the problems and demand changes from one side to attain a solution and offer no compromise. In the same situation, Chinese are far more inclined to reason that both sides have flaws and virtues, because we have a holistic awareness that life is full of contradictions and everything is changing.

b. Weaknesses of Dialectical Reasoning

We do not apply dialectical thinking to the physical material world, for example, we do not believe that the sun can rise in both the east and the west, although we believe A is good, and B is not bad. However, in tests of scientific thinking we, accustomed to dialectical reasoning, are really short. Asked to determine which statement is true in a survey—whether, for instance, national pay rise makes people enjoy stronger or weaker purchasing power—many Chinese respondents took the middle road, even when they believed one statement to be less true than another. The tendency to look for the middle way has hampered our efforts to seek scientific truth through aggressive argumentation—the classical Western method of identifying true and false answers. It may also have contributed to our willingness to tolerate corrupt officials and improper policies.

2. "Making Use of Advantages and Bypassing Disadvantages"

In fact there is no better mode in terms of reasoning. The best way is to use both—one mode for science and another for relationships.

In recent years, more evidence has been coming out to prove that we are not concerned with contradictions in the same way that Westerners are. We have a greater preference for compromised solutions and for holistic arguments and we are more willing to endorse both of the apparently contradictory arguments. On the other hand, the greater adherence to the principle of non-contradiction on the part of Westerners seems to produce no guarantee against questionable inferences. On the contrary, Western contradiction phobia may sometimes cause them to become more extreme in their judgments under conditions in which the evidence indicates they should become less extreme.

Therefore, it is necessary for us to make use of the advantages of the two reasoning modes and bypass their disadvantages (扬长避短)by learning from Western analytical methods for determining scientific truth in intercultural communication.

Further Reading

1. Hunt E.B. & Marin, J. P. & Stone, J. (1988). *Probabilistic Reasoning in Intelligent Systems: Networks of Plausible Inference.* Burlington, MA: Academic Press Inc.

2. Pearl, J. (1966). *Experiments in Induction.* San Francisco, CA: Morgan Kaufmann Publishers.

3. Nisbett, R. E. (2003). *The Geography of Thought: How Asians and Westerners Think Differently and Why.* New York: The Free Press.

4. Holland, D. & Quinn, N. (1987). *Cultural Models in Language and Thought.* London: Cambridge University Press.

5. 张培基(2006):《英译中国现代散文选》,上海:上海外语教育出版社。

6. 萧立明(2002):《英汉比较研究与翻译》,上海:上海外语教育出版社。

7. 饶尚宽译注(2006):《老子》,北京:中华书局。

8. 马玉珂编(1985):《西方逻辑史》,北京:中国人民大学出版社。

9. 罗素注,马元德译(1976):《西方哲学史》(上下卷),北京:商务印书馆。

10. 庞万里(2005):《中国古典哲学通论》,北京:北京航空航天大学出版社。

Unit 9　Holistic vs. Atomistic Visions

Listen to all parties and you will be enlightened (兼听则明,偏信则暗).

—Wei Zheng

As a chancellor for about 13 years during the reign of Emperor Taizong of the Tang Dynasty, Wei Zheng obtained far broader freedom to criticize others, particularly the emperor, than other officials. As a matter of fact he not only criticized but also gave advice to the emperor. For instance, he suggested the emperor listen to all parties. What led him to make such a suggestion?

Seize the day! Begin now! Each day is a new life. Seize it.

—David Powers

Do you think this suggestion may work for you? Why or why not?

I　A Detention Room Incident

In many American schools there is a detention room for children who have violated or rebelled against school rules and regulations to stay for two or three school days. My thirteen-year-old boy Minchang, an English beginner, picked up some bad language in the hallway during his first few weeks in the States and practiced it in the classroom. For this, he had to stay in the detention room for three days so that, in his teacher's words, "he can become a gentleman in the future." That man seemed to have completely forgotten what he said the other day— "Minchang is a sweet young man." I tried my utmost to explain Minchang's problem to his grandpa who believed that the school's decision smelled of racial prejudice. In China we focus not only on each of a boy's traits inferred from his past behavior, and situational factors influencing him will also be examined. But in the West, they are inclined to focus on each of his personal remarks, actions, or attitudes.

Minchang's detention room incident tells us much about two different visions of the world— the holistic and the atomistic one. On the one hand, people brought up in Chinese culture are likely to synthesize parts and examine the whole, paying special attention to the whole situation. On the other hand, people nurtured in Western culture tend to dissect things into parts, focusing on details and analyzing them one by one.

II   Prominent Attributes of Holistic and Atomistic Visions

1. A Brief Introduction to Two Visions

a. Atomistic Vision

Atomistic vision prevails in Western culture. Westerners are good at classifying things and arranging them systematically. Animals, plants, and objects are clearly divided, subdivided, and further divided according to their attributes. If you glance at the title, subtitles, and topic sentences of each paragraph of an English writing, you instantly know its content. When listening to a speech, you easily get the message by following the cohesive connectors signaling time sequence like *first, second, third, next, finally,* and so on, and words marking logical relationships such as *because, however, actually, supposing, although,* or *therefore.*

Atomistic vision is the only one accepted today among the scientists as well as medical practitioners. In their medical practice doctors of Western medicine treat their patients by examining parts of the body through tests, X rays and other medical appliances before making a diagnosis and prescribing medicine.

Atomistic vision involves frequent use of abstract concepts. Arguably, Westerners are relatively stronger in making use of abstract concepts for analytical judgment. Abstraction is synonymous with precision, exactness and clarity, which may help to explain why more theoretical works on science and technology have been produced in the West than in China.

b. Holistic Vision

Combined logical and intuitive thinking is holistic thinking. This synthetic vision predominates in Chinese culture, although analysis has never been rejected. We are accustomed to observing and judging things or people as a whole. When reading a classical Chinese article, the reader will find that the unity and harmony of the whole piece have been attached great importance and the correspondence between introduction and conclusion and the natural transition from one point to another have been given much attention.

Synthesis holds sway in Chinese society. Exposed to such a culture, many tend to dislike abstractions and science. Zhu Xi (1130—1200), the greatest Confucian scholar of the Song time, wrote commentaries upon almost all of the Confucian classics, engaged in political affairs, education, and agriculture. However, he had little interest in practicing his "investigation of the things(格物致知)" in the realms of natural and social sciences. A traditional Chinese medical practitioner exposed to this culture diagnoses a patient's disease by first looking at his complexion and tongue, smelling him, feeling his pulse and eliciting complaints, in order to form a correct judgment of the patient's general physical condition before prescribing medicine.

Confucianism also holds a holistic vision of a peaceful world, which rests on a carefully integrated program of personal self-cultivation, harmonized family life, and well-ordered states. At the heart of this vision is the sense of "the integration of Heaven, earth and man".

To sum up, the holistic vision is a dialectic mode of thinking with a flexible nature.

2. Attributes of the Chinese Holistic Vision

It happens that we peel an apple around and reserve the whole before biting it. Probably the secret behind this habit is associated with our holistic vision which has the following attributes.

a. Context-dependence

Chinese thought or vision is inclined to be more context-dependent. Holistic approaches attend to the entire context or background, emphasize change, and focus less on the object. The doctrine of ***yin-yang***, the Five Elements (***wu xing***), the Eight Diagrams(***ba gua***), traditional Chinese medicine, and even tea drinking employ a holistic approach, observing and depending generally much on the context. Take tea drinking for instance. Tea drinking is regarded as an art in China, so Chinese are so particular about the drinking atmosphere, source of water, aroma of the tea, shape of tea leaves, as well as the quality of tea leaves and their production place. While savoring a cup of tea in a quiet teahouse we are apt to imagine ourselves roaming among mountains and waters and integrating ourselves with nature. In this sense, tea means life. Therefore, it is unlikely for us to crush tea leaves into powder or tiny pellets like Lipton, the biggest tea exporter in the world.

b. Combination of Two or More into One

The holistic vision leads ordinary Chinese to combine two or more into one. The so-called perfect woman in a man's mind, for example, is able to play at least 3 different roles in his life—a wife to manage the household and finance, a lover for passion and a soul mate to share spiritual intimacy. This 3-woman concept is one of the most popular topics in the classmate get-together party in China. In philosophical terms, it can be said that we tend to combine two or more into one when making sense of the world. The well-known Tao (Dao), for instance, is simply the invisible, intangible, and indescribable whole which merges with all things in Heaven and on earth.

c. Acceptance of Contradictions

The Chinese holistic thought or vision inclines towards acceptance of contradictions. Both Chinese and Western people put emphasis on dialectics. However, Chinese dialectic is different from its Western counterpart in that it places more emphasis on contrary integration. Therefore, we are more likely to accept two obviously contradictory proposals and try to find a third way—the middle way.

d. Not Seeing the Trees for the Woods

The Chinese holistic vision tends to examine problems as a whole, so it is most likely to result in "not seeing the trees for the woods" in our vision of the world. For example, Chinese medical diagnosis is made by examining the patient as a whole if he or she feels dizzy. Often one herbal medicine is prescribed to cure many troubles.

e. Much Use of the Integration Concept

In ancient China, stress on integration or holism extended to a sense of the integration of human existence with natural and even supernatural things. There was a belief in a supreme deity *Tian* (Heaven) which ruled the world and took a personal interest in the affairs of mankind, a belief in the existence and power of spirits of nature and spirits of ancestors who had to be served and placated with sacrifices, a belief in the divine sanction of the political order and the great responsibility of a ruler to fulfill his moral duties to *Tian* (i.e. *tian ming* or the mandate of Heaven) and his subjects. It is the concept of the moral responsibilities of the ruler, and the way in which the ruler should carry out these responsibilities so as not to lose the favor and protection of *Tian*, which became a major concern of thinkers and one of the key problems of Chinese philosophy. For ancient Chinese, what happened on earth was believed to resonate with events in nature and in Heaven. The same is true of the Chinese today. According to Taoism which is still influential, animals, plants, natural objects, and even man-made artifacts have spirits that arise from nature. Therefore, advertisements that emphasize nature are more successful in China than in the West. Some Western carmakers have discovered this fact and started their advertising campaign for their products in China with scenes of nature—with just the brand name usually appearing at the end of the sequence. The holistic vision is also reflected in cuisine. Chinese food is usually prepared in bite-size pieces, but fish are often cooked and served whole. Whole fish culturally signifies wholeness of things as it has a proper beginning (head) with an end (tail).

3. Attributes of the Western Atomistic Vision

a. Dichotomy

A dichotomy is splitting one into two or more which are considered to be either contradictory or mutually exclusive. For example, the colors black and white represent a classic dichotomy: Either something is black, or it is white, with no room for overlap or alternatives.

Incidentally, Westerners tend to separate just as they divide an apple into parts before eating it, which is not strange, given the fact that dichotomy is common in their thought and their vision of the world. Lipton, the famous British tea company, breaks tea leaves into tiny pellets, puts them into very standardized small bags and makes big profits. For Westerners tea is composed of many elements that can improve human health, and drinking tea is to absorb those healthy elements before dumping the small tea bag into the garbage can instead of enjoying the aroma of the tea or admiring the shape of tea leaves.

b. Not Seeing the Woods for the Trees

The Western atomistic vision is inclined to place attention on parts of a whole. As a result, it is most likely to result in "not seeing the woods for the trees". For example, Western medicine often focuses on the single parts rather than the whole. If one has a headache, then the headache is to be treated; if there is pain in the foot, then the foot is to be treated; if there is a tumor, then open the body and remove it. And it's no secret that American women who don't see menopause as a celebratory transition into a new season of their lives (***geng nian qi***) experience more hot flashes during menopause than their Chinese sisters since a message they often get is clear and loud: "You have served your purpose. Now PLEASE STEP ASIDE."

c. Polarizing

The Western atomistic vision is apt to polarize and emphasize the debate between opposing forces so that the middle alternatives are virtually ignored. Therefore, when confronted with two apparently contradictory propositions, the Westerner tends to polarize his or her beliefs and insists on the correctness of one belief vs. another.

d. Discreteness-dependence

The Western thought or vision is inclined to be discreteness-dependent. The ancient Greek philosophers saw the world as being composed of discrete objects. It is true of today's Westerners. For instance, the question "does it have a backbone?" is often used to divide species into vertebrates and invertebrates. Beginning in the late eighteenth and early nineteenth century, some Western countries, especially America, began to apply the discrete approach to improve the efficiency in the worlds of manufacture and commerce. They invented assembly lines, broke down the production of everything from rice-cookers to planes into the most standardized parts possible and the simplest replicable actions, analyzed each component or each action of a worker, and made it maximally efficient so that products that had taken workers or craftsmen months to produce could now be produced within a few hours or minutes. They also set up profitable niche market ventures by addressing the need for a particular product or service that is not being addressed by the big providers.

III   Vision and Cognition

Cognition refers to the mental process of knowing, including aspects such as awareness, perception, reasoning, intuition, knowledge, and judgment. There is much evidence indicating that vision has much influence on human cognition.

1. Vision and Cognition of Factors Affecting Outcomes

For Chinese the factors affecting outcomes are extraordinarily complex. The practice of traditional Chinese medicine and *feng shui* for choosing building sites in China may encourage this idea, which in turn encourages the search for relationships in the context. This is quite different from the Western discrete and rule-based approaches. Consider, for example, the titles of the English books about approaches to education and self-teach—*How the Way We Talk Can Change the Way We Work: Seven Languages for Transformation* and *The Six Triggers of Persuasion*. In China, similar books are also popular but the titles betray a holistic vision, for instance, *Liu Yiting, a Harvard Girl* (《哈佛女孩刘亦婷》), *Zhang Zhaomu, a Harvard Boy* (《哈佛男孩张肇牧》), and *A Night's Talk with Sister Understanding* (《知心姐姐的话》).

Arguably, on the whole the Westerner is used to operating in an atomistic way, while the Chinese is more likely to emphasize relationships, including the environment or context. As a result, a child in the West who performs poorly in language is likely to be regarded as having little language ability. In China, such a child might be viewed as needing to work harder, or perhaps his teacher and parents should work harder, or maybe the setting for learning should be improved.

2. Vision and Language Cognition

We have learnt in our grammar books that nouns are more analytical, thinking-involving and logical while verbs involve a holistic understanding of humans and everything in nature. There are more nouns in English than in Chinese while there are more verbs in Chinese than in English. It is no coincidence that Western children learn nouns faster than verbs and Chinese kids acquire verbs just as fast as nouns since, for instance, " to write" involves the hand, the movement of the hand, the paper, the ink, the color of the ink, and the words written on a piece of paper. So for Chinese language cognition is very complicated, and hence a lifetime commitment.

3. Vision and Information Cognition

In the atomistic vision the information obtained from other people plays a crucial role. But in holistic vision, it has somehow to be integrated with the involved persons' own experience, intuition and creativity. When looking at the map of China, the Chinese can see that its shape appears uncannily similar to that of a rooster. Its head covers the three northeast provinces, its tail includes Xinjiang and Tibet and its wings spread over the resource-rich basins of the Yangtze and the Yellow River. The belly of this rooster is in the southeast, and Hainan and Taiwan islands are its feet. When I tried to transmit the information to my students from Calgary, Canada they closely examined the map but few could make out the image of the rooster.

IV   Vision and Language

1. Vision and Language Differences

Different visions of the world help produce different languages.

First, Chinese holism creates a highly "contextual" language. Chinese characters typically have multiple meanings and pronunciations, so to be understood they require the context of sentences. On the other hand, English words are relatively distinctive and besides, English speakers with atomistic vision are concerned to make sure words and utterances have as little context as possible.

Second, Chinese holistic vision allows people to look from the general to the specific and speak in a "topic-prominent" language. In Chinese, sentences have a position, typically the first position, that should be filled by the current topic, e.g. 这种脚,没地方买鞋穿 (literally, such feet have nowhere to buy shoes; freely, shoes are not available for such feet). While not obligatory from a grammatical standpoint, an idiomatic Chinese sentence usually starts with context, e.g.春季南京人爱去梅花山(in spring, Nanjing natives love visiting Plum Blossom Hill). English, however, as a "subject-prominent" language with an atomistic vision, starts with a subject. An idiomatic English sentence jumps immediately to a subject, and there must be a subject even in the sentence "It is snowing today (今天下雪)". Obviously English is preoccupied with focal objects as opposed to context.

Third, for Chinese one should adapt himself or herself to different situations since everything is in constant change, which is correspondent with his or her holistic vision. Therefore, there are many different expressions for "I" or "me" in ancient Chinese, e.g. *I* (草民, literally, grass-root man) in relation to the emperor, *I* (不孝之子, literally, your unfilial son) in relation to his parents, and *I* (学生, literally, your student) in relation to his teacher. It is difficult for ancient Chinese to think of properties that only apply to *I* or *me*, but much easier for them to think of properties that apply to I or me in certain settings and in relation to particular people. For Westerners, it is the self who does the acting based on an atomistic vision, e.g. *I am what I am. My name is John Smith. Call me John* (instead of saying "call your classmate John").

The fourth difference concerns raising proper questions. For instance, when inquiring as to whether one would like more to drink, eat or take, we ask, "再喝一点 (Drink more)?" but they ask "More tea?" in English. To Chinese speakers with holistic vision, it is obvious that it is tea that one is talking about drinking more of, so to mention tea would be redundant since the verb "喝(to drink)" itself involves all that contribute to the action including the action of drinking, the tea, the mouth, the hand, the lips, etc. To English speakers with atomistic vision, it's obvious that one is talking about tea, as opposed to any other activity that might be carried out with it, so it would be rather bizarre for the questioner to refer to drinking.

2. Vision and Argumentative Writings

The holistic vision seeks the integral and absolute knowledge, so it is qualitative (定性), not quantitative. Qualitative emphasis leads us to argue by induction. Our idea is to create a context that sounds powerful and convincing. In other words, what is said is not important; it is the context or the argumentative atmosphere that is important. Thus you will find much use of phrases employed to constitute a context of debate such as *we must, we should not, it is wrong to, it is absurd, cannot be denied,* or *resolutely demand* in Chinese argumentative writings.

The atomistic vision involves both qualitative and quantitative analysis(定性定量 分析), putting more emphasis on the study of the latter. The quantitative emphasis makes English writers develop their arguments in a deductive way. In an English argumentative writing, since context is less important and considerable stress is thus laid on making one's position clear, the tone is usually restrained, and the language is generally moderate to sound objective. In the writing process, therefore, native English writers tend to be less militant and more cautious in tone and language than traditional Chinese writers, especially those before China's reform and opening up. Their idea is to let the facts speak for themselves for they believe the facts themselves should be able to convince the reader.

However, in writing a thesis which involves qualitative and quantitative analysis Chinese writers often sound modest. In order to create a context of modesty, Chinese papers tend to have such titles as preceded by *A Superficial Discussion of..., An Attempt to Discuss..., Preliminary Analysis of...,* or *My Humble Opinions on...* To the English-speaking people all these sound uncertain and thus unconvincing.

3. Vision and Causation

Causation is a sociological term indicating the belief that events occur in predictable ways and that one event engenders another. The influence of different visions on causation is great. Let us consider the coverage of an American campus shooting case.

In early November 1991, Lu Gang, a Chinese post-doctoral student at the University of Iowa who had received his Ph.D. in Physics from the university earlier, submitted his dissertation at an awards competition, and lost to another Chinese graduate student Shan Linhua. He subsequently failed to obtain an academic job. On October 31, a snowy winter day, he walked into a seminar room and shot his adviser, the person who had handled his appeal, Shan Linhua who was to receive the award, several of his fellow students and bystanders, and then himself.

About this sensational case, different visions guided reporters from different cultures to focus on different aspects. The explanations for Lu's behavior in the American campus newspapers revealed an atomistic vision of causes, focusing almost entirely on Lu's presumed qualities—his bad personality characteristics(e.g. he was a *"darkly disturbed man"*, and had *"very bad temper"*) and wrong attitude (e.g. he had a *"strong belief that guns were an important means to redress grievances"*). Chinese reporters, on the other hand, emphasized causes associated with the context or environment to which Lu was exposed. Hence their explanations for this homicide almost entirely centered on Lu's poor people skills (e.g. *bad relationship with his adviser although he was a brilliant exchange student, envy of the slain student, isolation from the Chinese community, spoiled only-son in his family*), pressures from Chinese society (e.g. *no face to go back home to confront his family, a victim of the so-called "Top Student" educational policy in China*) and the American context (e.g. *Western violence culture, no gun control*).

Would Lu Gang commit the tragic murder if he had won the cut-throat competition, then?

Most of the Westerners who are used to dissecting things into parts before analyzing their relationships would say, "Yes!" "No, in many cases." would be the answer from most of us who pay special attention to the influence of context on people's behavior.

4. Vision and Communicative Behavior

Our vision controls our communicative behavior to some extent, which we cannot afford to ignore in our study.

a. Taking the Oath a Second Time

On January 21, 2009 American Chief Justice John Roberts delivered the oath to Obama at the White House again—a rare do-over. The surprise moment came in response to much-noticed stumble on the day before when Roberts got the words of the oath a little off, which prompted Obama to do so, too.

As for the messed-up oath at the inauguration on the 20th, some constitutional experts said the Constitution is clear about the exact wording of the oath and as a result, a do-over probably wasn't necessary but also couldn't hurt. Two other previous presidents had repeated the oath because of similar issues. Some observers said that right-wing nuts would be hinting darkly that Obama wasn't really president because he had not taken the constitutionally-mandated oath as written. Now, it turns out that reasonable people believed there was a potential problem and Obama did, in fact, take the oath a second time out of what White House counsel Greg Craig called "an abundance of caution".

Regarding Obama's second oath, many Chinese scholars echoed their Western counterparts' views. But some of my friends and students said among ourselves that his legality admitted of no doubt since Obama won the much-covered presidential campaign, took the oath of office as American President on the Capitol platform before the whole watching world, and above all, his group has replaced Bush's group. Yet we do understand it's a truly responsible act for Obama to take a second oath since most of his people hold the atomistic vision.

b. "Anticlimax!"

Here is a short Chinese text about a festival:

彝族人民的插花节

节日期间,彝族姑娘在门上和自己身上插花以示吉祥;给老人发上插花以示健康长寿;给心上人发上插花祝福白头偕老;在田边插花以示丰收;在羊角上插花以示六畜兴旺等。所有这些,都表现出彝族人民对幸福生活的向往。

For us, this text is well-written for it tells the reader what the festival is about and what people do on that special day before ending the description with a commentary remark as a concluding sentence, thus achieving the unity of the whole piece, which tallies with Chinese holistic vision. But after reading the English version translated by one of my graduate students, the comment a British professor made on the last sentence is "Anticlimax! (煞风景)" The English version is as follows:

Flower Festival of Yi Ethnic Minority

During the festival, young women paste flowers on the doors and insert some in their clothes for good luck. Old people wear flowers in their hair for health and longevity. Young men decorate their sweethearts' hair with flowers, praying for growing old together. People plant flowers by the side of the field for a good harvest and tie flowers to the sheep's horns for more domesticated animals. All these activities show that Yi people long for a beautiful life.

Westerners with atomistic vision like dissecting things into parts, so for them fact speaks louder than words, and hence it upsets them to be told as if they were pupils that "All these activities show that Yi people long for a beautiful life", which has already been explicitly implied in the text.

This case once again raises an age-old question for us to think about: What shall we do to reduce miscommunications caused by different thinking patterns?

V *Zhengshan Xiaozhong* and Lipton Black Tea

During my stay in Wuyi Mountain Nature Reserve ten years ago, I became addicted to a kind of black tea called ***Zhengshan Xiaozhong*** (正山小种). It has been confirmed that Lipton black tea originates from it. A story goes that one day in the 17th century a tea merchant purchased some freshly picked tea leaves, but unfortunately he ran into some bandits on his way home. In a hurry he hid his tea leaves in a safe place and ran for his life. A few days later he returned only to find his green tea leaves had turned black. As he couldn't afford more losses, instead of dumping the tea leaves into the garbage can, he processed the black tea leaves into black-colored tea never drunk before and thus not accepted by Chinese tea drinkers.

Later the black tea leaves were sold to some Dutch and Portuguese businessmen who sold them to British businessmen without expecting this kind of tea should become very popular with people in Britain. Later, some Englishmen visited Fujian many times to steal the processing technique of black tea as well as tea trees, some of which were planted by them in India and Sri Lanka so that the two Asian countries became big tea exporters years later.

In my home, there are some *Zhengshan Xiaozhong* black tea produced in China and Lipton black tea made in Britain. To be honest, when I first saw Lipton black tea thirty years ago I was surprised to notice the world famous tea consists of tiny pellets in standardized small bags. Tea in my mind used to look like tree leaves of different shapes! *Zhengshan Xiaozhong* black tea leaves are black, slim, and curly as if roasted while they were still tender buds, from which we can vividly see in our mind's eye how tea leaves look like in the mountains, bathing in the sunshine, drinking the dew drops, sleeping in the fog, dancing in the breeze... By tea we Chinese usually mean tea leaves of their original shapes and aroma, but to Lipton, tea is composed of so tiny pellets that at first sight you can never assume it is tea. However, it is said that the export of Lipton each year is much bigger than that of all the tea companies in China.

Chinese black tea and Western black tea have the same origin. But why does one remain unknown to many while the other is world-famous? It is said Lipton crushes tea leaves of all grades to powder in order to erase their differences so that the company can standardize tea. As a result, the shape of tea leaves becomes invisible and black tea is nothing but powder incorporating all tea grades. Consequently Lipton succeeds.

However, *Zhengshan Xiaozhong*, the ancestor of Lipton black tea, is still laboring in obscurity. Why don't we try breaking the leaves into powder or tiny pieces like Lipton and make big money, then?

Further Reading

1. Schumacher, E. F. (1973). *Small Is Beautiful: Economics As If People Mattered.* London: Blond & Briggs.

2. Nisbett, R. E. (2003). *The Geography of Thought: How Asians and Westerners Think Differently and Why.* New York: The Free Press.

3. Wechsler, H. J. (1974). *Mirror to the Son of Heaven.* New Haven: Yale University Press.

4. Brislin, Richard W. (1990). *Applied Cross-Cultural Psychology.* Newbury Park, CA: Sage Publications.

5. Holland, Dorothy & Naomi Quinn (1987). *Cultural Models in Language and Thought.* Cambridge, UK: Cambridge University.

6. 萧立明 (2002):《英汉比较研究与翻译》,上海:上海外语教育出版社。

7. 杜承南主编 (1994):《中国当代翻译百论》,四川:重庆大学出版社。

8. 刘彦生 (2007):《西方创新思维方式论》,天津:天津大学出版社。

9. 张隆溪 (2014):《阐释学与跨文化研究》,上海:复旦大学出版社。

Unit 10   Categorizing Objects by Relationships vs. by Attributes

"So you must take after peanuts," father continued, "because they're useful though not great and nice-looking."

"Then you mean one should be useful rather than great and nice-looking," I said.

"That's what I expect of you," father concluded.

We kept chatting until the party broke up late at night. Today, though nothing is left of the goodies made of peanuts, father's words remain engraved in my mind.

—Xu Dishan

Why did "father" single out the peanut rather than an actual person as his children's role model?

Pierre Mercier, a visiting French professor, went to a farewell tea party in honor of him. Professor Lu and his wife, whom Professor Mercier had gotten to know well, were also at the party. To his surprise, Professor Lu, two other professors and himself were arranged to sit at the same table while Professor Lu's wife sat at another!

— Anonymous

For discussion: Explain why Professor Lu and his wife were arranged to sit at different tables.

Out of clutter, find simplicity...
From discord find harmony...

In the middle of difficulty lies opportunity.

—Albert Einstein

Einstein was obviously not organized in the way we generally think of it. It seems the secret of being organized has nothing to do with how "neat and tidy" things are around us. Discover for yourselves what effect the previous beliefs of getting organized are having on your ability to lead an organized, productive, stress free, and successful life.

I Two Ways to Categorize One Person

Categorization is a cognitive process that allows us to relate to unfamiliar objects in an appropriate manner based on our familiarity with other objects that are similar to them. To live in an environment filled with many different objects, people, and animals, we must be able to categorize quickly. Generally speaking, we categorize objects according to their overall similarities. But in reality, similarities among objects do not always allow people from different cultures to categorize them in the same way.

Words came in December 2008 that Roger Y. Tsien won one-third of the Nobel Prize in Chemistry. The news soon produced a big sensation in China, where many people took great pride in him but soon felt a hit in the face from Roger, who was reported to have said, "I'm not a Chinese, but I hope my success can inspire more young people in China." Some Chinese just couldn't understand why Roger refused to admit he is Chinese since he is the Qian Xuesen's nephew, his parents are from China, and he looks like Chinese. This way to categorize a person according to his relationship originates from Chinese radiation thinking, a pattern of holistic thinking based on the principle of relationships.

Roger Tsien, despite his Chinese decent, has been exposed to American culture where one thinks of himself first as an American, then an American of Asian decent. Like other children of immigrants in America, his focus is more on the future, where he is going and what he will do in the future, but not on the past, nor on where his ancestors came from and what they did. What's more, Roger cannot speak good Chinese, he doesn't eat Chinese food, he lives in the American community, and of course it is natural for him to find a strong sense of belonging among Americans. Tsien's way to define himself arises out of the rule-based thinking, a pattern of analytical thinking focusing on the attributes.

II   Principles to Categorize Objects

Humans categorize objects—*persons, places, things, or animals*—for a great variety of reasons. Most often we group objects by following the principle of relationships, while Westerners are more likely to classify them by employing the principle of attributes.

1. Principle of Relationships

Guided by holistic thinking, a great majority of people in China judge an object to be more similar to a group with which it shares a close family resemblance, i.e. we often categorize by following the principle of relationships focusing on holism, mutual influences and change. In other words, isolated objects go to different categories, according to their relations with different things in fluid situations.

a. Focus on Holism

The principle's focus on holism supports the idea that nothing in China exists in an isolated or independent way. Instead, one thing has something to do with a multitude of different things and life is a constant passing from one state to another. To really know one object, we have to know all its or his relations. This principle of relationships indicates that the same thing is different in a different context and the same person is literally a different person in the family than in his role as a politician or professor.

b. Focus on Mutual Influences of Objects

According to the principle of relationships, shared attributes do not establish shared class membership. Instead, things are classed together because they are thought to influence one another through resonance. In the system of *feng shui*, metal, wood, wind, water, and earth all influence one another. Change in wind or water will affect all the others. And sometimes fire and smoke can be classed together, since there is no smoke without fire.

c. Focus on Change

This focus makes us believe that everything is changing all the time. Therefore, many of us hold that wealth means poverty is around the corner, and there is nothing to be happy about easy access to wealth or power, just as the proverb goes, "For this period of thirty years the Eastern Region of the Yellow River is prosperous, but for the next, it is the Western Region's turn."

2. Principle of Attributes

Guided by analytical thinking, the rule-based principle of attributes focuses on attributes, isolated objects as well as rules. In other words, following their attributes, isolated objects go to different groups according to relevant rules.

a. Focus on Attributes

Western thinking focuses on attributes. One reason why they stress attributes is that European languages, as inflectional languages, stress the importance of grammar and form—hypotaxis (形合) instead of parataxis (意合), and encourage a focus on attributes and on turning attributes into abstractions. Take English for example. The English adjective can be granted the abstract noun status by adding a suffix -*ness*: *white* becomes *whiteness*, *kind* becomes *kindness*. Western stress on attributes also owes much to the ancient Greeks. A routine habit of Greek philosophers was to analyze the attributes of an object and classify the object based on its abstracted attributes. It is true of Westerners today.

b. Focus on Isolated Objects

Ancient Greek philosophers regarded the object in isolation as the focus of attention and analysis. Most of them regarded a matter as particulate and separate—formed into discrete objects—just as humans were seen as separate from one another. For them the attributes of one object are salient; the attributes are the basis of categorization; the categories constitute the basis of rule construction; and events should then be understood as the result of objects operating in accordance with rules.

c. Rule-based Orientation

As is mentioned above, ancient Greeks habitually analyzed the attributes of an object and categorized the object on the basis of its attributes. They would then attempt to understand the object's nature and the cause of its actions in accordance with rules governing the categories. Rules at various levels of abstraction would be generated as hypotheses.

It is true of Westerners today. Categories are sometimes learned by applying rules to features. For instance, dogs are known to be mammals because a rule says that animals that nurse their young are mammals.

III   How to Categorize Objects and Why

1. How Objects Are Categorized

a. Categorization of Objects in Ancient China

For ancient Chinese, shared attributes did not establish shared class membership. Finding the features shared by objects and placing them in a class on that basis would not have seemed a very useful activity because the objects themselves were not the units of analysis. Instead, objects were grouped together because they were thought to influence one another. Let's take the system of the Five Elements as an example. Metal—wood—water—fire—earth are sometimes grouped in the order by which they produce one another: Wood gives rise to fire, fire gives rise to earth, earth gives rise to metal, metal gives rise to water, and water gives rise to earth; sometimes they are organized in the order by which they are conquered by one another: Fire is conquered by water, water is conquered by earth, earth is conquered by wood, wood is conquered by metal, and metal is conquered by fire.

The belief that the behavior of objects is due to the interaction of the objects with surrounding forces makes it natural for traditional Chinese to classify based on thematic relationships. When shown pictures of Bill Clinton, Barack Obama and Hillary Clinton, many of us will first of all justify our categorization in terms of relationship: Bill Clinton and Hillary Clinton are family.

The lack of interest in classes of objects with shared attributes is consistent with the basic scheme that the ancient Chinese had for the world. For them, the world consisted of continuous substances. That is why a part-whole dichotomy made sense to them, since the dichotomy does not encourage induction from a single case.

b. Categorization of Objects in Ancient Greece

Ancient Greeks, especially philosophers, had a passion for categories and used them as the basis for discovery and application of rules. This addiction to the categorization runs through Western intellectual history, where there has been a conviction that it is possible to find the necessary and sufficient conditions for any category.

For ancient Greeks, objects belonged to the same category if they were describable by the same attributes. So an one-many, individual-class dichotomy made sense to them, since the Greek world was composed of discrete objects. The Greek belief in the importance of the dichotomy was central to their faith in the possibility of accurate inductive inferences: Learning that one object belonging to a class has a particular attribute means that one can assume that the other objects in the same class also have the same attribute. So to speak, if one mammal is warm-blooded, it's a good bet that all mammals are warm-blooded; since one dog is warm-blooded, all dogs are warm-blooded. A focus on the one-many, individual-class organization of knowledge encourages induction from a single case, which encouraged the age-old Greek medical practice of dissecting human bodies into their component parts, treating the head if there is a headache, and treating the foot if there is a foot ache.

2. Why People Categorize Objects Differently

When shown a family album, we tend to see a family with interrelated members while Westerners are likely to see a collection of persons with attributes that are independent of any connections with others. Why do we categorize so differently?

First, we see the world through our own eyes. We see differently, just as Professor Stephen Covey said, "We see the world not as it is, but as we are." Indeed the world is composed of objects, but the point is Westerners are more exposed to objects and there are more object-dependent nouns that denote categories in Western languages. In contrast, Chinese are more exposed to relationships. Let us take the Chinese language as an example. There are more verbs in a Chinese sentence, and the context-dependent verbs denote relationships. Relationships involve, tacitly or explicitly, a verb. Learning the meaning of a transitive verb normally involves noticing at least two objects and some kind of action that connects them in some way, for instance, "to read" means to move your eyes from left to right and meanwhile use your hand to turn over pages. The action of "to read" might be successful on the precondition that all the body members that participate in this activity should be in good relationships.

Secondly, in the process of classification different thinking modes might be involved. Chinese people might depend on their radiation thinking mode and classify, while Westerners tend to be more rule-based and analytical.

Thirdly, when we categorize objects, we might use different principles. Chinese may categorize based on the principle of relationships, whereas Westerners may be focusing more on the attributes of the objects.

There might be more reasons behind the fact that we categorize so differently.

IV　Impacts of Different Ways of Categorization

Categorizing ways have influenced various aspects of human life, manipulating how objects operate. Such aspects as table manners, social life, family education as well as views of time and money are to be examined into in the following sections.

1. Impact on Views of Time and Money

a. Western Time and Money as a Category

Westerners group in accordance with class membership. For example, when shown pictures of an ox, a rabbit and a carrot, they may justify their classification in terms of the shared attribute: The rabbit and the ox are animals while a carrot is root vegetable. This way of categorization leads people to put intangible time and tangible money in one category, although it appears that they have nothing in common. In Western culture, actually "time is money" in many visible ways: minutely telephone rates, hourly wages, monthly salaries, and yearly budgets. These practices structure everyday activities in a very profound way so that Westerners act as if time were nothing but tangible money. Thus time can be spent, wasted, budgeted, invested wisely or poorly saved, or squandered—like money. Since money and time have the same attributes, it is natural for Westerners to place them in one category.

b. Traditional Chinese Time and Money Not as a Category

For many Chinese people, time is life, so in an emergency concerning life and death time is an order that one has no choice but to follow because life is priceless. For others, time is gold, but cannot be bought or sold, for instance, 一寸光阴一寸金, 寸金难买寸光阴 (literally, an inch of time is an inch of gold, but the inch of gold is not enough to buy an inch of time; freely, time is something more precious than money). Different definitions of time indicate that an attempt to understand time without appreciation of its context or relationships is futile in China.

2. Impact on Table Manners

We also categorize actions by relationships. At a Chinese dinner table, food is chopped to very small objects before being cooked. To send small bits of food successfully into the mouth, the hand needs support from the head, the neck, the body as well as the mouth; otherwise the small bits will fall onto the table cloth. Although the mouth is a taker at the dinner table while the hand is a giver and the other parts are assistants, there is an implicit division of labor in the actual process of eating. It is not rude for the mouth to reach for the soup when it is hot and it is not rude for the upper body to bend over bowls, for sometimes it is difficult to fetch the small food objects without stretching or bending. The mouth, the body, and the hand, because of their participation in the eating activity, should work together as a team. Therefore, the body parts and the steps in the process of eating are grouped into one category in China.

Westerners not only segment objects, but also segment an action into discrete parts. At the Western dinner table, the proper way is to chop food into small pieces, one-third of the mouth size before taking it all the way to the mouth, which is waiting to be served straight high above one's neck. To Westerners, it is rude to spit bones and other food scraps on the table since the mouth is a taker while the hand is a giver. It is considered bad table manners for the mouth to reach for the food for that is the hand's task. The division of labor is explicit so that the actions of receiving and giving food don't go to one category.

3. Impact on Social Life

Ancient Greeks thought of themselves as individuals with distinctive properties, as units separate from others within the society, and in control of their own destinies. Their social life was independent, full of verbal contention and debates.

For ancient Chinese the world was complicated, events were interrelated, and objects and people were connected. So Chinese social life was interdependent and it was not independence but harmony that really counted—the harmony of humans and nature for the Taoists and the harmony of humans with other humans for the Confucianists. Therefore their life was full of visits, family reunions, and parties which appeared very hot and noisy (*re nao*).

4. Impact on Early Childhood Family Education

An emphasis on relationships encourages a concern with the feelings of others. When a Chinese mother is with her toddler, she likes using such feeling-related expressions as *The fire will bite and hurt you if you touch it. Uncle Peasant feels bad if you do not eat everything mom cooked for you. The flower will say "ouch" and cry if you pick it. Brother A Fu* (the Wuxi clay figure) *is sad because you kicked him away.* Focusing on feelings and social relations helps children to anticipate the reactions of other people, with whom they will have to adjust their behavior.

When a Western mother is with her toddler, she tends to supply information about objects, e.g. *This is a car, It is bigger and faster than that car. That is a coat, It is blue and warm.* Concentrating attention on objects helps to prepare children for a world in which they are expected to act independently.

V   Causal Attribution Differences Arising out of Different Categorization Ways

A "causal attribution" is defined as the perceived cause of a given event or situation. One of the greatest and most remarkable misunderstandings we have about people arises from differences present in our causal attribution patterns established by people of different ways of categorization.

1. Causal Attribution Differences and Attention Focuses

The Westerner prefers categories and focuses on objects when explaining, whereas we are more likely to emphasize relationships, depending on the environment. So it should come as no surprise that Chinese people are more inclined to attribute behavior to context and the Chain of Causation(缘起说, i.e. the process of one thing leading to another), the core of Buddhism which stresses that birth, death and rebirth that take place according to laws of karma(报应) may also be repeated again and again, which process can only be stopped by achieving Nirvana, was quickly accepted when Buddhism was first introduced into China during the Han Dynasty. And it is not surprising that the Westerner is more apt to attribute the same behavior to the same actor, and what captures his attention is what he is likely to regard as causally important.

There is ample evidence that the causal attribution differences mirror the attention differences. When asked to explain why he or she supported Barack Hussein Obama to be US president, the American interviewee might explain in terms of presumed personality traits and other dispositions of his (e.g. *unique candidate, a path breaker, the new face of American Politics, "clean" candidate, the first African-American candidate for Presidency, the American dream of Martin Luther King, capable*). When asked to explain why former Premier Wen Jiabao is so dearly loved by ordinary Chinese people, we tend to explain in terms of contextual factors such as *He shows concern for the vulnerable group. As one of the top leaders of China, he is approachable and dependable. He, in spite of old age, went to the quake zone as soon as he got the news and shared the sufferings of Sichuan people.*

2. More than Preferences for Context or Objects

Differences in causal reasoning between Chinese and Westerners are broader than just preferences for environment or objects. Let us take for example how Chinese and American middle school teachers deal with historical events.

History teachers in China generally begin by describing the context of a given set of events in some detail. They then explain the important events in chronological order, making sure to link each event to its successor, i.e. putting emphasis on the initial event that serves as the impetus to subsequent events. Students are encouraged to imagine the mental and emotional states of historical figures by thinking about the analogy between their situations and situations of the students' everyday lives. The actions of historical figures are then analyzed in terms of these feelings, because the students cannot be regarded as having good ability to think historically until when they show empathy with the historical figures, including those who were the enemy of the Chinese people. Therefore "how" is frequently asked in the process of studying history. The answer to "how" presents events in cause-effect sequence, which is similar to process-oriented reasoning.

My thirteen year old boy Minchang did not do well in his history class during his stay in Texas partly because his history teacher adopted a different way to illustrate historical facts. Unlike his history teacher in China his American teacher would begin with the outcome (e.g. *The short history of the Texas Republic was troubled. Financing the new government proved to be difficult—foreign investors were leery about loaning money.*) rather than with the initial event or catalyst. In class, the chronological sequence of events was destroyed in presentation dominated by discussion of the causal factors assumed to be important (e.g. *The budding Texas Republic collapsed for three major reasons. The first one is...*). Students are not considered to have good ability to reason historically until when they are capable of citing evidence to fit their causal pattern of the outcome. So "why" is asked more frequently. The answer to "why" presents events in effect-cause sequence, which is similar to goal-oriented reasoning.

3. A Case of Miscommunication

Ian Brown, a colleague of mine from Canada, told me the other day, "Sometimes it is very difficult for me to understand my students' writings because I don't see any causality in them, and...the relation of cause and effect is elementary logic." He showed me a written request for leave of absence by one of his students. It goes as follows:

Mr. Brown, I have got a phone call from my family, telling me that my grandma is ill in hospital. I was brought up by my grandma. I cannot imagine a life without her. I must go home right away to be with her (in Hunan Province). I apologize for the inconvenience my absence from your class may cause to you.

Thanks!

Your student: Shelly

Ian was confused: What does she apologize for? Why does she think her absence may cause inconveniences? I can't see any logic in the written request! Moreover, "dear" is missing here, so Mr. Brown had the feeling that this student showed him no respect.

Further Reading

1. Graham, B. & Ashworth, G.J. (2000). *A Geography of Heritage: Power, Culture, and Economy.* London: Arnold, Oxford.

2. Nisbett, R. E. (2003). *The Geography of Thought: How Asians and Westerners Think Differently and Why.* New York: The Free Press.

3. Kolb, R. K. (1976). *Survival Kit for Overseas Living.* Yarmouth: Intercultural Press.

4. Covey, S. R. (2004). *The 8th Habit: From Effectiveness to Greatness.* Free Press.

5. Said, E. (1978). *Orientalism.* NY: Pantheon Books.

6. 马玉珂(1985):《西方逻辑史》,北京:中国人民大学出版社。

7. 周云之(2004):《中国逻辑史》,山西:山西教育出版社。

8. 周宁(2007):《世界之中国:域外中国形象研究》,南京:南京大学出版社。

Unit 11　Non-controllers vs. Controllers

... For misery, happiness is leaning against it; for happiness, misery is hiding in it. Who knows whether it is misery or happiness? There is no certainty. The righteous suddenly becomes the vicious; the good suddenly becomes the bad.

—King Wen and Duke of the Zhou

In the <u>I Ching</u> or the <u>Book of Changes</u> supposedly written by King Wen and Duke of the Zhou, there are many inspiring aphorisms. How do you understand this one?

The high risk of divorce doesn't seem to make Americans afraid to try marriage again and again. By middle age, about 95% of Americans have been married at least once. About 80% of those who get divorced eventually remarry. In fact, remarriage and the creation of new families are so common in the US that one American joke tells of a wife calling to her second husband, "Quick, John! Come here and help me! Your children and my children are beating up our children!"

—Anonymous

For further personal exploration and enlightenment: Read more and try to figure out Western stance towards life.

Several years ago, after I finished reading Leo Tolstoy's <u>Resurrection</u> with tears in my eyes, I wrote on its title page, "Life itself is a tragedy."

However, that is not how things are, for life is not a tragedy, but a "struggle". What do we live for? Or why do we live this life at all? The answer given by Roman Rolland is "to conquer life".

—Ba Jin

Are you satisfied with the answer given by the Nobel Prize Laureate Roman Rolland? Why or why not?

I   Too Early to Tell

When asked to comment on the impact of the French Revolution, PRC's first Premier Zhou Enlai (1898—1976) famously said, "It's too early to tell." The answer was not expected by Western reporters, but not surprising to Chinese given the fact that Zhou was nurtured in China where almost everybody knows the ancient Chinese parable about an old farmer who lived in the border area of north China. Here is the story:

One day, the old border man's only horse ran away. Knowing that the horse was the mainstay of his livelihood, his neighbors came to sympathize with him. "Who knows what's bad or good?" said the old man, turning down their sympathy. A few days later his horse returned, bringing with it a wild horse. The old man's neighbors came to congratulate him. Refusing their congratulations, the old man said, "Who knows what's bad or good?" As it happened, a few days later when the old man's son was trying to ride the wild horse, he was thrown off its back and one of his legs was broken. The neighbors came to show their sympathy because he had only one son and he was very old and in bad need of his son's help in the field. Rejecting their commiseration the old man said, "Who knows what's bad or good?" A few weeks passed. The government's army came to the village to conscript all the able-bodied men to fight a war against the invading Huns, but the old man's son was not fit to serve and thus was safe away from the bloody battlefield.

The story is interesting because nobody knows whether something is a blessing or not, which expresses a fundamental Chinese stance towards life: The world is constantly changing, full of contradictions and surprises, and hence uncontrollable.

II   Why So Different Stances Towards Life?

Zhou Enlai's response and the parable about the old border farmer (塞翁) indicate that we believe in uncontrollability rather than controllability, and hence most often we make no attempt to control. But facts like the high rate of remarriage in the West shows that Westerners are disposed to take actions and try to keep things under their control. Regarding the causes of this difference, some plausible explanations have already been provided.

1. Different Philosophies

a. Chinese Philosophical Emphasis on Change

Chinese life stance is shaped by the blending of three different schools of philosophy—Taoism, Confucianism and Buddhism. Each school is concerned with the constantly changing nature of reality.

Let's take the Taoist *yin-yang* theory for example. According to Taoism, *yin* (literally, the feminine, dark, and passive) alternates with *yang* (literally, the masculine, light, and active). *Yin* and *yang* exist because of each other, and when the world is in a *yin* state, this is a sure sign that it is about to be in a *yang* state. The diagram of the Great Ultimate—the sign of Chinese culture— consists of two forces in the form of a white and a black fish. The black fish contains a white dot and the white fish contains a black dot. "The truest *yang* is the *yang* that is in the *yin*." The *yin-yang* theory is the expression of the relationship that exists between opposing but interpenetrating forces that may complement each other, make each other comprehensible, or create the conditions for changing one into the other, thus making constant change possible. In this sense, the *yin-yang* doctrine is about change. Therefore, for the Taoists the weakest can become the strongest which can become the weakest. Even the weakest female, under the greatest pressure or if treated very fairly, might become the most vicious and commit terrible crimes.

Chinese Buddhism also stresses the need for change. According to Buddhists, an evil-doer can become a good person quickly if he is willing to repent. They believe that a butcher can become a Buddha the moment he drops his cleaver(放下屠刀,立地成佛).

Since change is constant, it is hard to keep things under control, but we firmly believe what Mencius said more than two thousand years ago, "Those who follow Heaven's will survive and those who disobey Heaven's will perish(顺天者存,逆天者亡)."

b. Western Philosophical Insistence on Stability

An important aspect of the Western philosophy is the belief that the world is basically unchanging and stable. Indeed, the great pre-Socratic Greek philosopher Heraclitus (540 BC—480 BC) emphasized change and famously said, "A man never steps in the same river twice because the man is different and the river is different." By the fifth century, however, the notion of change was put aside and the stability theory was established by Parmenides (b.510 BC) and other Greek philosophers, who maintained that motion was impossible because they believed that the world was static. For instance, Parmenides' pupil Zeno (490 BC—430 BC) proved in a few easy steps that change was impossible. He did this in two demonstrations. One was his famous demonstration with the arrow. The other was his demonstration with the object. Another Greek philosopher Aristotle also proved that all celestial bodies were immutable, perfect spheres and though motion occurred and events happened, the essences of things remained unchanged.

Since things generally do not change, it is easy to keep them under control by categorizing them according to their attributes, establishing rules, forecasting tendency or direction, and being future-oriented.

2. Different Views of Objects

Those who have had much cross-cultural communication are convinced that objects—persons, places, things, or animals—are literally viewed in different ways.

a. A Holistic View

An ancient Chinese farmer had to consult with *feng shui* (wind and water) and others about almost everything ranging from sowing in spring, weeding in summer, harvesting in autumn to planning in winter for the following year, or even when to hold the wedding ceremony and when to bury the dead. This made it natural for him to holistically look at objects and make no efforts to control over things or people. Such a holistic view of objects could have encouraged the ancient Chinese assumption of change as well as an assumption that things were out of their control.

Modern Chinese also view objects holistically—so much so that it can be difficult for us to visually separate things or people from their environments, which leads us to develop a sense of uncontrollability.

b. An Analytic View

An ancient Greek could plan a grape harvest, arrange for a new place to grow olive trees, or investigate whether it would be more profitable to sell wine somewhere without consulting with others. This made it natural for him to focus on the attributes of objects with an analytic view toward categorizing them and finding rules that would help to make prediction and thus exert control over their own behavior. For him, results were due to attributes of objects or his own actions. Such an analytic view could have encouraged the Greek to be goal-orientated and assume that change was under his control since things are stable.

Modern Westerners, like ancient Geeks, are not overly constrained by objects' relations and they view objects analytically, which leads them to have a sense of personal control, even when they are actually not.

3. Different Senses of Self

a. Ancient Chinese Sense of Self

An ancient Chinese assumed that self was in a network of relationships and thus habitually looked around him before taking actions, for instance, outward toward his counterparts and upward toward authorities. This assumption made it natural for him to view objects or actions in general as continuous and composed of relationships, which encouraged recognition of complexity, change and contradictions, strengthening his belief in uncontrollability. Therefore, it is not hard to understand why today's Chinese are disposed to size the situation in general and feel the need to attend to social relations—so much so that we have an inclination to think that objects are uncontrollable.

b. Ancient Greek Sense of Self

An ancient Greek had an impressive sense of self. He assumed that self was unique and individual. Equipped with this assumption, he kept his own life under control and felt free to act as he chose. This sense of personal control and freedom accompanied a stronger sense of self, which made the Greek view himself as a special individual with distinctive attributes and goals. Therefore, the sense of being personally in control is an important source of the Western well-being.

4. Different Power Distances

More power or higher status means more control. There is no society where everyone is precisely equal to everyone else.

a. Higher Power Distance in Chinese Culture

In the traditional Chinese thought, people are unequal at birth. Apart from this, the orthodox Confucianism encourages a highly hierarchical way of thinking based on one's position within society. Therefore, in traditional China, those in lower positions of power simply supported their bosses' ideas and showed great respect for their bosses as well as reluctance to criticize them. They would probably think that it was natural for the bosses to change their policy and decisions without consulting with people in lower positions, and the employees' task was to obey. An ideal boss was expected to be fatherly, brotherly, or at least approachable. Likewise, children at school were taught to respect and obey parents, teachers, and others in authority. Therefore, Chinese culture is usually grouped in the category of higher power distance cultures, in which one may find it hard to develop a sense of controllability since there is always somebody who is more powerful.

b. Low Power Distance Cultures

In some Western countries, it is believed that people are born equal. As for differences in power or status, they deem it necessary to eliminate, minimize or at least not to emphasize them. They are low power distance cultures.

In low power distance countries, those in lower positions in the hierarchy are likely to approach and criticize their boss. For them, the boss may be in a higher position, but that does not mean he deserves any privileges. As for children, they are encouraged to become adults as soon as possible by claiming the privileges of adults whenever possible and to learn how to keep things under personal control when they are little. In such a system, one may find it easier to develop a sense of controllability since people are fundamentally equal and independent.

c. Power Distances and Different Approaches to Teaching and Learning

A Chinese visiting scholar at New York University told me that she was impressed by the role of her American professors in the classroom. The professors didn't act as an authority who gives final conclusions, but as a researcher looking for answers to questions together with the students. She has also noticed one linguistic feature in their interaction with the students was that they used many modal verbs. When answering questions, they usually said, "This is my personal opinion and it could be wrong. It would be a good idea if you could read the book I mentioned the other day." "You could be right, but you might find this point of view also interesting." When making comments on students' performances, the professors usually said, "There might have been greater clarity if you had incorporated some of the ideas we discussed earlier this semester."

In China, authorities are always supposed to give wise decisions and correct directions. They usually say, "Keep this in mind." "It's dollars to doughnuts that..." "You must..." Therefore, students always expect the professor to give a correct answer to the question. Once Chinese students get the answer, they are sure about it. So the professor makes far more assertions and finds it difficult to use modal verbs for the function of modal verbs is to provide room for negotiation and different ideas.

To sum up, different power distances result in different approaches to teaching and learning, which also helps to develop different stance towards life.

III "Being" and "Doing" Cultures

If one is preoccupied with a sense of control, he or she will try to take actions, which may make himself or herself feel in control. Hence Western culture is also known as "doing" culture, since it lays emphasis on doing or actions, although too much doing can create a feeling of drowning in stress. On the contrary, there is much support in traditional Chinese culture for a human "being" rather than a human "doing".

1. "Being" Culture

When we were little, our parents used to tell us: If life is simple, you only have to open your mouth in order to achieve something; life as simple as that is naturally controllable. However, to us life in reality is complex and subject to changes without advance notice, and hence not easily controlled. Rather than attempting to control situations, we try to adapt to them or just let them be. That is why we have been encouraged to be humble and modest, to live in harmony with nature and at the rhythm of nature because of the assumption that everything has spirit obtained from nature and what is important is to remain balanced.

An American colleague of mine once commented, "Americans are more afraid of death and aging than many other people—we want to deal with it instead of accepting it." But this is not the case with us exposed to the "being" culture. Our matter of fact approach is illustrated in proverbs like *Human life is nothing but a stage over which the sun and the moon function as two spotlights* (人生一台戏, 日月两盏灯). *We live our lives in the same way as grass passes the seasons from spring to autumn* (人生一世, 草木一秋), and *There is no distinction between the old and the young among those on their way to the tomb* (黄泉路上无老少). Those proverbs exemplify Chinese belief that man is born to die and that life is merely a journey from womb to tomb, a natural process governed by an objective law that no one can escape. No matter what efforts one might make, everyone succumbs to mortality within a certain time span. Nothing can be done other than follow the natural process from birth to death. Therefore, the best policy is to let it be (顺其自然).

In short, "being" culture produces non-controllers who adapt and accept rather than controllers who take actions in order to keep things under their control.

2. "Doing" Culture

Westerners, although aware of the inevitability of death, try all means to stop or put it off instead of passively and philosophically accepting it like Chinese. This kind of effort can be found in the British heavy metal band Black Sabbath who sang in 1978 that "Never say die". The same maneuver is also reflected in George Washington, the first US President. During the American Independence War (1775—1783), he not only established the thought of "we can do it" as an integral part of the American spirit, but also exemplified the spirit after the war: Of the nine presidents who owned slaves, only he freed his; he resisted efforts to make him a king and established the precedent that no one should serve more than two terms as President; he voluntarily did what he promoted, setting up an example for the "doing" people.

Westerners are "doing" people, bent on achieving specific goals. They develop procedures, measure results and put stress on actions. For the "doing" people humans can be above nature. They try to make life comfortable and convenient. To them problems can be solved once they know the facts, so they remain objective and scientific.

"Doing" people are controllers who value predictability, so they emphasize inspecting the work that has been underway and controlling the procedures for producing quality work. They want things to be correctly done. Therefore, they value accuracy and precision in those they work with. Take former American Secretary of State Hilary Clinton for instance. As soon as she failed in her presidential campaign, she turned to support her rival Barack Obama and made it clear in her exit speech delivered at 4:34 PM Saturday, June 7th 2008 that "Life is too short, time is too precious, and the stakes are too high to dwell on what might have been. We have to work together for what still can be. And that is why I will work my heart out to make sure that Senator Obama is our next president. And I hope and pray that all of you will join me in that effort."

3. Distinctive "Being" and "Doing" Cultures

The biggest difference between "being" culture and "doing" culture, as evidence suggests, is that feeling in control is not as important for Chinese as it is for Westerners.

a. Different Definitions of Happiness

Feelings of happiness are enhanced more for us if we have other people around who might assist in providing control, while feeling in control of their lives is strongly associated with mental health for Westerners. We are satisfied that we are simply in the same boat with others, whereas Westerners are happy that they have direct, personal control.

b. Different Interpretations of Leadership

Westerners resent being told what to do or how to do. Leaders in the West usually make their requests as questions instead of commandments. For example, to tell a Westerner "Go to do it", even if you are the boss, will irritate him. "Could you help out?" will have the same effect without resenting him. Authoritarian leadership is much more tolerated in China since leadership is traditionally hierarchical, not team-based. When a Chinese boss orders one to do something, it means he is in control and responsible, not necessarily abusing power. Therefore, he is often heard using the imperative mood when making his requests.

c. Different Ideas of Modesty and Honesty

Westerners, as "doing" people, are not necessarily being dishonest if they openly say that they are accomplished at something they don't know. They believe, "it can be done as long as you do it." On the contrary, we are *keqi* about our skills, and will passively wait for someone to ask us to use our skills instead of volunteering our talents. I was told the following story shortly after I arrived in Houston in 2007:

Two friends, one American and the other Chinese, were asked which one of them could fix a fountain in the hallway. The American said, "Hey, no problem. I've done it many times and I can get it running in no time." The Chinese responded *keqily*, "I can give it a try but I am not that experienced." Undoubtedly the American got the job. He fiddled with the fountain this way and that for quite a while and then gave up. His Chinese friend then came up to the fountain, fiddled with it for a little while and got it fixed. The American got very irritated and shouted accusingly at his friend, "You are a liar!" And that brought an end to a friendship.

Keqi means being considerate, polite, and well mannered. It also represents humbleness and modesty. We often use *keqi* in the negative, as in "*bu keqi*," meaning "no, no, no. You shouldn't be so kind and polite to me." To be more specific, we tend to degrade ourselves to show modesty by negating complimentary remarks or our own abilities, and that makes Westerners think of Chinese to be dishonest and rude for they hate what they said being negated and they don't like negative people. They want to feel things are under their control and they like to make others have a sense of being in control by complementing or volunteering their talents.

IV   Manifestations of "Being" Culture and "Doing" Culture

1. Manifestations of "Being" Culture

In "being" culture, people do not try to be controllers; even though they do they will not care about the result, leaving the final decision for Heaven or authorities to make, which is clearly expressed in the following proverbs:

Man proposes and Heaven disposes (谋事在人,成事在天).

Submit to the will of Heaven. /Resign oneself to one's fate. /Trust to luck (听天由命).

Do not feel panic if the sky should fall, because the taller people would hold it up (天塌了,有高个子顶着).

"Being" people are very tolerant. Sometimes they are likely to take things for granted without making any complaints or efforts, which is revealed in the proverb "天下无不散之筵席 (i.e. all good things must come to an end; the best of friends must part; there is no never ending banquet under the sun)."

To adapt themselves to reality however harsh it is, people in "being" culture will say to themselves contentedly, "We are worse off than some, better off than many (比上不足,比下有余)," and "The table will turn in my favor (风水轮流转)." Meanwhile they keep encouraging themselves and saying when in trouble, "好事多磨 (i.e. good happenings, results, achievements, etc. must go through many trials and tribulations)." Confronted with the rapidly changing world, witnessing so many ups and downs, they manage not to be pleased by external gains, nor saddened by personal losses (不以物喜,不以己悲) and struggle to live in contentment.

In one word, non-controllers or "being" people recognize the necessity of human effort but also admit the futility of it. This dialectical attitude has a tendency to develop passive defensive tactics such as *Great things can be reduced into small things, and small things can be reduced into nothing*.

Life in "being" culture moves on, therefore, on the line of least struggle and least resistance. This develops a certain calmness of mind, which enables one to swallow insults and find oneself in harmony with others and not in control. However, in such a culture, there is strong hidden resistance to change, and those who pay no attention to self-cultivation are disposed to violate regulations and rules without any punishment.

2. Manifestations of "Doing" Culture

Who is the original author of the aphorism "Deeds, not words" is not important now. What matters is that this much-quoted saying shows that doing is more favored than speaking in Western culture. In "doing" culture, people try to be controllers, and for them doing is better than not doing. To feel themselves personally in control, controllers are not afraid of trying new things that are usually very challenging. Napoleon Bonaparte exemplified this spirit. He is remembered to have confidently said, "The man who has made up his mind to win will never say 'Impossible.'"

In such a culture where doing is highly favored, people don't judge a book by its cover, nor judge a person by his appearance. As the proverb goes, "We can't judge a person by what he says but by what he does." It is believed by Westerners that "easier said than done".

As is known to all, Western culture is heavily influenced by Christian culture. Many Westerners are Christians who declare to leave themselves in the hands of God, obeying Him, praising Him, and asking for everything from Him, but meanwhile the saying "God helps those who help themselves" is one of the most-frequently-quoted aphorisms in the West.

3. Impacts of Two Cultures on Daily Lives

Differences are present in almost every aspect of our daily lives. Two aspects are to be illustrated here.

a. Keeping Children Safe

When an American and a Chinese family spend a day together, the American toddlers are allowed to run around, and when they fall down, they stand up by themselves. The Chinese toddlers, on the contrary, are not allowed to play around and are watched for the whole time by their parents or grandparents. When they fall down, they are picked up, cleaned, and comforted. Thus it can be seen that Americans are less uncertain while Chinese are more uncertain and try their best to avoid uncertainties instead of controlling them.

In China, children from a so-called good family are not allowed to play with children of unknown origin. The children learn to identify who they are when they are very little. But in some Western countries, for instance the Netherlands, parents are not afraid to let their kids play with unfamiliar children. Children in this culture are told to learn by making mistakes. To Chinese parents, what is different might be dangerous. But to Dutch parents, what is different is curious and interesting. Evidently, Chinese people are more passive while Westerners are more active and more willing to actively cope with differences and uncertainties.

b. Waiting at the Train Station

In China, free timetables about all arriving and leaving times of trains are available in almost every waiting room of every railway station, but not many people go and get one, expecting anything could delay the arriving or leaving times of trains, since things are in constant change.

In Germany, there is in every train a magazine called Zugbegeleiter. This magazine contains all arriving and leaving times of trains. Everybody is looking at his watch and Zugbegeleiter when a train is arriving. Actually, this is a typical thing for controllers. The German people want to know precisely when a train arrives and when it leaves so that they know for sure that they won't be late for doing something according to their schedule.

4. When Chinese Meet Westerners

a. In Negotiations

As "doing" people, Western negotiators are more likely to do things such as changing their position in the middle of an argument and consulting with colleagues in the middle of a session. This flexibility can be explained as a desire to achieve the goal—an agreement or a contract. To reach the goal, the details can be changed, which makes them feel they are in control of the situation.

In "being" culture, decisions are usually made through consultation with several levels in a hierarchy, so Chinese negotiators may not be free to change their positions during actual face-to-face negotiating sessions, because they know even if they change things might not work. But after the formal session the negotiators will consult with all the important decision-makers and may change their position and some of the details.

David Jones, my 25-year-old colleague from America, learned this the hard way. When he first came to China, he tried to negotiate for improved working and living conditions with his immediate supervisor and expected her to be persuaded by his reasonable arguments. When his boss said "no", he felt upset. Later he came to realize that he would get better results by simply stating what he wanted, giving good reasons and then going away to give his boss a chance to discuss with her bosses. Often his boss would come back to him several days later with a decision—to both parties' satisfaction.

b. In Marriage

Michael White, a British businessman, married his soul mate Li Meimei in Nanjing several years ago. Despite cultural differences, he managed to have a sweet life with his Chinese wife. Unfortunately, they are now talking about a divorce. Here is an email from Michael:

Dear Jifang,

Meimei is spending a lot of her time with her daughter Jenny and her husband Tom in Shanghai and they want us to move in there and live altogether, Tom's parents and we two, something I will never agree to. So Meimei lately has been talking about a divorce and maybe it will be for the best if I let her divorce me, although on what grounds I do not know. In a house with six adults and a baby is not my idea of happiness, not what I got married for. We had four very happy years of togetherness and then this last 16 months or so has been very upsetting since Jenny gave birth to her baby. So we shall see.

Love and Kind Wishes

Michael

Meimei is a typical Chinese woman. Traditionally the Chinese woman is not a controller of her own life; she leaves everything even including where she lives for others to decide. By "others", I mean her father before she gets married, her husband after she gets married, and her son (or daughter) after her husband is gone. Meimei's first husband died of a car accident when her only daughter Jenny was little. She did not remarry until Jenny married Tom. Her marriage to Michael, although arranged by her daughter Jenny, had been very beautiful until 16 months ago when Jenny gave birth to a baby boy. Meimei who brought up her daughter as a single parent feels very happy to babysit her little grandson. To her great relief, her daughter and son-in-law kindly ask Michael to join their bigger family, seven now, including Tom's parents. It never occurred to Meimei that Michael, an aged step-father with many health problems, would refuse. "No! I don't want the baby to control my life," said Michael adamantly, "this is not what I got married for." Michael's response greatly perplexed Meimei and hurt her feelings. Suddenly Meimei found herself talking about divorce— in spite of herself.

c. In Job hunting

The most effective strategies to persuade a potential employer to offer you a job vary from culture to culture. Chinese applicants often think they should say that they are hardworking, creative and easy-going. This may be acceptable to a Chinese employer with "being" culture values, but a record of what you have accomplished with your hard work, creativity and people skills is necessary to persuade a Westerner from the "doing" culture. For a "doing" person, referring to your hard work is merely a statement of your character for him. He wants to know what you can do instead of what you are.

d. A Pet Peeve

There is a bigger pet peeve for Westerners not just in China, but in any culture where it is considered rude to give a plain and forthright "no" in reply to a question or request. That pet peeve is when foreigners are given the reply of "maybe" or "perhaps" when they really need a yes or no. Americans in particular prefer to receive a definite answer to a question even if the answer is "no". "Maybe" or "perhaps" is not an acceptable answer. Many Westerners feel that Chinese people often prefer to answer questions with "maybe" or "perhaps" so they are not committed. For them, it may be that you truly do not know the answer to a question. If that is the case, just say so. Then the listener can take actions and tries to keep things under control.

As a matter of fact, many cultures—including Chinese, go to great lengths not to be direct. The risk of disharmony with other group members is too uncontrollable for us to be outspoken. It's better to say "maybe" or "perhaps" and negotiate with them afterwards than to blatantly disagree or agree.

Further Reading

1. Davis, L. (2001). *Doing Culture.* Beijing: Foreign Language Teaching and Research Press.

2. Duiker, William J. (1978). *Cultures in Collision: The Boxer Rebellion.* Novato, CA: Presidio Press.

3. Hofstede, G. (1980). *Culture's Consequences: International Differences in Work Related Value.* Beverly Hills, CA: Sage Publications.

4. Hofstede, G. (1991). *Cultures and Organizations: Software of the Mind* (Revised and expanded 2nd ed.). New York: McGraw-Hill.

5. Ramo, J. C. (2007). *Brand China.* UK: The Foreign Policy Center.

6. 林语堂 (1998). *The Importance of Living.* 上海：外语教学与研究出版社。

7. 王钰 (2006).《权力与声誉：对中国在美国国家形象及其构建的研究》,上海：复旦大学出版社。

8. 周宁(2010).《世界的中国形象》,北京：人民出版社。

Part IV

Different Cultural Orientations

Cultural orientation (文化取向) *means a pattern or value system which this culture uses to respond to the world around us. It reflects the complex interaction of the values, attitudes, and behaviors displayed by the majority of the members of a particular culture. Individuals express culture and its normative qualities through the values that they hold about life and the world around them. These values, in turn, affect their attitudes about the form of behavior considered more appropriate and effective in any given situation. The continually changing patterns of individual and group behaviors eventually influence the society's culture.*

In this part, cultural orientation is broken down into 5 main dimensions:

- *The introvert-oriented vs. the extrovert-oriented*
- *Collectivism vs. individualism*
- *Femininity vs. masculinity*
- *Advocacy of Jing vs. Dong*
- *Implicitness vs. explicitness.*

Unit 12   The Introvert-oriented vs. the Extrovert-oriented

Chinese greet each other by holding hands of their own, whereas Westerners shake hands or hug when greeting others, for Chinese are introversive and Westerners are extroversive. The introversive Chinese uses one hand to hold the other of his own. However, the extroversive Westerner extends his hand to grasp the other person's hand as a greeting. Just as using chopsticks to send food to his mouth, so the Chinese uses his energy in an inward-directed fashion; just as using forks at meals, the Westerner employs his strength in an outward-directed fashion. One reaches out, the other in, and naturally the symbol of Western culture is Cross, and that of Chinese culture, Diagram of the Great Ultimate.

—Yi Zhongtian

For discussion: Study the patterns of Diagram of the Great Ultimate and Cross, and explain why they are accepted as cultural symbols.

Fine feathers make fine birds.

—An English proverb

This proverb is roughly equivalent to the Chinese one "人靠衣装，马靠鞍 (literally, beautiful clothes make beauties, and saddles make elegant horses; freely, clothes make the man)." What do you say to the two proverbs?

I   Personality Types

There is an old saying in Nanjing which goes, "一娘生九子，九子各不同 (literally, one mother gives birth to nine sons; the nine sons are different from one another)." Why are there differences between people from the same background?

1. Two Personality Types

Much of what happened around us can be explained when we look at the personality types, especially the notion of introvert-extrovert distinction. For instance, one of the biggest differences between people depends on whether they are introverts or extroverts. Extroverts are disposed to be interested and comfortable when they are working with people or things. They incline to focus on the outer world and are the talkers. Introverts are a different kind of people: They are quiet, and tend to be more involved and comfortable when they are working with ideas and concepts. These differences between introverts and extroverts are the biggest source of miscommunications, misunderstandings and communication breakdowns between those who sincerely want to get along. Extroverts tend to see introverts, because of their quietness, as closed, secretive, moody, and unresponsive. Introverts are likely to see extroverts, because of their love of being social, as exhausting, shallow, and noisy. Consequently, we get along easily with certain people while others drive us nuts.

2. A Blend of Introversion and Extroversion

Most people seem to be a blend of introversion and extroversion. One of the reasons is that there are two different ways of learning—abstract or concrete—and two different ways of making decisions—feeling and thinking. An extrovert's dominant or best-used function will be outward while an introvert's dominant function will be inward. But the extrovert will have an auxiliary second function which is introverted, and an introvert will have an auxiliary function which is extroverted.

It is important to note that while our root preferences stay the same throughout our lives, they can be affected by circumstances. An introverted child exposed to an extroverted culture may feel ridiculed and has to put on an extroverted mask while hurting inside. An outgoing child exposed to a more introverted culture may be criticized for being precocious or too noisy, and equally has to develop a protective suit. It can take years to recover from being forced to live outside one's preferences. Therefore, in reality all of us are a blend of introversion and extroversion.

II　Personality Types of Cultures

Many of the cultural differences can also be explained in terms of the personality types, particularly the notion of introvert-extrovert distinction.

1. A Historical Fact

During the period from 1405 to 1433, a treasure fleet under the command of the eunuch admiral Zheng He (1371—1435) made seven voyages throughout the China Seas and Indian Ocean, from Taiwan to the Persian Gulf and distant Africa. During the thirty years, China extended its sphere of influence through the Indian Ocean, half the world was in its grasp, and with such a formidable navy the other half was easily within reach—had China wanted it, but China chose not to.

Shortly after the last voyage of the treasure fleet, the Chinese emperor forbade overseas travel and stopped all building and repair of oceangoing junks. Disobedient merchants and seamen were killed. Within a hundred years the greatest navy the world had ever known willed itself into extinction and Japanese pirates ravaged the Chinese coast. The period of China's greatest outward operation in history was followed by a period of its greatest isolation.

In 1498 when Portuguese navigator Vasco da Gama (1469—1524) and his fleet of three battered caravels rounded the Cape of Good Hope and landed in East Africa on their way to India, they met natives who sported embroidered green silk caps with fine fringe. Village elders told tales of white "ghosts" who wore silk and had visited their shores long ago in large ships. But no one knew anymore who these people had been or where they had come from. It is da Gama and the other European explorers who started the wave of outward expansion that would change the map of the world.

2. The Introverted Character of Chinese Culture

a. No Intension of Outward Expansion

Because of its introverted character(内敛性), China in the Ming Dynasty had no intention of outward expansion at all.

Although we have been solemnly swearing, "人不犯我 , 我不犯人 ; 人若犯我 , 我

必犯人(literally, we will not attack unless we are attacked; if we are attacked, we will certainly counterattack)," this slogan actually denotes the age-old passive defense strategy. Even an ambitious ruler like Emperor Wu of the Han Dynasty had no intention at all to actively expand outward. He just ordered his great army to enter the area where the Hun stationed in order to stop the harassment by them to ensure his people's personal and property safety. A ruler as aggressive as the First Emperor of the Qin Dynasty, instead of expanding northward to drive away aggressors, had the Great Wall built to stop the northern barbarians who regularly raided the Chinese farming villages, leaving us a symbol of passive defense and introverted character.

b. Introverts and Extroverts in China

Traditional Chinese culture undoubtedly favors introverts. For instance, during the first visit to his future parents-in-law, a young man is expected to speak less, listen more, and answer politely, clearly and briefly. In the meantime he should sit like a bell and stand like a pine tree. So to speak, he is expected to appear more mature and steady so that his future parents-in-law will feel safe to let him take away their daughter. Most Chinese parents disfavor talkers because they appear immature and thus are not dependable. So there are many drawbacks to being an extrovert in China. An extrovert may have a harder time at school where academic success is the first consideration, for he will probably enjoy socializing with others more than reading books and taking notes in his classroom. So it's challenging for a parent to have an extroverted school-age child because of the large amount of solitary studying often required to do well. An extrovert in the office may appear very popular with his colleagues, but when it comes to promotion he will probably be "put aside" because of lack of the expected steadiness(欠稳重) and deep throat.

c. Why Chinese Are More Introversive

"Rome was not built in a day." It took many years for Chinese culture to become introversive, even to the extent that women's feet became notoriously smaller and smaller, and people found it harder to say "I love you" even to their family.

First of all, the orthodox Confucianism advocates introversive activities such as self-cultivation and self-criticism. For the Confucianists, self-cultivation is a lifelong process of cultivating a moral and spiritual character since the second sage Mencius favored "cultivating the great moral force (养吾浩然之气)". The *Great Learning*, one of the Confucian cannons, attempts to establish the value of self-cultivation in terms of accepted social norms, which requires a certain amount of self-criticism. Chinese schoolchildren are therefore taught how to practice self-criticism in order to live peacefully with others. This stance of perfectionism through self-criticism continues throughout life.

Secondly, Taoism encourages people to cultivate body by living far away from the noisy secular world in the mountain and by the riverside, and Buddhism, one of the three great teachings, has been used by people to nurture mind by meditating.

Thirdly, the ideal climate and rapid agricultural development of ancient China provided a good foundation for the formation of an agrarian economy of self-reliance and self-support, encouraging inactivity. Such an economy determined that Chinese culture is a culture of root deeply rooted in soil, blood-based relationships, and ancestor worship.

In one word, the introverted character is a legacy of about 2,000 years of history. Here only a few of the reasons why Chinese culture becomes introversive are mentioned, for it is hard to distinguish between cause and effect, just as it is difficult to solve the problem of what comes first, the chicken or the egg. The introverted character of Chinese culture may explain why China remains the world's longest continuous civilization in spite of various ordeals during its thousand years of development. On the other hand, this character has undoubtedly, to some extent, set back the development of China.

3. The Extroverted Character of Western Culture

a. The Inevitableness of Outward Expansion

Da Gama's voyage was followed by the establishment of one colony after another. This kind of outward expansion for the sake of profits and markets was inevitable given the extroverted character (外倾性) of Western culture. This character of Western civilization has long determined its direction of development—expanding externally, and expressing its desires through practical actions, and discouraging inactivity. Later with the development of its capitalist economy the West became much more extrovert-oriented, transcending restrictions and obstacles on its way of development. For instance, in science scientists focused their attention on changing the nature and society and benefiting from them; in medicine they used external means such as medicine and medical devices to treat patients; in politics, economy, and military, they invaded, pillaged and resorted to arms.

b. Introverts and Extroverts in the West

Western culture seems to favor extroverts, despise and devalue introverts. Since their school days, Westerners have celebrated sportsmen and cheerleaders more than they have celebrated the studious, bookish type.

In Western countries, particularly in the United States, the extrovert is considered socially superior to the introvert, as he genuinely enjoys the company of others in large groups. The extrovert is often perceived as engaging and exciting. On the contrary, introverts are so widely disfavored that knowing how to raise one can be challenging for a parent.

c. Why Westerners Are More Extroversive

What have been helpful for the formation of the extroverted character of Western Culture?

First, Western culture originates from ancient Greek and Roman cultures as well as Hebrew culture. The three cultures have one thing in common, that is, they are developed on the basis of sea trade, transportation, and colonization because of want of ideal agricultural environment. These professions require those who are involved in them to be extroverted, outward-looking and fearless.

Second, Western society encourages liberty and openness and favors out-going people, which orients the culture further towards extroversion.

Third, Western philosophy, eager to acquire new concepts to enrich itself, encourages people to be extroverted, stretching out, expanding, conquering, controlling, and looking outside.

Fourth, Christianity has endowed Westerners with a strong sense of mission—

spreading God's message across every corner of the world, which makes Westerners more extrovert-oriented.

Arguably, the extroverted character is a legacy of many years of history.

III Effects of Personality Types on Pattern Preferences

"One's fate is determined by his personality."(Heraclitus) This aphorism vividly accounts for the importance of personality. As a central dimension of human personality, introversion and extroversion also find expressions in the thinking modes—introverted thinking and extroverted thinking. The former has helped to form the circle culture with circle patterns like the Diagram of the Great Ultimate as its logo, and the latter has played an important role in the formation of the grid culture with grid patterns like the Cross as its symbol.

1. The Circle and Grid Patterns in People's Life

a. The Circle Pattern

"The empire, long divided, must unite; long united, must divide. Thus it has ever been." With this characterization of the inevitable cycle of Chinese history, *Romance of the Three Kingdoms* begins and meanwhile defines the circle pattern which characterizes Chinese history. It is really incredible how many facets of Chinese life the pattern touches. Most of the cities and towns of China, for instance, are arranged in the circle pattern. Take Beijing for example. Beijing's urban transport is dependent upon the five "ring roads" that successively surround the metropolis, with the Forbidden City area marked as the geographical centre for the ring roads. The 1st Ring Road is not officially defined. The 2nd Ring Road is fully located in Beijing's inner city areas. Ring roads tend to resemble expressways as they progressively extend outwards, with the 5th Ring Road and the 6th Ring Road being full-standard National expressways—linked to other roads only with interchanges. Expressways to other regions of China are generally accessible from the 3rd Ring Road outward.

In the circle pattern important things are usually located at the center and everything else is drawn toward the center. In Jiangsu Province, for instance, almost all major roads lead to Nanjing, the capital city, and most mileage signs tell you how far you are from Nanjing.

The circle pattern is also visible in the social and political life of China. In rural areas, Chinese farmers live in villages where the ancestral hall is at the center. In a Chinese family picture the oldest male (i.e. the patriarch) sits at the center, and you can tell how important one is in the family by how far he is from the center or whether he sits, stands, or squats on the heels. In his ward, a new patient can tell immediately who is in the authority among a group of doctors in white who are doing their morning inspection— just by observing who is surrounded by the medical team.

b. The Grid Pattern

The grid pattern touches many facets of American life. Most of the cities and towns of the United States are arranged in a grid pattern. If you look at the map of Manhattan the grid pattern is very clear: The streets running east and west are numbered in sequence. The north-south streets are also numbered in sequence but are called avenues. The naming and numbering system varies from city to city, but the basic grid pattern is the same. With a pattern like this it is difficult to get lost, because the address of any building locates it in a specific place on the grid. This is a pattern that provides easy access even to strangers. The visitor does not need to rely on a knowledgeable local to find his way. I stayed for a week at #5601 Hollywood Blvd in Los Angles. In fact this place is not in the area of Hollywood, but far out close to downtown Los Angles. The grid pattern has been extended to the hotel, so anyone can easily find it.

This same pattern can be seen in the interstate highway system that covers the country with a grid of regularly numbered highways. The odd numbered roads run north and south and the even numbered roads run east and west. Interstate 45 will take you from Houston to Dallas and Interstate 44 will take you from west to Wichita Falls, Texas or east to St. Louis at Interstate 55. Anyone can go where he likes with the aid of a map.

The large farms of the mid-western America are arranged in a similar way. After the War of Independence the United States acquired large tracts of unsettled land from

England and promptly divided it into regularly shaped states, counties, townships, and farms. Each farm was a regular rectangle and one plot in each township and a larger tract in each state were set aside to meet the educational needs of the area. This pattern encouraged settlers to move west, because the grid provided a path for them to follow. It ordered and civilized the wilderness. From the airplane you can easily notice that the boundaries of many states are straight lines. And you can also find the same pattern in the characteristic American suburban sprawl. Those who rise in social class and income move out from the city into newer and more expensive housing areas far from the city. Older areas in the inner city are taken over by new arrivals. They live there until their fortunes improve, at which time they will follow the grid out to more desirable housing on the outskirts. This pattern has no fixed center. Any point on the grid can become important depending on what is located there. It can just as easily disappear into obscurity if economic development or public taste favors another location. New cities grow up at the intersections of the interstate highway system while the centers of older towns die from neglect. People want to know what opportunities they will find as they move out across the grid. Any corner can become a center.

c. The Cultural Patterning of Space

The circle and the grid cultures have caused two major systems for patterning of space. The Chinese system connects all points and functions. If you look at a map of China that shows the railway system, the circle pattern is clearly visible, and different lines repeatedly come together at places of interest like Beijing, Wuhan, Shanghai, and Guangzhou. But the Western grid system separates activities by stringing them out. China is a series of circular networks that build up into larger and larger centers. Each small center has its own channel to the next higher level. Generally the roads between centers do not go through other towns, because each town is connected to others by its own roads. This is in contrast to the American pattern of stringing small towns out like beads on a necklace along the routes that connect principal centers.

Both systems have advantages and disadvantages. For example, a mistake in direction in the circle system becomes more serious the farther one travels. In the grid system, baseline errors are of the 90-degree or the 180-degree variety and are usually obvious enough to make themselves felt even by those with a poor sense of direction. If you are traveling in the right direction, even though you are one or two blocks off your course, the error is easily rectified at any time. Nevertheless, there are certain inherent advantages in the circle system. Once one learns to use it, it is easier to locate objects or events in space by naming only one point on a line. Thus it is acceptable to tell a first-time visitor to meet you at the Qinhuai River Amusement Park(水木秦淮) not far from the Caochangmen Bridge west of Nanjing. That is all the information he needs. In contrast, the grid system involves at least two lines and a point to locate something in space. In the circle system, it is also possible to integrate a number of different activities in centers in less space than with the grid system. Thus, residential, shopping, marketing, commercial, and recreation areas can meet and be reached from central points.

2. The Circle and Grid Patterns in Political Life

a. The Collective Leadership with Comrade Xi Jinping as General Secretary

Power in the circle culture is likely to become over-concentrated. And history tells Chinese people that over-concentration of power is liable to give rise to arbitrary rule by individuals, thus hinders the practice of socialist democracy, impedes the progress of socialist construction and prevents us from taking full advantage of collective wisdom. Therefore, today we often read or hear remarks like "Let's unite closely around the Party Central Committee with Comrade Xi Jinping as general secretary, immerse ourselves in hard work, strive to fulfill the various tasks of next year's economic and social development, and create a new phase in reform, development and stability on our journey to building a relatively affluent society in an all-round way." It turns out that the collective leadership with President Xi Jinping at the center is very effective, which further proves the proper use of the traditional circle culture can benefit today's Chinese political system.

b. Separation of Powers in the West

Separation of powers is the Western political doctrine under which the executive, legislative and judicial branches of government are kept distinct to prevent abuse of power. The grid model for the governance of democratic states was first developed in ancient Greece and came into widespread use by the Roman Republic as part of the un-codified Constitution of the Roman Republic. Under this model, the state was divided into branches or estates, each with separate and independent powers and areas of responsibility. However, today no democratic system exists with an absolute separation of powers or an absolute lack of separation of powers. Nonetheless, some Western systems like American political system have been evidently founded on the principle of separation of powers. This U.S. form of separation of powers is also known as "checks and balances".

3. Co-existence of the Circle Pattern with the Grid One

Interactions with the West enable the circle pattern to co-exist with the grid pattern in China today. Here let's consider buildings in Beijing where traditional architecture is based on the circle pattern and appears introverted in style with emphasis on the enclosing walls. Enclosing walls have two main functions: One is to protect the buildings inside; the other is to indicate that the buildings inside are very important and treasured. The ancient buildings in Beijing that have survived to this day fall roughly into three categories: palaces, temples and private houses. The Forbidden City is the largest and best preserved ancient palace complex now extant. It is the most representative ancient palace in China. On each of its four sides are high walls which protect the buildings inside. The Yonghe Palace Lamasery, popularly known as the "Lama Temple", is one of the most famous temples in Beijing. All the buildings in the temple are surrounded by a high wall. There are many courtyards inside. The entrances to all the courtyards are in the south, whereas the most important buildings are all in the north. The buildings in the Lamasery form many layers. Only by going through layer after layer of courtyards can the tourists see the centre of the Lamasery—the Sacred Hall of the Wheel of the Law(法轮殿). In the old alleys known as hutong we can also see the characteristic traditional Chinese architecture. The walls on both sides of the alley are very high and they serve to protect the private houses behind and highlight their importance. The private houses are mostly courtyard houses, with the most important room situated in the north of the courtyard. The center of a private house is protected by lower inner walls and other buildings as well as by the outer walls.

While traditional buildings are introverted in style, modern ones are extroverted in Beijing. The layout of Zhongguancun is a good example. There are no enclosing walls in the Zhongguancun Square, which is completely open so that it is very easy for passers-by to enter the square. Hotels and apartment blocks face the streets, not surrounded by other buildings. It is said that the three most famous construction projects in Beijing are the Olympic Stadium and Gymnasium, the National Grand Theatre and the new China Central Television Station. Their design purpose, which is to attract the attention of passers-by and make people want to get in, is completely different from that of the high walls of the Forbidden City.

IV   A Contrast of Cultural Phenomena

Culture consists of a great many phenomena. These phenomena, like the cells that contain the secret of life, contain the genetic code—a nation's cultural code.

1. Candle Bundles (蜡烛包) and Baby Clothing

The custom of tying up newborn babies is very popular in many parts of China, especially the area on the middle and lower reaches of the Yangtze River. Parents usually put their nude baby in a small quilt, wrap it up and tie it up tightly with a cloth rope into something like a candle which is widely known as "candle bundle", because they believe tying up the baby can make it quiet, self-disciplined, and not hyperactive when it grows older. Arguably, Chinese self-cultivation and introverted character start from the tied bundle, a Chinese baby's first clothing.

However, Western parents neither tie up their babies tightly, nor let them be without any clothing. They choose soft fabrics as their newborn baby clothing, leave their babies' four limbs free of any restraints, enjoy watching the free movement of their babies, and are happy to see that their new baby is so active and outgoing.

2. Acting Classes and Piano Lessons

Chinese are apt to be introverted while Westerners are extroverted. The difference is not as simple as the assumption that Chinese speak less and Westerners speak more, but lies in whether one can better speak his mind, appear more confident, especially when making a public speech. It is known to many that one can speak very little and still attract listeners' attention. So most rich American parents take their children to acting classes to learn how to speak in public, what to say to appeal to listeners, how to behave, and how to cooperate with others in their acting rather than merely encourage them to join the show business. No wonder Western children with acting education are as relaxed as they are at other times when interviewed or making a speech in public.

However, rich Chinese parents take their children to piano, painting, calligraphy, or chess lessons to allow their kids to have a better chance of self-cultivation. As a result, Chinese children are publicity-shy, and it is very challenging for some of them to speak in public. Even if they do, they appear nervous and awkward, scratching their head, not knowing how to stand properly. For these reasons, some of them become aloof from public places and shun communication with others.

3. Body Touch

a. Guy-girl Friendship

Extroverted Westerners can have affectionate guy-girl friendship without any romantic interest. If you are not kissing or holding hands, you're probably not dating. Chinese tend to have a much lower threshold of what is considered a relationship because most of us express ourselves in an introversive way. What Westerners might consider a normal guy-girl friendship can be read as definite interest in the other person by Chinese. In particular, spending time alone with someone of the opposite sex is a strong sign of interest.

b. Hugging

Our introversion blocks us from explicitly expressing our kindness and closeness to others by using our body movement and gestures. Psychological research shows that children who are often touched and hugged are psychologically healthier than those who get less touch and hugs. Everyone has a need for human touch. Chinese children get far less hugs and kisses than Western children after they are more than 10 years old, almost no hugs and kisses are from parents, not to mention from other sources. Except holding hands, standing shoulder to shoulder or walking by linking arms, we don't have body touch with others until we are old enough to start dating. In other words, within a decade or even longer, we don't have very intimate body touch.

Meanwhile in the extroversive Western culture, parents and their children, siblings, and good friends never stop hugging or kissing each other. It is widely known that any speech cannot replace the expressions of our body. Body touch is highly recommended by both sociologists and psychologists. But we still rarely use body touch to transfer our intimate feelings and share our emotions. Is the fact a result or reason of our introversive culture?

4. Covering-up and Showing-off

Extroversive Westerners seem disposed to show off while introversive Chinese cover up.

Chinese ***Erhu*** can produce beautiful music with the whole instrument closed from inside, while its Western counterpart violin is hollow, with a very big round open door.

Chinese buns are closed without showing their contents, whereas an Italian pizza displays its content on the surface so that the consumer can make his decision by merely looking at the top.

The Chinese university campus is encircled with a high wall in order to create a serene and quiet atmosphere, while a Western one is open and accessible to anybody.

My summer in 2007 in Houston left me smiling a lot. After taking in the unfamiliar sight of girls in their shorts and short skirts and tank tops, I was astonished by how comfortable women felt displaying their cleavages. Imagine a young lady strutting her stuff like that on the street of Nanjing! She would attract lingering glances for sure. Not that I hadn't seen bare body or some cleavage in Nanjing. Magazines and movies are full of them, with more and more entertainers daring to bare a lot. But spotting common women on the street in low-cut blouses is a bit tricky.

5. Modesty and Confidence

When I was growing up I had a hard time responding to others' compliments. At the time I did not know one could just say "thank you" and accept all the compliments in the West. Complements made me feel good and proud, and I knew I welcome it. But I had to be modest and correct others that I was not that good for I was told that there will always be someone better than you, and you have to learn to be humble and modest. To a certain extent, there is truth and value in that. Some Chinese do manage to be modest to avoid unnecessary jealousness. Imagine 100 people around you value high grades as good, and you have got it, they can be so jealous and just want to isolate you to feel better themselves. Can you handle that? At the same time some Chinese can be very self-deprecating. It is not unusual for a man to introduce himself as "a silly old egg" to show his modesty.

The cultural divide in modesty is very real. American kids, exposed to an extroversive culture, are taught "Confidence will get you places(自信使人进步)". Chinese kids, at least my generation, were taught "Modesty will get you places". Both people follow their respective cultural training to make progress.

6. Handling the Deceased's Belongings

I have attended two burial ceremonies in my life. One is Chinese and the other is American.

At the Chinese ceremony, I saw my tutor set fire on his deceased wife's personal belongings such as her expensive beautiful clothes, handbags, purses, and pictures before putting her jewelry into her casket and locking it. In this way almost all the traces she had left in this world were erased by her dear husband, a sad lonely widower now.

At the American ceremony (not very typical), we gave thanks for the deceased's life and witness, sang songs, and then carved up some of his belongings. Every mourner had a share and went back home with a beautiful memory of the deceased and something once owned by him as a memento. As for his widow, she was grieved but was already talking about her plan for future.

7. Answers to Questions like "Would You Like Something to Drink?"

"Would you like something to drink?"

A typical reply from a polite Chinese is "no, no, thank you" although he is very thirsty. A hospitable hostess should keep offering drinks until her guest says as if embarrassed, "OK. I'm sorry to trouble you."

A typical reply from a polite Westerner on this occasion is "yes, please" if he is thirsty, or "no, thanks" if he is not.

This cultural divide has caused many jokes. One of them is about an American gentleman's first visit to a traditional Chinese family. When he was served the first cup of tea, he drank it up and said, "Nice tea!" Seeing that he liked the tea, his hostess said, "Then drink more, please." and she refilled his cup out of hospitality before he had time to say "no, thanks." No longer thirsty, he still bottomed it up out of politeness. The hostess hastened to put another big glass of fresh tea before him, assuming he must be a big drinker. The American said, "No, no more." But his hostess insisted that he drink it up, assuming that he was refusing out of courtesy. Although he was unable to drink any more, the American poured the water down his throat and felt he was really full. His hostess was very happy to see his guest enjoy her tea so much and smilingly put another cup of tea before him and said, "Drink slowly (i.e. take your time)." But believing it's a waste not to drink it all up, the man ended up going home with a stomach full of tea!

V   The Trend of the Introvert-oriented Culture

The world is becoming more extroverted and less introverted. To account for this tendency, two possible reasons are presented as follows:

First, man is a social species, so extroversion obviously helps him to socialize with others.

Two, the globalization process increases the need for people who are able to interact with others, which requires people to be extroverted, or at least calls for people who are able to put on the suit of extroversion.

However, due to the deep-rooted introverted character, it is hard for Chinese culture to become predominantly extroverted. Chinese culture as a whole will remain fundamentally introvert-oriented in many years to come.

Further Reading

1. Hall, D. L. & Ames, Roger T. (1995). *Anticipating China: Thinking Through the Narratives of Chinese and Western Culture*. Albany, NY: State University of New York Press.

2. Thomson, L. (1998). *Personality Type*. Boston, MA: Shambhala.

3. Kroeger, O. & Thuesen, Janet M. (1989). *Type Talk: The 16 Personality Types That Determine How We Live, Love, and Work*. New York: Dell Publishing Company.

4. Levathes, L. E. (1994). *When China Ruled the Sea: The Treasure Fleet of the Dragon Throne*. New York: Simon & Schuster.

5. Menzis, G. (2002). 1421: *The Year China Discovered America.* US: HarperCollins.

6. Myers, L. B. & Peter B. Myers (1980). *Gifts Differing: Understanding Personality Type*. Palo Alto, CA: Consulting Psychologists Press.

7. Carreau, J. (1981). *The Nine Nations of North America*. Boston, MA: Houghton Mifflin.

8. 易中天 (2006):《闲话中国人》,上海:上海文艺出版社。

9. 乐黛云、张辉(1999):《文化传递与文学形象》,北京:北京大学出版社。

Unit 13   Collectivism vs. Individualism

Private interests are vested in the group, that is, in the family or in the community, and not in the individual. True self-fulfillment for the individual lies in fulfilling social responsibilities to the greatest extent possible. In fact, the establishment of harmonious social relations is seen as an absolute necessity, without which any development is impossible.

—Jean Brick

Jean Brick, as an outsider who has come inside for some time, has observed the group-oriented Chinese value with keen cross-cultural awareness. For further thoughts: Discuss the satisfactions and difficulties of being a member of a group in China.

There is no such thing as society. There are individual men and women.

—Margaret Thatcher

What can we conclude from what former British Prime Minister Mrs. Thatcher said in a speech in 1987?

I   An Embarrassing Habit

Foreigners can observe many things we Chinese have taken for granted for so long. Introduction is one of them.

Tracy L. Steele is an American historian. I met her when she was a visiting scholar in Nanjing University ten years ago and soon we became friends. In 2007 she stayed with my family for the Spring Festival, during which I took her to pay New Year visits to some of my professors, introduced her to them and she enjoyed talking with them. My apartment is on the fifteenth floor of a tall building for the university teaching faculty only, and we have to use the elevator a lot. Every time we got in the elevator, we would run into some of my school colleagues whom I greet whenever I see them. To be frank, I have been doing this for more than twenty years, but have never tried to make any self-introduction and they have never asked me to do so, either. We indeed do not feel uncomfortable about the situation that two people on nodding or speaking terms don't know each other's name. It happens everywhere. Neighbors, colleagues, acquaintances, or people from the same martial art class greet each other and chat a while when meeting on the campus or in the shopping mall or classroom but they won't bother to know each other's name. That's truly the case. We do feel quite reluctant to ask others their names. However, it doesn't necessarily mean knowing someone's name isn't important in China. Only we feel it is a little bit impolite to ask acquaintances their names. When we run into someone whose name we don't know, we'll later ask others. Then we will proudly say his or her name the next time we meet. Knowing others' names without asking them indicates we take them seriously. Usually foreign professors will give us their names the first time we meet in the classroom. But the Chinese professor won't. The students are supposed to find that out themselves. That is not because names are sacred in China.

Every time my colleagues soon started talking to me, seemingly ignoring Tracy, I could feel how upset Tracy was. Not until then did I realize how embarrassing a custom it is not to make introductions in intercultural communication. I tried to get Tracy into our conversation by introducing them, but refrained from doing so in case I should embarrass my colleagues by asking them their surnames after having known them for so many years! Tracy told me later that she felt awkward not to be introduced and be a part of the conversation although she knew Chinese are not good at introducing people to each other, but the elevator was so small a space. Moreover, she felt it was an interesting incident because in her country it is nearly impossible that someone could know and interact with another person for twenty years, and not know their names.

This experience serves to highlight an interesting difference between Chinese and

Western cultures. Western culture is often said to be individualistic, whereas China emphasizes collective, group relationships. One of the results of this difference is our reluctance to ask people their names and be asked by others. Another impressive consequence is that people in China are more often addressed according to their role in a group such as *Director Zhang, Master Liu*, and *Secretary Wu* or their relationship to the person they know like 敏畅妈妈 (Mama Minchang, i.e. Minchang's mum) and 晓兮奶奶 (Grandma Xiaoxi, i.e. Xiaoxi's grandma). In the West, people are more likely to simply address the other person by his or her first name—the symbol of their individuality.

II   Collectivism and Individualism as Cultural Orientations

1. Collectivism

In China importance has been attached to collective interests, which can be divided into those of the small circle (blood-based), the intermediate circle (nation-based) and the large circle(world-based). In many cases collective interests are placed above the individual's if they are in conflict.

a. Blood-based Groups

China is a country with a massively large population where people live in groups based on biological and marital relations. Family loyalties and an emotional commitment to the village or the kin group take precedence over any sense of nationhood. The small interest groups present in all the workplaces (***dan wei***) are nothing but an extension of such a group.

b. Nation-based Patriotism

Patriotism has been highly praised since ancient times. The patriotic spirit has been inspiring Chinese people to put national interests above the groups' especially when the nation is in danger. Wang Fuzhi (1619—1692), a Confucian philosopher with great patriotism and an uncommonly strong sense of national consciousness, raised an army to support the remnants of the Ming Dynasty when Beijing fell to the Manchu. Finally realizing the hopelessness of such efforts, he retired to his native place and spent the remainder of his life there, refusing to serve the Manchu, a people whose origins were beyond the Great Wall. Gu Yanwu (1613—1682), another famous Qing scholar, spent almost most of his life traveling about and conducting researches, because he was asked by his foster-mother not to serve the Manchu government in any official capacity when she starved herself to death, refusing to live under the foreign rule after the fall of her native city. Moreover, Gu Yanwu is better remembered for his motto—"everyone has a share of responsibility for the fate of his country (天下兴亡，匹夫有责)." As the end of the 19th century approached, many Chinese people, witnessing the aggressive behavior of the foreign imperialists, began to be more conscious of themselves as a nation and more determined to be united as one, and their fight against foreign invasion has been recorded in history books read by school children today.

c. World-based Great Harmony

We have always been educated in the spirit of patriotism as well as internationalism. "A public spirit should rule everything under the sun and a gentleman should put others' interests above his own when the great Way prevails(大道之行，天下为公)," said Confucius more than two thousand years ago. An ancient Chinese gentleman would consider it his primary aim in life "to cultivate his own moral character, put family affairs in order, administer state affairs well, and pacify the whole world(修身、齐家、治国、平天下)." A couplet from a Ming Dynasty academy of classical learning says, "The sounds of wind, rain, and reading each come into my ears; the affairs of family, state as well as world are all kept in my mind."(Gu Xiancheng) Fan Zhongyan, the Song Dynasty poet, expressed his desire "to show concern over state affairs before others in the world and enjoy comforts after them."

Obviously the interests of the small circle, the intermediate circle and the large circle come above one's own, and one has to cultivate and exert himself in order to achieve the goal of serving the human community. In present-day China, collectivism remains an orthodox value, despite our changed attitudes toward the individual's role in society, social behavior, and values as a result of individualism introduced from the West. For example, many of us don't like to be separated from crowd, solitude is still the most terrible punishment, and the collectivist saying "Extend your respect for your aged parents to all the aged, and extend your love for your own children to all children" is often on our lips. People in China are generally reserved with strangers and might not initiate conversations with adults we don't know, but the rules for children are different. Children are all affectionately called "little brother" and "little sister". So in a way, everybody in the world is family in China.

2. Individualism

Western priority has been given to developing individual potentialities, realizing individual objectives and seeking individual interests. In the West, individualism is undoubtedly a positive core value; competition and independence are highly valued.

a. Competition and Success

In Western culture an individual is moving forward continuously in his self-chosen direction for the sake of self-fulfillment. Suppose different people run parallel to one another, they will each smoothly attain their own aims in life. In such a society, maybe people are "selfish", but they stay out of each other's way and feel happy. However, if they stand in one another's way, the stronger must make the other go out of his way to keep moving on himself, conforming to the law of the survival of the fittest. Guided by the competition-oriented individualism, everyone seeks independence and self-reliance, and everyone feels insecure and makes unremitting individual efforts to achieve success.

b. Independence and Friendship

Among the ancient Greeks, many were able to make a living that didn't depend too strongly on others (such as those independent grape growers and wine producers). Today independence remains the Westerner's preference.

Emphasis on independence makes Westerners conclude that friendship is mostly a matter of providing emotional support and spending time together, so they feel uncomfortable in a relationship in which one is giving more and the other is dependent on what is being given. Chinese friends give each other not only emotional support and concrete help, even give each other money and might help each other out financially over a long period of time. This is rarely part of Western friendship, because it creates dependence and thus violates the principle of equality.

3. Attitudes Toward Collectivism and Individualism

Not all Westerners are happy with individualism and not all Chinese are satisfied with collectivism, but in general Chinese attach more importance to collectivism, whereas Westerners focus more on individualism.

a. Pro-collectivist Chinese

For Mao Zedong, individualism is evil and equal to selfishness. The selfish behavior that Mao condemned is not necessarily at the expense of others. It is to place personal interests above those of the group or simply to devote much attention to one's own interests. Mao's anti-individualist, pro-collectivist attitude is deeply rooted in Chinese tradition, although Taoism pays much attention to the individual pursuit for "cultivation of body and life" and individual freedom. After all, the value system of Taoism has not been the mainstream one. Since Confucianism became the orthodox ideology, a stress on the value of groups has been clearly reflected in the advocacy of *ultimate public with no consideration of self* (大公无私) and proverbs like *Two heads are better than one*. But Chinese collectivism does not denote a negation of the individual well-being or interests. It maintains that the group's well-being is the best guarantee for the individual interests.

b. Pro-individualist Westerners

Cultural preference for individualism does not mean Westerners' neglect of the collective strength in the workplace. Recently *ji ti* (集体, literally, the group or the collective) in Chinese vocabulary has been replaced by ***tuan dui*** (团队, literally, team or teamwork), a concept introduced from the West. Teamwork refers to a joint action by two or more people or a group, in which each person subordinates his individual interests and opinions to the unity and efficiency of the group. This does not mean that the individual is no longer important in Western culture; however, it does mean that effective and efficient teamwork goes beyond individual accomplishments. Today's Western businesses and organizations often go to great lengths to coordinate team building events in an attempt to get people to work as a team rather than as individuals.

Likewise, the choice between individualism and collectivism at the level of society has considerable implications for many of the Western theories, especially economic theories. Economics as a discipline was founded in Britain in the 18th century. Among the founding fathers, Adam Smith (1723—1790) stood out above the rest. Smith assumed that the pursuit of self-interest by individuals through an "invisible hand" would increase the wealth of nations. This is an individualist idea from a country that even today ranks high on individualism. Since him, economics has remained an individualist science, and most of its leading contributors have come from strongly individualist nations such as Britain and the United States. However, we cannot afford to forget the fact that it is the individualist West that produces the concept of "teamwork" that exhibits the collectivist spirit.

III　Collectivism and Individualism in Cultural Anthropology

To more clearly describe the two cultural orientations, it might be better to examine them within the context of anthropology.

1. Collectivist Culture

According to Dutch cultural anthropologist Geert Hofstede, "Collectivist culture is a term used to designate the cultural trait of giving primacy to the goals and welfare of groups in the view of the world related to relationships with other humans." In other words, a culture in which the interests of the group prevail over the interests of the individual is collectivist. In this culture, the first group in one's life is the family into which he was born and grows up. There may be a number of people living under the same roof, for example, great-grandparents, grandparents, uncles, aunts, cousins, sisters, and brothers. This is the extended family where the child soon learns to think of himself as a part of "we" group or in-group. The in-group is the major source of one's identity and the only secure protection one has access to against the hardships of life, hence it is a good policy for one to remain loyal to it for a lifetime, and becoming disloyal is one of the worst things one can do. The "we" group is distinct from other people who belong to "they" group or out-group. The concepts of in-group and out-group have gone beyond families into many other departments such as workplaces, officialdom, and the neighborhood in a roughly group-based collectivist country.

Therefore, in a collectivist culture education aims to enable a child to live more harmoniously with others in a group. Everyone, however rich in wealth and high in social status, is in need of help and assistance at a certain point in time to live a good life, since in a collectivist society people are interdependent, finding it hard to live without help from others.

2. Individualist Culture

Based on cultural data he collected in the 1970s from people working for IBM in over 40 countries, Geert Hostede assumes that cultures in which the interests of the individual prevail over the interests of the group are individualist. In these cultures, most children are born into families consisting of one or two parents and, possibly, other children, while their relatives live elsewhere. This is the nuclear family where children soon learn to think of themselves in terms of "I". This "I" — their personal identity, is distinct from other individuals and these other individuals are classified to their group membership according to their individual characteristics or attributes rather than their relationships. The concept of "I" has gone beyond families into many other departments. So to speak, an individualist society is roughly individual-based.

Therefore, education in an individualist culture aims to enable children to be independent. No psychologically and physically healthy person should be encouraged to be dependent.

3. Differences and Cultural Discomforts

Different nations have different cultural traits just as different people have different characteristics. Key differences between the collectivist and individualist societies are summarized below:

In collectivist societies, one is integrated from birth into strong, cohesive groups that protect him in exchange for unquestioning loyalty. In the groups, opinions are sometimes predetermined by group membership, collective interests often prevail over individual interests, the state dominates the economic system, companies are largely owned by families, collectives or the state, private life may be invaded by groups, law and rights may differ by groups, human rights rating is usually lower, the principle of egalitarianism often prevails over that of individual freedom, harmony and consensus tend to be ultimate goals, and patriotism is a noble ideal.

In individualist societies, one looks after himself or his immediate family first, everyone is expected to have his own opinion, individual interests prevail over collective interests, the role of the state in the economic field is restrained, companies are often owned by individual investors, everyone has a right to privacy, laws and rights are supposed to be the same for all, human rights rating tends to be higher, the principle of individual freedom usually prevails over the principle of equality, every individual is goal-oriented, and autonomy is an ideal.

Cultural differences are often responsible for discomfort in intercultural encounters. For instance, Westerners are not expected to share snacks that they have with their friends. It is not considered rude to buy a bar of chocolate and eat it around your friends. In China people consider it bad not to share treats with friends and feel uncomfortable. During my stay in America, I noticed the most remarkable thing about visiting American households is that everyone is always thanking everyone else: "Thank you for reminding me. Thank you for passing me the salt. Thank you for teaching my son." To be frank, they sounded very hypocritical to me, though I knew I was wrong, but I just couldn't help feeling that way, because every family member in China has the obligation to serve and help at home and you don't have to thank them so frequently for carrying out their obligations.

IV   Collectivist and Individualist Perspectives of "Self"

Differences between collectivist and individualist cultures are also present in their different perspectives of "self".

1. Chinese Sense of "Self"

a. Chinese View of "Self"

Chinese view of "self" is deeply rooted in the collectivist culture. First, Chinese view of self has been around for many years. "In the Confucian human-centered philosophy man cannot exist alone; all actions must be in the form of interaction between man and man."(Hu Shih) In other words, one exists within particular situations where there are particular people with whom one has relationship of a particular kind.

Second, Chinese sense of self is mainly knitted into the cultural context. That is why we understand ourselves in terms of our relation with, e.g. the family, *dan wei* (workplace), or society. There is a Chinese expression that reflects a cultural prejudice against individualism: "The peg that stands out is pounded down." Individual distinctiveness is not particularly desirable. For us, feeling good about ourselves is likely to be tied to the sense that we are in harmony with the wishes of the group to which we belong. Since all actions are in concert with others, or at the very least affect others, harmony in relationships becomes a chief goal of social life, which requires one to forget his individual interests and think in terms of collectivist interests.

Third, the self is connected, fluid, and conditional. Just like the Chinese character "仁 (*ren*, literally, humanity)" which denotes humanity of one for another, this self involves at least two persons. In ancient Chinese there are many expressions for I, depending on the speaker's relationship with the listener. When a minister spoke to the emperor, he customarily used *chen* (literally, your humble subject), which is closest to the trans-situational I; when a man referred to himself in the presence of his parents he might say *hai er* (literally, your child); when a father talked to his son, he employed *wei fu* (literally, your dad) which is equivalent to I.

Fourth, equal treatment is not assumed as desirable, since there are the concepts of in-group and out-group. People tend to be closer to in-groups and more trusting of them. However, Westerners tend not to draw distinctions between in-group and out-group.

b. Modern Chinese Debate over Self and Group

In modern China, the debate over self and group seems to be quite confusing sometimes. On the one hand, the stress on individualism is unprecedented because of acceptance of Western demands such as individual freedom and respect for individual rights, although individualism is undoubtedly against collectivism and holism. On the other hand, the group interests are still emphasized because of a need for harmony. In some sense, modern China is characterized by making attempts to unite the interests of individuals and those of groups. For example, Li Dazhao (1888—1927), the great Chinese politician, provided a theory of Great Harmony with individual freedom and thus won much applause from many people.

2. Western Sense of "Self"

Western view of "self" originates from ancient Greece. The ancient Greeks had a remarkable sense of self. They viewed themselves as unique individuals with distinctive attributes and goals. To modern Westerners, one has attributes or characteristics that are independent of circumstances or particular personal relations. This self can move from group to group and setting to setting without significant change. As beneficiaries of the ancient Greek civilization, modern Westerners have the same remarkable sense of self, as can be seen in all of the following statements made by them on different occasions:

- Each individual has his unique distinctive attributes. Moreover, each individual needs to be distinctive in important ways.
- Each individual is in control of his own life and feels better when his choice and personal behavior determine outcomes.
- Each individual is passionate about personal success and achievements, and finds that relationships and group memberships sometimes get in the way of realizing their goals.
- Each individual strives to feel good about himself by achieving success through his own efforts.
- Each individual prefers equality in personal relations or when relationships are hierarchical, he prefers a superior position.
- Each individual should not be singled out for special treatment because of his

personal attributes or connections to VIP.

3. Manifestations of Different Senses of "Self"

a. In Self-introduction

Here is a typical Chinese self-introduction: "My name is Zhu Jifang. I'm Sharon White's friend. Sharon's carpool friend Tracy Snow brought me here." It is obvious that the focus is on relationship.

A typical English self-introduction is: "My name is Jane Will. I am a stay-at-home mom with a 5-year -old daughter Leah and I am married to Tom. I recently received a referral for a beautiful 9- month- old girl and I am headed to China to bring her home." Evidently, the focus is on I.

b. In Self-description

"Tell me about yourself." A straightforward request, isn't it? The kind of answer largely depends on the society you are exposed to. Westerners will tell you about their personality traits (e.g. *loving, out-going*), role categories (e.g. *banker, salesperson*), and activities (e.g. *I go boating a lot*). Their self-description almost has nothing to do with the context. But our self-description depends much on the context (e.g. *I am on the teaching faculty of Hohai University, I am not a good mother because I am fun-loving with my friends, I am Joan Quin's pen pal*).

c. In Children's Primer

Americans over a certain age remember their primer *Daisy and the Doll*. It depicts a little girl Daisy, the only child of color in her classroom. Daisy was both embarrassed and angry when the teacher, in assigning poems to read and props to hold for a school program, singled Daisy out by giving her a doll with a black face. That moment was the first time someone had treated Daisy differently due to her skin color, and Daisy had trouble making sense of this experience. Ultimately, Daisy was able to use her courage and her talent as a poet to show her teacher, classmates, and the community the importance of speaking out about race and racial equality. This would seem the most natural sort of basic information to convey about kids—to the American individual thinking.

The first pages of the primer for many Chinese of the same period depict a little boy handing out bigger pears to his brothers. The first sentences are: "Little Kong Rong gives bigger pears to his elder brothers. He says, 'I'm younger. Of course I should have a small one.' Then he gives his younger brothers bigger pears and keeps the smallest one for himself, saying, 'I am growing up. Of course I should give up bigger pears.'" The primer is about relationships with others, which seem important to convey in a child's first encounter with the printed words— natural for Chinese collective thinking.

d. About Distinctiveness

When North Americans are asked about their attributes and preferences, they report themselves to be unique, whereas Chinese are much less likely to do so.

It isn't that we feel badly about our own attributes. Rather, there is no strong cultural obligation to feel that we are unusual. Plus, we don't like to be separated from crowds. The goal for the self in relation to society, as taught by our teachers and parents, is to achieve harmony and to play one's part in achieving collective interests.

Instead of teaching children how to blend harmoniously with others, American parents encourage their children to be special and unique at schools in which each child gets to be a "VIP" for a day.

V   Interdependence vs. Independence

Collectivism or individualism as cultural orientation may lead people to value either interdependence or independence.

1. Interdependent Chinese and Independent Westerners

Traditional Chinese are disposed to be interdependent, taking friends, family, the prosperity of the state, and even the world harmony as sources of happiness. "There is an old saying, 'The world is the state.' As a matter of fact, the foundation of the world lies in the state, the foundation of the state the family, and the foundation of the family the individual (人有恒言，皆曰"天下国家"，天下之本在国，国之本在家，家之本在身)." (Mencius)

Westerners tend to be independent, taking independence as a great source of happiness.

In reality, every society and every individual is a blend of interdependence and independence. Therefore, it is quite easy to bring one or another orientation to the fore. And it is very possible that even if one's upbringing had not made him incline in one direction or another, the cues that surround him would make the person living in China behave in generally interdependent ways and the person living in Western societies behave in generally independent ways.

2. Early Training for Independence and Interdependence

The training for independence or interdependence actually starts in the crib. It is common for Western babies to sleep in a cradle separate from their parents, or even in a separate room. But that is rare for Chinese babies. The Chinese baby is almost always with his/her mother and sleeping in the same bed with her. The close association with mother is what some Chinese apparently would like to continue indefinitely, which is reflected in the interdependent relationship between mother and child, i.e. the child is dependent on his/her mother for care, love, food, money, advice, etc., and in turn the mother will be dependent on her child for psychological and practical help when she is old and sick in the future, just as the saying goes, "Rear children for old age."

Independence for Western children is often explicitly encouraged. Western parents constantly require their children to do things on their own and ask them to make their own decisions, "Would you like to go to MGM or Magic Kingdom first" so that both mothers and children are capable of living independently and having fun when children are around 18 years old.

3. Targeted Ad Campaigns

An important business implication of the differences that exist between independent and interdependent societies is that advertising needs to be modified for a particular cultural audience. Scholars have found that American advertisements emphasize individual benefits and preferences (e.g. *Obey your thirst. Don't leave home without it*), whereas Chinese ads are more likely to emphasize collective ones (e.g. *Feichang Cola, our own cola. Tianxiang Paint will give you a sweet home*). The individualist advertisements are evidently more effective with Westerners and the collectivist ones with Chinese.

4. Everybody, Somebody, Anybody and Nobody

Here is an English story copied from *wenweipo*.com on Oct. 18, 2008:

Everybody, Somebody, Anybody and Nobody

This is a famous story about four people named Everybody, Somebody, Anybody and Nobody. One day there was an important job to be done and Everybody was sure that Somebody would do it. Anybody could have done it, but Nobody did it. Somebody got angry about that, because it was Everybody's job. Everybody thought Anybody could do it, but Nobody realized that Everybody wouldn't do it. It ended up that Everybody blamed Somebody when Nobody did what Anybody could have done.

Read it and you may smile understandingly and soon think of the two famous Chinese proverbs 人人负责,等于无人负责 (i.e. Everybody's business is nobody's business) and 一个和尚挑水喝,两个和尚抬水喝,三个和尚没水喝 (i.e. One boy is a boy, two boys half a boy, three boys no boy). Smiles can be used to express happiness. Probably your smile at this moment may mean more after you finish reading the story.

Further Reading —————————————————————————————

1. Brick, J. (2000). *China: A Handbook in Intercultural Communication* (2nd Edition). Sidney: NCELTR Publications (National Centre For English Language Teaching and Research).

2. Hofstede, G. (2005). *Cultures and Organizations: Software of the Mind.* New York: McGraw-Hill.

3. Medearis, M. & Medearis, A. S. (1983). *Daisy and the Doll.* Middlebury, VT: A Vermont Folklife Center Book.

4. Kluckholn, Florence & F. Strodtbeck (1961). *Variations in Value Orientations.* Evanston, OH: Row & Peterson.

5. 陈立夫 (2008):《陈立夫解读〈大学〉》,北京:中国友谊出版公司。

6. 张忠利、宗文举 (2002):《中西文化概论》,天津:天津大学出版社。

7. 范仲淹 (2010):《范仲淹全集》,南京:凤凰出版社。

8. 梁羽生 (1999):《名联谈趣》,上海:上海古籍出版社。

Unit 14   Femininity vs. Masculinity

Chinese culture is apt to be feminine. The Chinese mind is akin to the feminine mind in many respects. Femininity, in fact, is the only word that can summarize its various aspects.

—*Lin Yutang*

Is what Mr. Lin Yutang says a proper definition of Chinese culture? If not, what constitutes a proper description?

A man's chief quality is courage.

—*Cicero*

For Confucius, however, a man's chief quality is humanity. Do you side with Cicero or Confucius? Why?

I   Gender Traits

1. Gender Traits of Advertising Language

The now-famous advertising blurb "Just Do It" was freely translated as "想做就去做 (literally, do it if you want to)" when it first appeared in Hong Kong, a Chinese community where self-discipline is favored. The ad slogan, though well-received in America where personal freedom is valued, soon spread its reputation as a bad influence among many Hong Kong consumers who complained that it encouraged the youth to act imprudently. This complaint forced the advertiser to change the translation into "应做就去做 (literally, do it if you should)." The change from the more active "想 (want to)" to the less active "应 (should)" turns out to be a good decision.

Chinese garment makers are very careful when drafting their ads, which is one of the reasons why they have been doing well both at home and in the international market. For instance, to Chinese senior citizens they promise their clothes can make them look *graceful, noble, younger, comfortable, calm, dignified and steady.* To Western senior citizens, those adjectives are replaced by *young, unique, tasty, fashionable, energetic*, etc.

Note the vocabulary in Western ads. Zillions of book blurbs, radio ads and TV commercials emphasize the categories we commonly gender-code "masculine". Meanwhile the big stress in China is on qualities associated with those of femininity.

2. Gender Traits of Answers to the Question "What Makes a Man?"

What makes a man?

The answer which is widely accepted by Chinese people is humanity. Humanity means "the quality of being humane and kindness". According to Confucius' teachings, if a man is not humane and kind, he is not a man. If he is a man, he has to be faithful to his boss, filial to his parents, kind to his brothers and sisters, friendly to people around him, and nice to strangers. For many years, humanity, a quality which is usually associated with that of femininity, has been regarded as a man's bottom line.

Meanwhile the answer given by Westerners sounds more masculine. Take, for instance, the famous poem "What Makes a Man" composed by American realist Hamlin Garland:

Do you fear the force of the wind,

The slash of the rain?

Go face them and fight them,

Be savage again.

Go hungry and cold like the wolf

Go wade like the crane.

The palms of your hands will thicken,

The skin of your cheeks will tan

You'll grow ragged and weary and swarthy,

But you will walk like a man!

II   Feminine Chinese Culture

1. Femininity of Chinese Culture

Many activities in the traditional Chinese society display feminine traits.

a. Cognitive Activities

Chinese cognitive activities, like the feminine cognitive activities, often involve common sense. For this reason, traditional Chinese educators take it for granted that there is no need to say too much about paternal and maternal affection since such a love is as natural as *Water flows downwards instead of upwards*. Instead, the affection for parents and grandparents is more in need of being taught. The same common sense also serves as a good comforter to guide people in the direction of optimism. For instance, when their children are not so good at academic work at school and thus have lost self-confidence, Chinese parents will say to themselves, "When the little tree is older it will naturally become straight. As long as you have a seedling, you don't need to worry that it will not grow up." They then go on optimistically encouraging their children to work harder for they hold that their children, though a failure at school, are likely to be successful in society as long as they grow up healthily. Children in turn are convinced by their parents' positive attitude that they can be successful as long as they try harder because their parents are always right since "they have crossed more bridges than we have crossed streets!"

b. Literary Creation

What Chinese scholars create out of their imagination exhibits varying degrees of femininity. The most characteristic creatures of Chinese imagination are the lovely female ghosts and spirits such as those portrayed in the *Strange Stories from a Chinese Studio* written by Pu Songling (1640—1715) in classical Chinese during the early Qing Dynasty. The stories are about the female fox spirit who is in love with a man and ready to die for the guy, the female ghost who falls in love with an indecisive poor young scholar, the dead sweetheart who returns to her lover and bears him children, the female ghost of a wronged woman who possesses the body of some young woman and takes revenge on the living, etc. These stories with human warmth have touched many Chinese people, for those female ghosts and spirits are wonderfully awesome: They boldly love, hate, and live an ordinary human life. The proper use of imagination has given beauty and charm to Chinese imaginative activities.

c. Thinking

Chinese people more often use intuitive thinking, a kind of creative and constructive right-brain thinking which is associated particularly with qualities of females. As a result, Chinese logic is highly personal like women's logic according to Lin Yutang.

Chinese way of thinking, characterized by its concreteness associated with traits of femininity, is prevalent of proverbs and metaphoric expressions, like women's conversations. For example, when faced with adversities, we comfort ourselves this way: "The moon cannot always be round; the flowers cannot always look so fine and good friends cannot often meet." When faced with a promotion, we won't feel overjoyed and say to ourselves, "For this period of thirty years the Eastern Region of the Yellow River is more important, but for the next thirty years it will be the Western Region's turn." The concrete thinking way is vividly revealed in these frequently used proverbs.

d. Chivalry to the Vulnerable Group

Chinese show much feminine tenderness to the sufferings of others. The early Chinese chivalry was manifested not toward women and children, but toward the old people. "The people with grey hair should not be seen carrying burdens on the street (颁白者不负戴于道路矣)," said Mencius and he also described the four classes of the world's most helpless people as "the widows, widowers, orphans and old people without children (鳏寡孤独)." Of these four classes the first two were to be taken care of by a political economy, which should be so arranged that there would be no unemployed men and unmarried women. In one word, Chinese chivalry is a special privilege given to the vulnerable group.

e. Great Love

There is no explicit distinction between "state" and "family" in China. "State" means in Chinese "*guo jia* (literally, state-family)". In this sense, the state is a big family and the individual family is a small one. In the family-centered society both the big and small families are loved. The love for the big family is known as "great love", the love for the small one "small love".

The year 2008 was a year full of troubles. It started with a terribly heavy snowstorm hitting many provinces. However, the snow and ice did not chill Chinese people's warm hearts to help each other. The country got over "cold injuries" in a very short time with relief efforts across China.

On May 12, 7.8-magnitude earthquake centered on Wenchuan County jolted Sichuan Province. In the face of disaster, Chinese people united as one to fight against hardships. The mass of ordinary citizens at home, the overseas Chinese, and compatriots from Taiwan, Hong Kong and Macao voluntarily made donations. In many cities of China, people waiting to donate blood stood in long queues.

Misfortunes and calamities could descend upon people any time, but we believe "big disaster is followed by great love(大灾之后必有大爱)" and "much distress regenerates a nation(多难兴邦)." The compatriot affection of the great Chinese family surpasses the interest-based and blood-based relations. The idea to "extend love for my own seniors to that of others; extend love for my own children to that of others(老吾老,以及人之老;幼吾幼,以及人之幼)" has been once again proved to be very relevant today.

f. Femininity Worship

Most Chinese school children can recite the following lines:

"Of all things yielding and weak in the world,

None is more so than water.

But for attacking what is unyielding and strong,

Nothing is superior to it,

Nothing can take its place(天下莫柔弱於水。而攻坚强者,莫之能胜)."

"He who knows the masculine but holds fast to the feminine,

Will become the stream of the world.

Being the stream of the world,

He lives in constant virtue,

And returns to the state of a baby (知其雄,守其雌,为天下溪。为天下溪,常德

不离，复归于婴儿)." (Lao Zi)

Ever since Lao Zi, Chinese people have been in love with the striking use of symbols such as water, the symbol of a humble, self-effacing force that is in the end all-powerful(e.g. 水能载舟，亦能覆舟, i.e. water might move the ship, but also could sink it), the female and the mother, the symbols of passivity and creation (e.g. 恩逾慈母, i.e. enjoy more affection from somebody than from one's own mother), or the weak, the symbol of purity (e.g. 赤子之心, i.e. as pure and innocent as a baby's mind). Chinese strong belief in these appealing qualities makes Chinese culture impressively feminine, which can explain why we do well in such Olympic game events as table tennis, weightlifting, and diving. These events involve more tenacity and skills (韧力和技巧)—attributes characterizing femininity, but less explosion and speed (爆发力和速度). For this reason, there are disadvantages for Chinese athletes to compete in events like track and field, footfall and swimming that require for high speed and explosion which characterize masculinity.

g. Lifestyle

Chinese lifestyle is apt to be feminine, too. One of the most popular Chinese ways of spending time is to have some tea, melon seeds, and small talk while playing cards, chess or *ma jiang*. It seems that the sipping of tea at home, the interminable talking and eating of melon seeds in a teahouse, and the fun in playing *ma jiang* have consumed much of our time.

2. Femininity of the Chinese Language

Chinese language and its grammar show feminine qualities. Its form, syntax and vocabulary reveal a love of simplicity and concreteness.

a. Love of Simplicity

Our love of simplicity is associated with the economy of syntactical relationships, as in the expression 坐吃山空 (literally, sit eat mountain empty) which to us clearly means that "If you only sit, eat and do nothing, even a fortune as big as a mountain will vanish" and as in the classical Chinese poetic line 春蚕到死丝方尽 (Spring silkworm till its death spins silk from love-sick heart). The latter, an example of how a few words can be used to convey a lot of meaning, is from To *One Unnamed (Wu Ti)*, a love poem by Li Shangyin (813—858). It compares the poet's love to spinning silk of the spring silkworm which does not cease its spinning silk until death. However, the connection between the image of "spring silkworm spins silk" and the theme of faithful love are clearly achieved through the homophonic pun images created by only two characters 丝(silk) and 思(love), which resort to the auditory sense of the reader before leading the reader to imagine how love is endless like the silk spun by the spring silkworm.

b. Love of Concreteness

With the Chinese as with women, concrete imagery always takes the place of abstract terminology. Take, for instance, a Chinese doctor who has had adequate basic scientific training in Physics, Chemistry, and Mathematics. To explicitly explain why it is best to have an apple in the morning every day, better to have one in the afternoon, and improper to have one in the evening, he might say in a concrete way, "The apple is golden in the morning, silver in the afternoon, and rotten in the evening."

The Chinese concrete way of expressing can also be illustrated by the nature and use of its abstract terms: An abstract notion is often expressed by the combination of two concrete qualities, e.g. *big-small* for *size*, *long-short* for *length*, and *broad-narrow* for *breadth*. Even *long* and *short* refer to the right and wrong of parties in dispute.

English abstract endings like -ly and -ness are unknown in Chinese. We simply say, "the white of a white horse is not the same as the white of a white man (白马之白也，无以异于白人之白也)." (Mencius) This has a bearing on our lack of analytic thinking.

The dislike of abstract terms is further seen in our classifications. We always seek the most expressive names for different categories. Therefore, when we talk about different methods of writing, we love mentioning the method of *releasing a captive before capturing him* (欲擒故纵) instead of its equivalent expression *playing about a subject*, the method of *showing a dragon's head without showing its tail* (神龙见首不见尾) instead of *freedom of movement and waywardness of thought*, the method of *a sharp precipice overhanging a ten-thousand feet ravine* (壁立千仞) instead of *abruptness of ending*, the method of *letting blood by one needle prick* (一针见血) instead of *directness*, the method of *going straight into the fray with one knife* (单刀直入) instead of *direct opening*, the method of announcing a campaign on the east and marching to the west (声东击西) instead of *surprise attack*, the method of *side-stabs and flanking attacks* (旁敲侧击) instead of *light raillery*, the method of a *light mist hanging over a gray lake* (烟锁云湖) instead of *mellow and toned down style*, the method of *layers of clouds and hilltops* (层峦叠嶂) instead of *accumulation*, and the method of *throwing lighted firecrackers at a horse' buttocks* (鞭马而驰) instead of *final stab toward conclusion*. (Lin Yutang) This profuseness of concrete images has great influence on the writing style and consequently on thinking ways. On the one hand, it makes for vividness; on the other, it may easily degenerate into a senseless decorativeness without exact content, which has been the besetting sin of many periods of Chinese literature and against which Han Yu in the Tang Dynasty set up a revolt.

3. Much-praised Strength of Femininity

There exists in China a much-praised strength—the strength of femininity (阴柔的力量). Xia Yan(1900—1995), the famous Chinese author, wrote, "Someone asked, 'What has the greatest strength on earth?'... All the answers turned out to be wide of the mark. The mightiest thing on earth is the seed of a plant." He continued to write that the bones forming a human skull are so tightly fit together that all anatomists, hard as they try, are powerless to take them apart without damaging them. But once some seeds of a plant are placed inside a human skull awaiting dissection before heat and moisture are applied to cause them to grow, they let loose a terrible force to separate all the skull bones, leaving each of them intact. The seed metaphor is employed by Xia in his writing to praise the strength appreciated by Chinese people—a feminine strength, seemingly weak but matchlessly powerful.

Yi Qi's story is widely known in China. Yi Qi refers to the brothers Bo Yi and Shu Qi who grew up as sons of Guzhu Jun or the Lord of Guzhu. The father wanted his youngest son Shu Qi to inherit the princedom, so the eldest son Bo Yi ran off to avoid conflict. Shu Qi then also ran off because he thought Bo Yi was entitled to the position. Later the middle son inherited. Joining up and having heard of the virtues of King Wen, Bo Yi and Shu Qi went west to Shanxi. However, when they found that King Wen had died and his son King Wu was about to attack his lord Zhou(纣), they ran off in great disappointment again, this time to Shouyang Mountain where they did not allow themselves to have any food of the newly-established Zhou Dynasty and starved themselves to death. What kind of strength was powerful enough to support them to die that way? The strength of femininity! There are many celebrities in Chinese history who have exemplified this strength. Qu Yuan, the patriotic poet, drowned himself in the Miluo River in order to wake up his compatriots and Sima Qian, the great Han historian, chose to live in shame rather than die—for the sake of his unfinished cause.

III　Masculine Western Culture

Western culture as a whole is apt to be masculine. In such a culture, emphasis is on success and achievement is pursued, so people live to work. They are goal-oriented, ambitious and eager to excel.

1. Masculinity of Western Culture

Western culture is inclined to be masculine in many aspects.

a. Personal life

The Western head, like the masculine head, is full of desire for control at least over their own personal life. Once they feel things are out of their personal control, they will become uncomfortable and sometimes depressed. They feel good about themselves only when they are independent and can keep their own personal life under control.

Despite the unhappiness caused by losing control over his life, it's not a loss of dignity or face for a man to depend on a woman financially. When a couple gets divorced in America, the court may require the woman to pay her former husband a monthly sum of money called alimony if the woman is working and earns a good salary. About 10% of American women out-earn their husbands. If the woman has totally supported her husband during the marriage, the court may decide that she must continue to support him after the divorce. For Westerners it is acceptable for a man to get alimony from his former wife since man and woman are equal.

b. Imaginative Activities

"The masculine imagination lives in a state of perpetual revolt against the limitations of human life." (Wystan H. Auden) The Western imagination shows this masculinity. The most characteristic creatures the Hollywood film directors spin out of their imagination are ET in *Star War* directed by Steven Spielberg and *The ET Reunion* directed by Laurent Bouzereau; the most attractive creatures created in Hollywood are Superman, Batman, Spiderman and Captain American, who fight against evil forces and help the weak and helpless by wearing a very cool masculine mask or cloak. Films like *Star Wars, The Empire Strikes Back* and *Return of the Jedi*, and the Special Editions of the three films are regarded as modern-day fairy tales. The fast-paced action adventures set in a new and exciting universe, feature grand design and boundless fun. These films have inspired countless viewers with themes that are universal and timeless, the conflict between good and evil, and the dispute between technology and humanity, the celebration of heroism, and the limitless potential of the individual. The proper use of imagination in Hollywood has given a masculine charm to the Western imaginative world.

c. Logic Thinking

Logical thinking is generally considered as being analytical, objective, and associated particularly with qualities of males. Westerners depend largely upon their logic for solving almost all nature's mysteries and human affairs. Take Hillary Clinton for instance. Although disappointed that she did not make it to the "top" because her campaign opponent Barack Obama was too powerful, she decided to suspend her campaign and endorsed Obama, a Democratic party member like her, and hence displayed the masculinity of putting aside the past and looking into the future. Her logic in the exit speech delivered on June 7th, 2008 was very clear: "Now, I understand—I understand that we all know this has been a tough fight, but the

Democratic Party is a family. And now it's time to restore the ties that bind us together and to come together around the ideals we share, the values we cherish, and the country we love."

d. Addiction to Sports

Westerners like sports and some of them are even addicted to sports, which have consumed much of their spare time, energy and money. What is impressive is that in the excitement of athletic competition most sports teams choose masculine mascots that reflect their "fighting spirit". Typically, these representatives are personified by warriors, predatory creatures or machines, e.g. *Houston Rockets, Phoenix Suns, San Antonio Spurs, Seattle Supersonics, Dallas Mavericks,* and *Sacramento Kings*.

2. Masculinity of the English Language

English shows qualities of masculinity exactly because this language, in its form, syntax and vocabulary, reveals a love of expanding sentences, complexity of syntactical relationships, an abstract way of thinking, and tougher daily expressions.

a. Complicated Syntactical Relationships

"The amalgamation of characters makes a sentence; the accumulation of sentences makes a text(积字成句;积句成章)."(Liu Xie) It means that the Chinese sentence is always ready to accumulate as a female is. In contrast the English sentence usually centers around a verb, always ready to expand like a male. Take 坐吃山空 for instance again. This idiom's English version may expand this way:

Sit.

Eat.

Sit, eat and do nothing.

If he sits, eats and does nothing, a fortune will vanish.

If he sits, eats and does nothing, a fortune as big as a mountain will vanish.

If he sits, eats and does nothing, even a fortune as big as a mountain will vanish.

Sister said if he sits, eats and does nothing, even a fortune as big as a mountain will vanish.

My sister said if he sits, eats and does nothing, even a fortune as big as a mountain will vanish.

I heard my sister say that if he sits, eats and does nothing, even a fortune as big as a mountain will vanish.

Yesterday I heard my sister say that if he sits, eats and does nothing, even a fortune as big as a mountain will vanish.

The day before yesterday I heard my sister say that if he sits, eats and does nothing, even a fortune as big as a mountain will vanish.

What is interesting is that the sentence can go on expanding infinitely, showing a tendency to expand and radiate in all directions with the verb as the center, becoming longer, fatter, and more complicated.

b. Western Love of Abstract Terminology

The abstract way of thinking leads men to revel in using abstract terms. This has been proved by an analytic study of the vocabulary of men authors. With Westerners as with men, abstract terminology always takes the place of concrete images. First, there are in English abstract endings like -*ly*, -*ness*, and -*y*, which are unknown in Chinese. Second, this love of abstract terms is seen in the Western classifications such as *the developed and the underdeveloped, and the rich and the poor.*

c. Tougher Daily Expressions

1) Questions

Chinese people do not regard it rude to ask strangers their birth year, marital status, and wages. Our questions like *How old are you, Are you married, How much do you make every month*, and *Do you go to church* reflect the cultural trait of tenderness. Westerners avoid this kind of questions by asking questions typical in Western culture with the trait of toughness.

2) Greetings

When people run into acquaintances or friends, they usually greet each other. The purpose of greeting is to establish or maintain social contact, so formulaic expressions are used. In China, people often employ the following concrete greetings like *Have you eaten yet, What are you going to do*, and *Where are you going*. Westerners treat them as real questions. But the fact is those questions in Chinese are used to show kindness and politeness and nothing more, which is a reflection of tenderness. In the

West, people often employ the following expressions to greet each other: *Good morning/evening/afternoon. Fine day, isn't it. How is everything going?* These greetings are polite, but sound a little bit tough to Chinese ears.

3) Partings

In China, we always use very concrete expressions like *Walk slowly, Watch your legs*, or *It is dark, so be careful* when we see our guests off while the Westerners do it in a different way. They will say Bye, *Thank you for coming, See you tomorrow*, and sound independent and very much in control.

IV   Why So Different?

Why do we appear so different in so many aspects? Six reasons are presented below:

First, we see differently. Traditionally, Westerners tend to clearly see objects ignoring the context while Chinese see both. Chinese notion of "the empty and the full (*xu shi*)" is a case in point. Ancient Chinese found the empty is correlative to the full, hence advocated "replenishing the empty (*bu xu*)". Westerners have developed a masculine culture which favors the visible, tangible, and discrete while we have created a feminine culture stressing both the visible and invisible. Therefore, they have invented the solar calendar, whereas we have created the lunar one and use both forms of calendars.

Second, we worship different objects. We have a tradition of worshipping what are commonly categorized as "feminine", for instance, the perished such as our ancestors, the soft such as water, the night such as the moon, the weak such as the baby, and the female such as the mother. Westerners have a tradition of worshipping what are commonly categorized as "masculine", such as heroes (e.g. brave warriors, great orators, and famous athletes), the sun (e.g. Apollo, the symbol of masculine charm), and the machine.

Third, we have different thinking modes. As discussed above, Chinese thinking is associated with qualities of femininity: intuitive, holistic, and context-friendly while

Western thinking is apt to be male: rational, analytic, and individual object-centered.

Fourth, we have different ethical values. The Four Virtues in China and the West embody our distinctive cultural spirit and characteristics. The Chinese Four Virtues, elaborated on in the Confucianist doctrines, are humanity, righteousness, propriety and wisdom, which endow Chinese culture with female characteristics. For instance, men do not need to be very ambitious or competitive; quality of life is more important than material success; being slow and small is valued; interpersonal relationships are stressed and supported; being kind and caring matters most to people; failure is not considered a disaster; conflicts are resolved through a middle way. The Four Virtues of ancient Greece are wisdom, justice, temperance, and bravery. Modern Western ethical values arise from the Four Virtues, which may help to nurture people of masculine characteristics, who are logical, intellectual, rational, objective, practical, dominating, independent, free, individualistic, demanding, success-oriented, ambitious, aggressive, proud, egotistical, moral, trustworthy, decisive, competitive, uninhibited, adventurous, etc. To sum up, guided by their Four Virtues, masculine cultures value achievement, assertiveness, heroism, and material wealth, while feminine cultures value relationships, and care for the less fortunate and overall quality of life.

Fifth, we have the deep-rooted concept of face similar to English "dignity". The concept of face is so important in China that losing it most often means "no face to live in the human world". For instance, it is a loss of face for men to depend on women financially. In Chinese the character "男(man)" has a "田(field)" above and a "力(strength)" below, symbolizing that men are born to do manual labor and support the family. Females are generally assumed to be more concerned about face since cosmetics always sell well. As a matter of fact, males are found to be more passionately in love with their face. The most famous story about man's love of face involves the infamous Ming general Wu Sangui. When he got the news that his concubine Cheng Yuanyuan was raped by one of Li Zicheng's subordinates when Beijing, the Ming capital, fell to Li— the head of the peasant uprising, he felt his face was stripped off. To seek revenge for loss of face, he ordered his men to open the gate of Shanhai Pass for the great Manchu troops so that they could successfully launch an attack, dominate the whole country and set up the Qing Dynasty. To be frank, it is hard to find an equivalent expression to Chinese "face" in English. Prussian philosopher Immanuel Kant (1724—1804) said that being human means having dignity. Given the similar role dignity plays in Western life, face is roughly translated as dignity on many occasions.

To distinguish between the two concepts, let us consider a business negotiation. In the middle of such a session a Westerner might readily change his bargaining position in order to reach an agreement. He does not experience a loss of dignity in doing so. His personal dignity is likely to rest on a contract. He might lose dignity if his boss accused him of being too inflexible to do what needed to be done to complete the business deal. A Chinese in the similar situation might think he would lose face if he should change his position in a bargaining session. His face is more likely to depend on being loyal to his principles and strong and firm when facing opposition. In one word, Chinese stress on face which is attentive to the process may have resulted in a culture with more feminine characteristics, while Western emphasis on dignity which focuses on results may have helped to form a more masculine culture.

Sixth, we live in different environments. Chinese are born to be part of a blood-based group. How to build a harmonious relationship is our first lesson to learn. To be successful we need to be good at networking, and hence we have to spend lots of time and energy outside our goal or career otherwise we will achieve nothing. There are many virtuous people in Chinese history, who have functioned under great pressure. These celebrities were talented but employed by none or envied and attacked by those with less or no abilities. However, they managed to achieve something in spite of ill treatments, distrust, persecution, or even the threat of death, and showed a great feminine strength which is helpful in the formation of a feminine culture since many take them as role models. On the contrary, a Westerner's first lesson is individualist. Western education aims to teach children to be independent and take care of themselves. They need to be personally successful to be respected, and hence they are goal-oriented. In such a society, who you know is not so important. What counts is what you can do, which manifests a great masculine strength.

If you are interested in reasons why one culture is apt to be feminine and the other is disposed to be masculine, observe more closely and you will find more.

V. The Trend of Cultures and Its Potential Impact

You must have seen professional women wear high heels without stockings, but you've never seen professional men wear leather shoes without socks! And that was not the case for women several decades ago in China! Does that mean our culture is more masculine and less feminine than before? Read the article below, and you may foretell the trend.

Livin' Large

You could look it up. The total U.S. Food Supply provides 500 more calories per day per person than it did in the 1970s, an increase of 24 percent, according to the Department of Agriculture.

In the 1960s, the average chicken at slaughter weighed about three and a half pounds; by the mid-1990s, it had gained a pound. In 1966, a commercial cow at slaughter averaged 1,011 pounds; by 2006, it weighed 25 percent more, or 1,275 pounds.

In fast-food restaurants, portions are two to five times larger today than in the 1980s.

In the 1964 edition of *The Joy of Cooking*, a recipe for chocolate chip cookies was said to yield 45 servings. In the 1997 edition, the same recipe was said to yield only 36 servings.

According to the latest federal health statistics from the Centers for Disease Control and Prevention, the average adult weighed nearly 10 percent more in 2003 than in the 1980s. Males grew from 142 to 152.

Over roughly the same period, the average 5-year-old boy gained 9 percent in weight, rising from 43 pounds to 47. The average 5-year-old girl gained 7 percent, rising from 42 pounds to 45.

The International Journal of Obesity totaled 509 pages in 1993, its first year. In 2006, it filled 2,322 pages.

It the past ten years, the standard movie seat has grown more than 10 percent, from 19 to 22 inches wide, according to *Irwin Seating of Grand Rapids*, Michigan.

The Casket & Funeral Supply Association of America reports that standard caskets have grown from about 22 inches wide in the 1970s to 26 inches today.

The average TV screen is growing at the rate of one inch per year, the Consumer Electronics Association reports; the 2006 average was 27 inches. Today, U.S. households watch TV for an average of 8 hours and 11 minutes a day, up from 6 hours and 45 minutes in 1980, according to Nielsen Media Research.

From 1996 to 2006, the average motor vehicle made in the United States gained 500 pounds, reaching 4,142 pounds, mostly because of bigger engines and more options.

In 1991, some 10 percent of new houses came with a three-car garage, says the National Association of Home Builders. That number doubled by 2005.

In 1950, the average new house provided 290 square feet per family member, reports the *Journal of Industrial Ecology*. By 2003, that number had tripled, to 893 square feet per family member.

Since 1980, the standard refrigerator has expanded 10 percent, to 22 cubic feet, and the standard clothes washer 25 percent, to 3 cubic feet, says the Association of Home Appliance Manufacturers.

The first Wal-Mart, which opened in 1962 in Rogers, Arkansas, was 16,000 square feet. Today, there are 1,238 Wal-Mart Supercenters in the United States, and each one is 100,000 to 220,000 square feet.

The Energy Information Administration reported in 2006 that the average American produces 4.5 pounds of solid waste per day (including such things as paper, container, food and law clippings), a 150 percent increase since 1960.

When the National Association of Professional Organizers (people hired to organize personal belongings) was founded in 1985; it had five members. It now has 4,000.

Overstuffed Americans increasingly exercise another option: The Self-Storage Association says the number of self-storage facilities in the United States has increased ninefold since 1984, from 6,601 to 59,657.

(From p.128, September 2007, *Smithsonian*)

The trend is obvious: America is more and more masculine. Given the fact that over the years we have been greatly influenced by American culture, Chinese culture seems less feminine than before and I assume (maybe I am wrong) the alarm clock of a great economic crisis has already rung and the balance of **yin** (the feminine) and **yang** (the masculine) has been destroyed for quite a while. Actually, over the recent 300 years, the world has become more masculine and less feminine. No wonder some of us feel uncomfortable since our internal balance has been upset and we are experiencing the unhappiness generated by this disequilibrium. The present global financial crisis that originated from the American Wall Street shows that, to keep the global balance, it is necessary to rejuvenate feminine culture and check masculine culture. The world without feminine culture or masculine culture is doomed to end up in disaster, just as a marriage without woman or man will inevitably end up hurting all the people involved.

Further Reading

1. Clinton, H., Saturday (June 7th 2008). "Hillary Clinton's exit speech". www.Asiaing. com.

2. Hofstede, G. (2005). *Cultures and Organizations: Software of the Mind.* New York: McGraw-Hill.

3. (September 2007). *Smithsonian.* Washington DC.

4. Kluckholn, Florence & F. Strodtbeck (1961). *Variations in Value Orientations.* Evanston, IL: Row & Peterson.

5. 林语堂(2000):《吾国吾民》,北京:外语教学与研究出版社。

6. 杨伯峻注(1980):《论语译注》,北京:中华书局。

7. 王先谦撰(1988):《荀子集解》,北京:中华书局。

8. 饶尚宽译注(2006):《老子》,北京:中华书局。

9. 范文澜 (2001):《文心雕龙注》,北京:人民出版社。

Unit 15   Advocacy of *Jing* vs. *Dong*

Chinese college youths are considerably more mature than American students of the same age, for even young Chinese freshmen in American universities cannot get interested in football and motorcars.

—Lin Yutang

Why do Chinese youths appear more mature than their Western counterparts?

One should seek serenity to cultivate the body, thriftiness to cultivate the morality. Seeking fame and wealth will not lead to noble ideals. Only by seeking serenity will one reach far (夫君子之行：静以修身，俭以养德；非淡泊无以明志，非宁静无以致远).

—Zhuge Liang

Is what Zhuge Liang, the wisest man in Chinese history, advocated still relevant today when fame and wealth seem to be criteria of success and many are trying all means to become famous and make big money?

Stop to smell the roses along the way.

—An old English saying

For further study: Look for more similar catchphrases in Chinese.

I   Introduction to Two Concepts

1. *Jing* (静) and *Dong* (动)

Jing means *non-action, motionlessness, stillness, serenity, quietness, stasis, tranquility, silence, smoothness, repose,* etc. and **Dong** denotes the same with *action, motion, movement, dynamic, activeness,* etc. **Dong** and **Jing** are basically understood correlatively. It is believed that where there is **Dong** there must be **Jing**; where there is **Jing** there must be **Dong**. For instance, in both Chinese and Western garden scenery, serenity is lodged in motion and motion arises from serenity. As one sits in repose in a pavilion, the clouds are floating, the water is flowing, birds are flying, and flowers are falling. And still water is in repose, but fish in it are moving. As stillness and motion interweave, they naturally create an aesthetic interest. For another instance, in our circle of friends, you may find some quieter on some occasions and more active and talkative on other occasions.

Regarding **Jing** and **Dong**, different cultures have different preferences. Some advocate that it is better to be **Jing** while others hold that it is good to be **Dong**.

2. *Jing* Advocacy

Some cultures advocate **Jing**, and are inclined to maintain an unchanging nature. In these cultures anything that might unbalance or disturb their equilibrium is discouraged. Instead, consensus-building, cooperation, togetherness, in-group, mass experiences, social sanctions and social regulation, structured socialization, peer loyalty, nation loyalty, sense of belonging, homogeneity, identity formation through allegiance to a group, etc. are encouraged. To keep static or peaceful, these cultures employ numerous self-preservation mechanisms, strict hierarchy, obedience, discipline, and even discrimination (in gender, age, and familial affiliation). People exposed to these cultures prefer **Jing** and are inward-directed or introverted, valuing the peaceful co-existence of their inner world with the outside.

3. *Dong* Advocacy

Some cultures advocate **Dong** and prefer to be pluralistic or heterogeneous. To keep dynamic or active, they encourage conflict as the main arbiter in the social, political and economic spheres (e.g. *the invisible hand of the market and the American "checks and balances"*), and favor contractual and transactional relationships, partisanship, utilitarianism, heterogeneity, self-fulfillment, fluidity of the social structures, freedom, rule of law, and democracy.

People brought up in these cultures are apt to be outward-directed or extroverted and show an unusual love of actions.

II   *Jing* Advocacy of China

A distinct aspect of Chinese culture is its ***Jing*** advocacy. Chinese love serenity, seeking a poetic pastoral quiet life. The quietude, peace and harmony described in the *Peach Blossom Land* by Jin Dynasty scholar Tao Yuanming have been pursued by Chinese people, some of whom meanwhile love ***re nao*** (hot and noisy) on occasions like parties and holidays.

1. Preconditions for Chinese *Jing* Advocacy

A good living environment, stable family life, agrarian economy, doctrines of the three traditional Chinese teachings, etc. may have helped to determine Chinese love of *Jing*.

a. A Good Living Environment

A good living environment is one of the preconditions necessary for ancient Chinese to maintain an unchanging nature and live a quiet and uneventful life. In very ancient times, cold currents from northern Siberia used to rush southward, carrying with them billions of tons of sand from the Mongolian Desert all the way to the south. When they reached the Yellow River, their power lessened, causing adequate rain to fall together with lots and lots of sand which deposited about 150-meter deep fertile topsoil for the Central Plains Region, the cradle of Chinese civilization and birthplace of Han nationality. With such a fertile plain and a favorable climate, this region became a food-barn, which enabled the ancient Chinese to settle down in one place for many generations.

b. An Ultra-stable State-family

Living in one place for many generations was one of the preconditions for families to become larger and larger, especially in the Central Plains Region. One of the hundred surnames or ***bai xing*** constituted one big family—the foundation of the state established much earlier in China than in the West. Hence, there has been in Chinese the concept of *guo jia*, which implies that the state is an extended family in which interdependence and hierarchy are natural and essential. Running the state composed of many families therefore depended on the rulers' ability to keep peace within the ultra-stable family-state.

c. Agrarian Economy

Traditional Chinese culture arises from agriculture which has long been regarded as the basis of economy. The rural-based agrarian economy relied on farming, hand labor, and manufacturing at home. This self-reliant and self-supporting economy resulted in an isolation and introversion in need of a spirit of opening up and transcending limitations.

d. Confucian Emphasis on *Jing*

Chinese advocacy of *Jing* is a part of the Confucian tradition. It is manifested in the doctrine of filial piety which traditionally limited Chinese travels and confiscated Chinese desire to leave home seeking more fortune outside by taking risks and adventures, for Confucius said, "A man does not travel to distant places when his parents are living, and if he does, he must have a definite destination(父母在,不远游, 游必有方)." His disciple Zengzi defined the filial child this way: "He does not climb high, and does not tread on dangerous places(孝子不登高,不履危)." In one word, a filial son should live a quiet and safe life to please his aged parents.

The Confucian ideal family life has always been a quiet one, in which men are supposed to spend half of their time studying and half of their time tilling the field while women are supposed to spin and weave. The dream life is actually the "assumed" life of the early Zhou Dynasty when life was the simplest and the needs of man were fewest. The worship of the ancients then became similar to the worship of simplicity and serenity, for the two notions in Chinese are closely related as in the phrase *gu pu* (literally, ancient and simple).

According to the theory of virtue, another important Confucian doctrine, *Jing* is the basis of exemplifying virtue. The *Great Learning*, one of the Four Confucian Classical Books, begins with the following sentences: "What the Great Learning teaches is to clearly exemplify illustrious virtue, to love the people, and to rest in the highest excellence. Only when one knows where to rest can he determine the object of his pursuit. Only with an object of pursuit can he achieve calmness of mind. Only with calmness of mind can he attain a tranquil repose. Only in tranquil repose can he deliberate carefully. Only through careful deliberation can he reach the desired goal (大学之道,在明明德,在亲民,在止于至善。知止而后有定,定而后能静,静而后能安,安而后能虑,虑而后能得)."

Dong Zhongshu, the famous Han Confucian scholar, drew widely from the other schools and held that "the vastness of the Way arises from Heaven; Heaven is unchangeable and the Way is unchangeable (道之大原于天,天不变道亦不变)", and encouraged the formation of an ultra-stable society where many generations could live in the same place so that the sense of deep root provided the kind of life ancient Chinese sought, which could create the feeling of being quiet, harmonious, stable, peaceful, and thus happy.

In order to remove selfish desires that may influence self-cultivation, Wang Yangming, the Ming Neo-Confucian scholar, suggested that one practice his type of meditation which he called "sitting still (静坐)". Obviously he got inspired by the practice of Chan meditation in Buddhism. The purpose is to cultivate one's mind and nature so as to realize the inner peace and balance with the outside world.

e. Taoist Cultivation of *Jing*

Lao Zi put forward the doctrine of "keeping quietude, valuing the supple, respecting the femininity, and taking no action(守静,贵柔,尊阴,无为)", based on which he came to the conclusion, "The heavy is the root of the light, and the quiet is the master of the unstable. Therefore, the sage travels all day, without putting down his heavy load. Though there may be spectacles to see, he easily passes them by. This being so, how could the ruler of a large state be so concerned with himself as to ignore the people? If you take them lightly you will lose your roots. If you are unstable, you will lose your rulership (重为轻根,静为燥君。是以君子终日行不离轻重。虽有荣观燕处超然。奈何万乘之主而以身轻天下。轻则失根,燥则失君)." The conclusion denotes that stability dominates the instability. Zhuang Zi, the second important figure of Taoism, is famous for his concept of mind's house (心斋), through which one is brought into harmony with nature and achieves peace by sitting and forgetting(坐忘). In *Human World* (《人间篇》) he stated, " Only the Way can accumulate vacancy; the vacant is the mind's house (惟道集虚，虚者心斋)," believing only by maintaining the quiet and vacant mind can one attain the Way, because he held that the practice of "sitting and forgetting" could integrate one with nature.

Based on their observation and studies, both Lao Zi and Zhuang Zi favored the notion of *Jing* as the natural disposition of sages. After the fall of the Han Dynasty there arose the Neo-Taoist movement. Its central objective was to enjoy a long and serene life which, as taught by Lao Zi, may be attained through simplicity and tranquility, and as illustrated by Zhuang Zi, through integration with nature, spiritual freedom, and indifference to life and death. This Neo-Taoist Movement assumed momentum in the third century BC and has continued to the present time.

f. Buddhist Emphasis on Inner Silence

Ancient Chinese followed the life pattern of "using Confucianism to run the state, Taoism to cultivate body, and Buddhism to nurture mind(以儒治世，以道养身，以佛修心)". A silent mind, freed from the onslaught of thoughts and thought patterns, is both a goal and an important step in spiritual development according to Buddhist philosophers. Inner silence is understood to be able to bring one into contact with the divine or the ultimate reality of this moment. The Buddhist tradition implies the importance of being quiet and peaceful in mind and spirit for transformative and integral spiritual growth to occur.

2. Chinese Preference for *Jing*

Chinese people, especially scholars, like to enjoy a calm and serene life. We are apt to think of calm persons as being intelligent and dependable. And we prefer a quiet stay at home after a long workday. If given a choice, we would like to lead a quiet life and attend to our own business.

a. *Jing* as a Name of Objects

Maybe you have noticed the fact that Chinese parents like naming their children *Jing*. Take Wang Jing (a famous singer) and Wen Jing (a renowned CCTV anchor) for instance. They do this in the hope that their kids will appear serene and quiet because serenity is a good quality. A young lady who is serene and quiet will be favored by her teachers, parents, supervisors, friends, etc. and a quiet boy will probably be good at his academic work at school.

In order to create a good environment for booklovers to do some reading and shopping, book distributors employ *Jing* to name their stores, e.g. *Jing Zhai* (literally, Serenity Studio) and *Le Jing Zhai* (literally, Studio of Happiness in Quietude).

Garden administrators use *Jing* to name their gardens in order to attract more visitors who need a break from work, e.g. *Jing Yuan* (literally, Serenity Garden) and *Le Jing Yuan* (literally, Garden of Happiness in Quietness).

The public sign "静 净 敬 (*jing jing jing*, freely, please be quiet, polite, and keep clean)" can be seen on many campuses, calling on students to keep quiet in public places, to be environment-friendly, and to respect parents, teachers and people who are older than them.

Despite the surface changes in custom, women's clothes, people's reading habits, the rhythm of life, etc., Chinese today retain a sneering smile for the hot-headed young person who is noisy, active, and in love with adventures and changes.

b. Chinese Idioms Denoting *Jing*

There are in Chinese many idioms denoting *Jing*. They are used to express good wishes for stillness, quietness, stability, tranquility, settlement, safety, peace, etc., as can be seen in idioms such as 岁月静好(freely, Enjoy a tranquil and comfortable life), 安邦定国 (freely, Bring peace and stability to the country), 安居乐业 (freely, Live and work in peace and contentment), 安家落户 (freely, Settle down in one place), 安然无恙 (freely, Be safe and sound or Be uneventful), 故土难离 (freely, Be attached to one's native land and unwilling to leave it./Hate to leave a place where one has lived long), 安身立命 (freely, Settle down and get on with one's pursuit), 安然而至 (freely, Expire peacefully), 以静制动 (freely, Use quietude to control motion), 以不变应万变 (freely, Be prepared for everything with no change), 文静 (freely, Be gentle and quiet), and 稳重 (freely, Be steady). A Chinese parent or teacher might use the expression

Hold your tongue (静一静) to quiet a noisy child.

c. Power of *Jing* in the Ancient Music

The ancient Chinese music is expected to create a sense of tranquility, serenity, peace, safety as well as beauty. The monophonic music reflects ancient Chinese concern for unity and harmony. Singers would all sing the same melody and musical instruments play the same notes at the same time. The famous "Empty City Scheme" is about how Zhuge Liang saved an empty city by playing the zither, an ancient musical instrument. During the Three Kingdoms period, Zhuge Liang was in the city of Yang Ping. He sent his general Wei Yan with the majority of the Shu soldiers to fight against the 200,000 strong Wei army led by General Sima Yi, leaving only 10,000 men behind to defend the city. However, due to miscalculation, the Shu army missed the Wei army. When the Wei army was about 60 miles from the city, Sima Yi learnt from his spy about Shu's strength that was left in the city. Zhuge Liang also received the news that the enemy was near, but it was too late to summon Wei Yan back. The town was in panic but Zhuge Liang remained calm. He ordered his soldiers to keep all the army flags flying and not to leave the tents without permission. He then ordered men to open the gates and pretend to sweep the ground next to the gates. When Sima Yi arrived, he was shocked by what he saw. He knew Zhuge Liang was a good strategist with many tricks up his sleeve. So when he saw that the gates were opened up, he suspected that Zhuge Liang might have laid an ambush, waiting for him. His suspicion was further aroused when he saw Zhuge Liang was sitting leisurely on top of the city wall playing the zither and sipping tea. Sima Yi paid attention to the chords played by Zhuge Liang and they were placid and calm, showing no signs of a troubled mind. He therefore concluded that the empty city was definitely a scheme to lure his troops in. Sima Yi ordered his men to turn around and retreat. Thus Zhuge Liang salvaged the situation.

Incidentally, Buddhist music is also meant to create a sense of serenity, in which one is expected to be able to be gradually or suddenly enlightened. Hence, the simple recitation of Amitabha's name in company of the same melody and musical instrument becomes the most common of all Buddhist practices in China and a tool popular with millions who seek liberation from the sufferings of this world.

d. Chinese Preference for Steady and Taciturn Candidates

In selecting talents to leading positions, Chinese prefer to see first of all whether the candidates are steady and taciturn or not, which has been a tradition since Zhou Dynasty, the so-called Golden Age.

According to the *Yao Dian and Shun Dian*, Emperor Yao was reverential, intelligent, accomplished, thoughtful, and mild. When Fang Qi recommended his son to be his successor, saying: "Your heir-son Zhu is highly intelligent." Yao said, "Alas! He is insincere and noisy. Can he do?" Later Shun was recommended to him because "although he is the son of a blind man, his father is obstinately unprincipled, his step mother deceitful, and his half brother Xiang arrogant, he has been able to live in harmony with them and to be awesomely filial. He has controlled himself and has never done any evil." And above all, he was steady and taciturn (稳重寡言), and thus dependable. It turned out that Shun was chosen to be in Yao's position.

e. Chinese Wish for *Jing*

"Calm seas and tranquil breezes (风平浪静)" is a best wish for fisherman, or for the safety of a traveler or a person who is ready to travel. Jinghai Temple in Nanjing was built in 1402 when the famous navigator Zheng He came back from his second voyage to the Indian Ocean. In praise of his achievements in navigation and exchanges with the other peoples and cultures, Emperor Cheng of the Ming ordered to build Jinghai Temple (literally, Calm-sea Temple), praying for the peace of the whole world. The temple was also built to show his gratitude and appreciation for the Sea God's protection of his great fleet, to ask for more mercy on travelers and to wish his people a tranquil and quiet life.

3. *Jing* as a Theme Popular with Chinese Poets

Jing is traditionally used by Chinese literati as background in which they express their homesickness, ambition, pride, and uniqueness. Take ***Jiang Xue*** (Fishing in Snow) by Tang Poet Liu Zongyuan (773—819) for instance.

　　　江雪
千山鸟飞绝，
万径人踪灭。
孤舟蓑笠翁，
独钓寒江雪。

Fishing in Snow

From hill to hill no bird is in flight;

From path to path no man is in sight.

A lonely fisherman afloat

Is fishing snow in a lonely boat.

(Tr. by Xu Yuanchong)

　　Born in the Tang capital Chang'an, Liu Zongyuan was promoted very rapidly in the civil government. He supported the reform efforts of Emperor Shunzong, fell into disfavor with the authorities when the emperor suddenly abdicated in 805. In exile, Liu Zongyuan turned his attention to literature. His autobiographical poem *Jiang Xue* composed during his exile is considered an example of how a few words can be used to convey a great deal of meanings such as his ambition, his uniqueness, and his perseverance. The poem has been the subject of numerous landscape paintings to exhibit the serene background, ambition and pride which characterize decent talented scholars or scholar-officials.

　　Jing is also employed by Chinese literati as a subject in which they express their idea of what the best life is, as demonstrated in this poem:

松下问童子，
言师采药去，
只在此山中，
云深不知处。

I asked the boy beneath the pine.

He said to me, "The Master's gone

Herb-gathering somewhere in this mount.

Cloud-hidden, whereabouts unknown."

This feeling for nature and stillness overflows in almost all Chinese poetry, and forms an important part of the Chinese spiritual heritage. Even as late as today, a call for the return of the traditional appreciation of the static beauty of harmony would be answered by many, because every Chinese has a desire for this beauty since we are exposed to poems featuring serenity.

III   *Dong* Advocacy of the West

A distinct aspect of Western culture is its advocacy of **Dong**. Westerners tend to be more active, incessantly reaching out, creating and discovering. A life of such is a life of strength and discovery for them.

1. Ancient Greece and *Dong* Advocacy

a. Ancient Greek Climate and Its Economic Activities

Ancient Greece could not possibly be as agriculturally productive as China. For one thing, there is the Mediterranean climate: hot dry summers and cold rainy winters, and the average annual rainfall in Athens is only 15.9 inches, and for another, there are few rivers in Greece, and most of the country is broken up into islands and peninsulas that cannot receive the runoff of wetter mountains. Ancient Greece was thus wealthy off something else—sea trade, transportation, and even piracy, which led those who were in these professions to live a restless life by visiting different places, experiencing alien cultures and facing rapidly changing situations.

b. Sea Trade of Ancient Greece

Long coastline and being surrounded by water on three sides made it possible for ancient Greeks to develop sea trade and transportation. To engage in trade, anyone needs something to get started, and Greek agriculture could provide a couple of starter products. Olive trees grow well in Greece. Olives must be soaked in brine to be edible, but more importantly they can be pressed for olive oil. The oil is not very perishable, and could be stored and shipped easily to be sold at distant locations in exchange for food, fuel oil, or other purposes. Grapes as well grow well in Greece. Grapes can be pressed and fermented to produce wine, another product that is not very perishable and can be stored and shipped.

Trade as a way of life would foster considerable independence, being far away from all authorities at home, and it would involve dealing with all sorts of strangers, cultures, practices, and ideas.

c. Commodity Economy of Ancient Greece

Ancient Greece took advantage of its ecology and geography to develop its commodity economy, so commodity production and exchange characterized its economy. The Greek commodity economy helped to meet each other's needs, possessing the characteristics of openness to the outside, independence and equality, on the basis of which Western culture of extroversion was set up. Settled agriculture came to Greece almost two thousand years later than to China, but it quickly became commercial. Since commodity economy arose out of equality and independence, this economy brought equality and democratic ideas to Western culture which advocates dynamic activities like discovery, invention, and adventures.

2. Scholars and *Dong* Advocacy

Western love of *Dong* owes much to Western philosophers and scientists, too.

a. Heraclitus

Greece has given Westerners more philosophy than any other place in the West by producing many philosophers. Heraclitus (540 BC—480 BC) is one of them. The best-known aspect of Heraclitus' ideas is the omnipresence of change(一切皆流). There is, he said, nothing static in the universe, the mind, or the soul. Everything is ceasing to be what it was and becoming what it will be. This was a new idea. "All things flow; nothing abides," he wrote and "we are and we are not." His best-known remark is, "You cannot step twice into the same river, for other waters are ever flowing on to you." His system contains other hypotheses, but this is the most fruitful, and the one which commended itself most to his followers and successors.

b. Cratylus

If the world was in such a constant flux that streams could change instantaneously, then so could words. Thus, Heraclitus' disciple Cratylus found communication to be impossible. As a result of this realization, Cratylus renounced his power of speech and limited his communication to moving his finger.

c. Nicolas Copernicus

Nicolas Copernicus (1473—1543) was the first astronomer to formulate a scientifically based heliocentrism, a theory that the sun is at the center of the solar system. His book, *On the Revolutions of the Celestial Spheres*, is often regarded as the starting point of modern astronomy that began the scientific revolution which encourages discovery and invention of new ideas.

3. Western Preference for *Dong*

a. Ancient Olympic Games

Ancient Greeks loved sports. What is astonishing, even to us today, is that during a celebration of the Games, an Olympic Truce was enacted to enable athletes to travel from their city-states to Olympia in safety; the entire Greek nation laid down its tools—including its arms if city-states were at war with one another—to participate in the Olympics as athletes or audience. The prizes for the victors were laurel wreaths, palm branches, woolen ribbons and sometimes even food for life. The modern Games held every four years is a continuation of the ancient Greek Olympics.

b. Ancient Greek Love of Fun

There is an ancient theater at Epidaurus in Greece. It can hold fourteen thousand people. Built into a hillside, the theater has a good view of mountains and pine trees. Its acoustics are very good after so many years. According to historical records, Greeks from the sixth to the third century BC traveled for long periods under very difficult conditions to Epidaurus merely to see plays and listen to people read poetry. They used to stay in the theatre from dawn till dusk for several days in a row and had great fun from the poetry reading and stage performance.

c. American Presidents' Hobbies

Like us all, presidents need relaxation. Over the years, American Presidents have participated in a great variety of sports and hobbies while in the White House. Some were famous for their hobbies, such as Dwight Eisenhower for his golf, Ronald

Reagan for horseback riding and John Kennedy for sailing and touch football. Gerald Ford even played football for the University of Michigan in the early 1930s. He was selected as Most Valuable Player in 1934 and was named an All-American, the only President to win this distinction. After college, he was offered contracts by several professional teams. President Barack Obama's favorite sport is basketball and he played varsity basketball in high school.

George Washington, true to the times and his class, enjoyed fishing and horseback riding. He found great relaxation in the out-of-doors, and enjoyed getting away from the pressures of office.

Washington's successor, John Adams, apparently had no specific hobbies during his term as President, and engaged in no sports. That may have had something to do with the portly Adams' nickname of "His Rotundity".

d. Western Preference for Active People

"All work and no play make Jack a dull boy" is one of the most often quoted proverbs, denoting that without time off from work, a person becomes bored and boring. If you work all day in this culture, few will be deeply impressed by your hard work. Instead, people will think you are a person of no life, a poor guy, and an overly introverted person.

e. Western Love of Adventures and Pursuit of Material Wealth

Traditional Western culture, composed of Greek, Roman and Christian cultures, holds that everything could be achieved through action and one's value could only be found in action. During the 1400's, some Europeans began to wonder what lay across the great oceans. Many decided to make dangerous journeys across the oceans in order to explore new lands for themselves, and one of them was Christopher Columbus.

In north China, there is a bridge called Marco Polo Bridge(卢沟桥). Marco Polo was an Italian businessman. He traveled to China as a teenager and had spent 17 years here. Upon his return he wrote a book that describes all the wonders of China. Columbus read this book titled *The Travels of Marco Polo*. He too wanted to travel to the East. Columbus made four voyages across the Atlantic Ocean between 1492 and his death. During this period, new countries, a new continent and new civilizations were discovered for the very first time. As for why there were so great geographic discoveries in Europe, below are some possible reasons:

They wanted to explore new lands.

They intended to become rich by finding gold and silver.

They hoped to find new lands for their country to control.

They expected to find new people to convert to the Christian religion.

They wanted to prove that the world was round.

But for the majority of ordinary sailors, it was just a job. In one word, Western culture favors motion in the form of outward expansion or long distance travel.

IV Differences and Discomforts

1. Different Translation Strategies

In China, the best life or the most beautiful memory is experienced in a static state while in the West, in a dynamic setting. Chinese culture as a whole tends to be still, so anything relevant to stillness could be encouraged and hence prospers, which may illustrate why stillness is a favorite topic with classical Chinese poets and painters. Western culture as a whole is one of motion, so anything relevant to motion could be promoted and hence flourishes. This difference might probably account for why Western translators adopt free translation to render classical Chinese poetry which is the aggregate of the Chinese cultural heritage, and sometimes go so far as to change the original theme of stillness into that of motion. *Jing Ye Si* by Tang poet Li Bai is one of the first poems most Chinese pre-school babblers can recite. Below are its two English versions translated by two scholars of different cultural and educational backgrounds.

A Tranquil Night

Abed, I see a silver light,

I wonder if it's frost aground.

Looking up, I find the moon bright;

Bowing, in homesickness I'm drowned.

(Tr. by Xu Yuanchong)

The Moon Shines Everywhere

Seeing the moon before my couch so bright

I thought hoar frost had fallen from the night.

On her clear face I gaze with lifted eyes:

Then hide them full of Youth's sweet memories.

(Tr. by W. J. B. Fletcher)

Obviously the first version by Xu Yuanchong, a famous Chinese translator, is more faithful to the original. Xu chooses expressions like *tranquil* and *homesickness* in his version since **Jing** is traditionally used by Chinese literati as background in which they express their homesickness or ambition. However, the second version translated by Fletcher appears understandably unfaithful. Given the fact that a word-for-word translation into Chinese of **Goodbye** which literally means "God be with you" according to English etymology may not be recognized as a parting in Chinese and the word-for-word translation into English of **zai jian** which means "See again" may not be regarded as a parting, it seems reasonable for the Western translator to translate by using dynamic expressions such as *shine* and *fallen* in accordance with his own culture in which tranquility is not associated with homesickness and serenity is not so strongly advocated.

2. Cultural Discomforts

In a normal discussion, Westerners (especially North Americans) usually appear active by interrupting each other. They find silence uncomfortable and rude in conversations. Chinese do not generally interrupt each other. In group discussions, pauses and silence are valued. For some Westerners, Chinese silence is confusing, and sometimes upsetting.

My friend Dr. Nancy Bush was invited to work for half a year at a Chinese university. She told that her students were very attentive in her classroom. They applauded warmly every time her lecture ended. However, Dr. Bush was a little bit disappointed for no one asked her any questions, although she kept encouraging them to say something or anything. Somehow her students chose to sit back smiling or giggling but saying nothing. And they didn't avoid eye contact with her as she tried to persuade them to stand up and speak something! She grew upset and confused. Dr. Bush's experience reminds me of what happened to me when I was a freshman in Central China's Normal University twenty-five years ago:

One day Mr. Brock who taught us Western Culture was ill. His wife came instead to teach us. In order to activate the atmosphere, she played a piece of music and suggested us dancing to the music together with her, but all of us just sat there watching her and blushing with embarrassment. Then, she asked us to stand up and dance. Although we stood up, few of us followed her. Most of us felt shy, so we fell silent, and I could see that Mrs. Brock was very frustrated.

Actually what Dr. Bush and Mrs. Brock experienced in China characterizes some Chinese students in their American lecture rooms. A few years ago, Li Ying, a graduate student studying psychology at an American university, became upset because of constant demand from her instructors that she should be more active by speaking or doing something in class. She was told repeatedly that failure to speak up could be taken as an indication of failure to fully understand the material and that speaking up and hearing the reactions from the instructor and classmates would help her to understand better. Li Ying refused to believe it. Instead, she felt that she and her fellow Chinese students would not benefit from being active in class because their way of understanding is not verbal, but silent. There is an age-old tradition in China of equating quietness rather than speech with digesting and accumulating knowledge, just as the aphorism goes, "He who knows does not speak, he who speaks does not know."

Further Reading

1. Wu, Jian (1990). *Encountering the Chinese*. Yarmouth, Me: Intercultural Press.

2. Stewart, Edward C. & Milton J. Bennett (1991). *American Cultural Patterns: A Cross-Cultural Perspective*. Yarmouth ME: Intercultural Press.

3. 罗素著,马元德译(1976):《西方哲学史》,北京:商务印书馆。

4. 张忠利、宗文举(2002):《中西文化概论》,天津:天津大学出版社。

5. 林语堂(1998):《生活的艺术》,北京:外语教学与研究出版社。

6. 饶尚宽译注(2006):《老子》,北京:中华书局。

7. 杨伯峻译注(2006):《论语》,北京:中华书局。

8. 陈鼓应译注(2001):《庄子》,北京:中华书局。

9. 许渊冲译(2003):《中国古诗精品三百首》,北京:北京大学出版社。

Unit 16　Implicitness vs. Explicitness

二十岁的时候,老妈打电话,不等说完三句就恨不能挂了电话。三十岁之后,一听到妈的声音就禁不住哭出声来:"妈呀,您老的所有担心现在都应验了……"

—*Anonymous*

The English version of the above is as follows:

At the age of twenty, while talking with my mother over the phone, I wanted to hang up before my mother had finished a few words. After thirty the voice of Mom invariably triggers my crying, "Mom, your worries about my marriage have all come true..."

Why does the translator have to turn what is implied in the original into the explicit marriage reference in the English version?

Good prose is like a window pane.

—*George Orwell*

Do you agree with the British novelist and essayist George Orwell? Why or why not?

I　"Half a Story"

In North America, it seems everything has to be explicitly talked about. Even the littlest thing has to be "Why, why, why? How, how, how? What, what, what?" It's the speaker's or writer's responsibility to give definite and detailed answers to these questions instead of waiting for the listener or reader to come up with them.

At the end of 2007, as soon as I came back to my host university in The Woodlands, Texas with my son Minchang from our trip to New York City I went to see my colleague Jane Summers who arranged the trip for us.

"Juliet and Nathan have been worried about you and Minchang. People feel I'm the person responsible for your safety here in America."

Noticing a change in Jane's tone, I was kind of surprised and confused, "Why?"

"They say New York is not The Woodlands. You told them only half a story, Jifang. Why didn't you tell them the whole story? You should have told them you have a friend in New York, you have family there too, and you also have my brother and his family in case anything should happen to you."

"But I had no time to give them more details about our plan. I just asked them about the ferry to the Statue of Liberty and told them this is my first trip to New York. Wait a minute. Did I have to tell them all?"

As a matter of fact, I knew I would not depend on anybody if anything should happen to me and my 13-year-old son in New York, because those Jane mentioned don't belong to "we" group. My friend Amy once worked in Hohai University as an English teacher, but we hadn't seen each other for four years. My so-called family in New York is my husband's sister-in-law's sister who had migrated to New York two years before by marrying an American of Chinese descent who is much older than her, and I had seen her only once. And Jane's brother? I had never seen him and his family.

"Exactly. Everybody here thinks that I should be responsible for you. Half a story is misleading. They would judge me. Chinese seem to like telling half a story. "

I said nothing (I regret not saying anything more to her. I hope I can do better next time). I was thinking. Actually I have been thinking about the seemingly offensive comment made by Jane— "Chinese seem to like telling half a story."

Now I feel there is some sense in what she said. I remember how Jane added information to my remarks when I talked to people who don't know much about China. I remember she added, "Jifang's father was a doctor" when I told my new friends "my father refused to give my son any medicine for his ADHD." I remember she explained, "Nanjing is the capital city of east China's Jiangsu Province" when I told my new friends "I'm from Nanjing." Having consulted many sources, I find myself on the journey to a new (at least for me) dimension—implicitness vs. explicitness.

II　Implicitness and Explicitness of Language

Steven Pinker, a prominent Canadian-American experimental psychologist, cognitive scientist and author of popular science, acknowledged that language is not adequate to account for all of our thoughts. He indicated problems of ambiguity (i.e. implicitness), lack of logical explicitness, etc. as examples. What he said is true of Chinese language which is oriented to be implicit or ambiguous.

1. Implicitness of the Chinese Language

A word, term, sign, symbol, phrase, sentence, or any other form used for communication, as a consequence of being implied or indirect, is called implicit if it is open to different interpretations and can be understood in diverse ways. The implicitness of Chinese may arise out of our distrust of words and layered expressions—a direct result of our synthetic thinking mode.

a. Chinese Distrust of Words

"The Chinese distrust of logic begins with the distrust of words, proceeds with the abhorrence of definitions and ends with instinctive hatred for all systems and theories."(Lin Yutang) Our distrust of words is revealed in what our parents taught us when we were little, such as 听话听声, 锣鼓听音 (literally, When you listen you should pay attention to the tone just as you should pay attention to the sounds when you listen to the gong; freely, You should figure out what is implied.) and 察言观色 (literally, Observe one's face color; freely, Learn what one is thinking by studying his face). When we write something we are reminded to remember the policy of 只可意会, 不可言传 (literally, It can only be implied, not expressed in words) to increase the readability. The distrust of words is also displayed in pop lyrics such as 一切尽在不言中(literally, Everything is expressed in silence; freely, No words means many words), and present in aphorisms like 会听是金, 会说是银 (literally, The ability to listen is gold; the ability to speak is silver) because many Chinese believe "醉翁之意不在酒 (literally, The drinker's heart is not in the cup; freely, Many kiss the baby for the nurse's sake)." Therefore, for the sake of convenience or to save time, polite or shrewd people love saying "随便 (literally, Do whatever you want)," leaving the other party to figure out for himself, and hence "客随主便(literally, I am your guest and I will do whatever you want me to do)" becomes a polite pet phrase.

Distrust of words is one of the reasons why some Westerners find it difficult to learn Chinese.

b. Layered Expressions

Many of the popular Chinese expressions are "layered". The superficial message becomes apparent immediately, but as one re-reads, he discovers deeper meaning. The following proverbs may help to explain why Chinese is regarded as ambiguous:

千里之堤,毁于蚁穴(An ant may well destroy a whole dam.)

不做亏心事,不怕鬼敲门(A clear conscience never fears midnight knocking.)

儿不嫌母丑, 狗不嫌家贫 (A dog won't forsake his master because of his poverty; a son never deserts his mother for her homely appearance.)

玉不琢不成器(The finest diamond must be cut.)

Read and re-read the above proverbs and you will find them open to different interpretations and can be understood in different ways.

c. Chinese Synthetic Thinking Mode

Closely associated with intuition and thinking in terms of images, the synthetic or holistic mode of Chinese thinking, has determined the quality or state of implicitness, which is synonymous with *ambiguousness, cloudiness, equivocalness, indefiniteness, nebulousness, obscurity, uncertainty, unclearness,* and *vagueness.*

Intuitive thinking is a special process of obtaining knowledge about the whole situation. This thinking takes place very quickly with much information, transcending the restrictions imposed by the pursuit of clarity. It seeks the integral and absolute knowledge, so it is qualitative, not quantitative. Lack of quantitative analysis results in ambiguity, which features Chinese, for instance, the concept of Tao (Dao or Way) is ambiguous since, according to Lao Zi, Tao is invisible and indescribable.

Thinking synthetically helps to form the habit of communicating through symbolic expressions, hints and allusions expecting listeners and readers to grasp the meaning by reading between lines. Many readers may have read a public sign which says 记得绿罗裙,处处怜芳草 (literally, My love, when you miss me, look at the green grass which is me; freely, Keep off the grass.)

The ambiguity of thinking encourages neglect of logical clarity and lexical-semantic "accuracy", which makes combination of linguistic units in Chinese very often appear casual. There are many expressions used by many including linguists in spite of logical ambiguity such as 开心 (literally, to open heart; freely, to be very happy) and 救灾 (literally, rescue disaster; freely, disaster rescue). Obviously only a few representative words combined together are enough. Therefore, the basis of Chinese grammatical rules is meaning, not form; thus we like to say, "He who says the least says the most (懂得最多的人说得最少)."

Synthetic thinking mode instructs us not to depend very much on quantitative instructions. For instance, we learn cooking not by following recipes with precise quantitative descriptions, but by intuitively acquiring our mothers' or our masters' technique after repeated imitations, so we don't use measuring cups. Another example is traditional Chinese paintings. We seek close resemblance in spirit when we paint instead of accurate likeness in appearance. In fact, intuitive feeling and fuzzy beauty are held in great esteem in almost all forms of Chinese art such as poetry, drama, and painting.

2. Explicitness of the English Language

A word, term, sign, symbol, phrase, sentence, or any other form used for communication, is called explicit if it can be interpreted in only one way. Therefore, explicitness is synonymous with *certainty, clarity, clearness, definiteness, explicitness,* and *lucidity*. Comparatively speaking, English is explicit. Its explicitness may arise out of Western logical thinking, the opposite of Chinese holistic or synthetic thinking. Logical thinking is a learned mental process, in which one uses reasoning consistently to come to a conclusion. Problems or situations that involve logical thinking call for structure, for relationships between facts, and for chains of reasoning that make sense. The basis of all logical thinking is sequential thought. This process involves important ideas, facts, and conclusions. To think logically is to think in steps, involving both qualitative and quantitative analysis, but putting more emphasis on the study of the latter. The quantitative emphasis endows English with explicitness and accuracy. For instance, they like using idioms such as *Don't beat around the bush. Let's get down to business. Let us be clear, and Get to the point.* They write explicitly in the public sign *Keep off* rather than 小草微微笑 , 请君走便道 (literally, Little grass is smiling sweetly, so please use the road instead of the grass) or 小草有生命 , 脚下请留情 (literally, Little grass has life; please let your feet show them some sympathy). Westerners, exposed to relatively explicit languages, try to get at things very clearly, asking or explaining what, why and how much while we show more interest in dealing with things using metaphors or intuitive comparisons.

Many Westerners believe that God has made man a creature of time and therefore, a creature of number, so they tend to depend on very explicit words and exact quantitative instructions. For instance, they learn cooking by following recipes with precise quantitative descriptions. They are trained how to make their case in 30 seconds or less. They seek accurate likeness in appearance when working on oil paintings, e.g. every inch of canvas is filled up and even the wrinkles on the dress can be seen.

III   Implicit Chinese

The implicitness or ambiguity of Chinese has been much discussed by scholars at home and abroad. Some of them hold that implicitness is producing a country of lazy-bones while others advocate using implicitness in creative work.

1. Beauty and Ugliness of Implicitness

a. Beauty of Implicitness in Classical Chinese Poetry

Implicitness, sometimes known as "plurisignation" or "multiple meaning", is a central concept in the interpretation of poetry. Oriental Studies Master Ji Xianlin defended it as a source of poetic richness rather than a fault of imprecision during an interview in 1996.

Chinese, as a language of parataxis(意合), does not stress the form, its structure can be incomplete, and its verbs are not so salient, especially in classical Chinese poetry which requires the reader or listener to involve his own personal experience in Chinese poetry interpretation and appreciation. Take for example "鸡声茅店月，人迹板桥霜(Standing near the hut in the moonlight, I hear the cock crowing, and get a sense of some steps of passers-by before me on the bridge) " composed by Tang poet Wen Tinjjun (812—866). We can understand the two lines on the basis of our own experiences and see a man who, away from home, misses his family in late autumn. This understanding owes much to the free and ambiguous expressions employed by Wen. Suppose the expressions are clear and explicit, our aesthetic fancy might be greatly reduced. Wang Guowei (1877—1927) in *Comments on Ci* (《人间词话》) brought up with **yi jing** (literally, poetic excellence) and **gu ya** (literally, classical grace) theory, coining phrases like 有我之境 (literally, context with me; freely, context with an explicit actor) and 无我之境 (literally, context without me; freely, context without an explicit actor) employed in classical Chinese poetry. According to him, "采菊东篱下，悠然见南山" provides a "context without me", and its beauty lies in the ambiguity of the actor. If translated into English, however, the actor should be added as in "While picking asters' neath the eastern fence, my gaze upon the southern mountain rests", otherwise the translation will not make any sense to the target reader, thus leaving no imaginative space and decreasing the original poetic beauty of vagueness.

As a great example of literature highly succinct in writing, classical Chinese poetry is full of vivid images in limited space of lines that produce pictures in the minds of readers or listeners, so it is essential to exert our imagination when reading and appreciating a classical Chinese poem. Take for instance two lines from a poem by Wang Wei (701—761): "劝君更尽一杯酒，西出阳关无故人(I would ask you to drink a cup of wine again; West of the Sunny Pass no more friends will be seen)." Obviously the second line is the cause and the first one is the effect, but there is no word in the lines to join them, so we have to comprehend these two lines by firing or unfolding our imagination. The following is a lyric by the Yuan poet Ma Zhiyuan (1251—1321), entitled **Qiu Si** (Autumn Thoughts):

枯藤老树昏鸦，

小桥流水人家。

古道西风瘦马，

夕阳西下，

断肠人在天涯。

Autumn Thoughts

Over old trees wreathed with rotten vines fly evening crows;

Under a small bridge near a cottage a stream flows;

On ancient road in the west wind a lean horse goes.

Westward declines the sun,

Far, far from home is the heartbroken one.

(Tr. by Xu Yuanchong)

Old trees, rotten vines and *evening crows* arranged one after another in a sequence in the original, give us much freedom of thinking and great enjoyment. The implicitness is not bad, is it? Only two verbs can be found in the original poetry, 下 (set down) and 在 (stand, be), which is unimaginable in English. The famous American poet Ezra Pound, influenced by Chinese poetry, composed poems in the Chinese way, became very popular for a period of time and then went into oblivion because Chinese poetic lines without verbs appear ambiguous and thus beautiful, but English, as an inflectional language, stresses the importance of grammar and form—hypotaxis and thus lines without verbs are ambiguous and hence undesirable.

Ancient Chinese poets used implicit language to produce vivid images for aesthetic purposes. Take for instance the two famous lines of poetry 问君能有几多愁，恰似一江春水向东流 (freely, How much sorrow, pray, can a person carry? Like the spring torrent flowing eastward, without tarry). The two lines are from a ci poem composed by Li Yu (937—978), a poet emperor of the Later Tang Dynasty. In this poem spring water in the river implies the endless melancholy.

As an art of language, Chinese poems use words in extraordinary ways for expression and description. A story goes about Wang Anshi (1022—1086), a famous poet and statesman of the Song Dynasty, who racked his brains for perfection in the choice of words. Originally, he used words explicitly in the line of his poem and it was read as "春风又到江南岸 (freely, The vernal wind has reached the southern shore again)." But he did not feel satisfied for its explicitness. After looking desperately for the right word, he found that the adjective "green" should be the best one for his choice because it is so colorful and imaginable a description of "the southern region of the Yangtze" in spring when being tentatively used as a verb, much better than any explicit verbs such as *dao* (reach), *guo* (pass by), and *ru* (enter) he had weighed. In this way he finalized the line as "春风又绿江南岸 (freely, The vernal wind has greened the southern shore again)."

There are many implicit, typical and poetic expressions in classical Chinese poetry which can arouse rich literary associations. For examples, *the moon* (明月) can be associated with homesickness; *weeping willows* (杨柳依依) may evoke memories of departure. And there are also some culture-loaded words that can call forth specific feelings among Chinese people and their implicitness can't be reproduced in any other language. So it is unimaginable to separate classical Chinese poems from Chinese language. In this sense, Chinese poems cannot be translated into any other language. As a carrier of culture classical Chinese poetry reflects the history, tradition and civilization of China and the living environment, thinking mode, values and tastes of its people in ancient times. Its beauty is rooted in the fertile soil of Chinese culture, brimming with Chinese scent.

b. Ugliness of Implicitness

The reader or listener responsibility system which was born out of the implicitness works against efforts, offering ambiguous explanations, which has created many negative effects.

Wang Yangming (1472—1529), the leading figure in the Neo-Confucian school of Mind, is regarded as one of the four greatest masters of Confucianism in history along with Confucius, Mencius and Zhu Xi because of his contribution to the revival and development of Confucianism. Nevertheless, the language in which he expressed some of his ideas was so ambiguous that almost immediately his school diverged on some basic issues.

Buhaoyisi, one of our pet phrases, is open to many interpretations, but it is safe for us to use it and it can save us a lot of trouble in countless difficult situations. When we're late for a meeting, we can say *buhaoyisi* (Sorry. I am late). When we reach for the last cookie on the plate while others are watching, we say *buhaoyisi* (Sorry, but I need one more). When we bump into someone on the subway, we say *buhaoyisi* (Sorry for bumping into you.). When we are caught beating the traffic light, we say *buhaoyisi* (Sorry for breaking the traffic rule). When we take things that don't belong to us, like taking briberies, we say *buhaoyisi* (Sorry for this). *Buhaoyisi* has created many people without bottom lines. With *buhaoyisi* as a pretext, many of us put away all rituals or our faces and do what we really want to do such as enjoying help or kindness from others. The intention is to use the phrase as a smoke screen to hide the bad scars in our body.

Arguably, the implicitness of language has ruined many dreams since ancient times. The legend of Liang Shanbo and Zhu Yingtai is a case in point. The story is about a young woman named Zhu Yingtai from Shangyu, Zhejiang, who disguised herself as a man traveling to Hangzhou to study. During her journey, she met Liang Shanbo, a scholar from Kuaiji in the same province. They felt like old friends at the first sight. Therefore, they gathered some soil as incense and took vows of brotherhood in the pavilion of a thatched bridge. For three years at school, they shared the same room where there was only one bed and two quilts. Yingtai slowly fell in love with Shanbo, but Shanbo did not see any traces of female characteristics in Yingtai. Time flew by quickly. One day Yingtai received a letter from her father asking her to return home. As a filial daughter she had no alternative but to pack her belongings immediately and bid farewell.

Liang Shanbo, being Yingtai's sworn brother, accompanied Yingtai for 18 li to send her off. On the way, Yingtai implied to Shanbo that she was female. For example, she compared themselves to a pair of mandarin ducks (love birds), but Shanbo did not catch on to her hidden meaning. Finally Yingtai had an idea: She told Shanbo that she would be a matchmaker and match Shanbo with her sister. Before the two parted, Yingtai reminded Shanbo to pay a visit to her home so that he could propose for marriage. Liang Shanbo and Zhu Yingtai reluctantly took leave of each other at the pavilion where they had first met.

When Shanbo arrived at Yingtai's home, he discovered her true gender, but it was too late. Yingtai told Shanbo that her parents were forcing her to marry Ma Wencai, a rich spoiled young man although she had hinted to her parents about her love for Liang Shanbo and her determination to marry none but him. Liang Shanbo was heartbroken. His health slowly deteriorated until he died in his office as a county magistrate.

On the day Yingtai was to be married to Ma Wencai, whirlwinds prevented the wedding procession from escorting Yingtai beyond Shanbo's tomb. Yingtai left the procession to pay her respects for Shanbo. She begged the grave to open up. Suddenly there was a clap of thunder, and the tomb opened. Without hesitation, Yingtai leapt into the grave to join her beloved Shanbo. A pair of beautiful butterflies emerged (the spirits of Zhu Yingtai and Liang Shanbo) from the tomb and flew away, which symbolized the union of the couple.

Westerners find it difficult to understand *The Butterfly Lovers*. It is hard for them to imagine the life of young ladies from rich or academic families, not to mention the implicit way they expressed themselves. Zhu Yingtai, an ancient woman restricted by the time she lived, could do nothing but imply to Shanbo about her real gender and feelings and hint to her parents about her own plan.

2. Impacts of Implicitness

Implicitness plays a mixed role in China. Co-existing with its ugliness, its greatest beauty lies not only in producing many touching poems but also in creating social harmony.

a. Social Harmony

We often hear people say something like *Whatever we do, it's OK to be just about right. What is the use of being precise and accurate? It's better to be a confused man, just as Zheng Banqiao said.* Yes, Qing poet and painter Zheng Banqiao (1693—1765), a representative of the Eight Eccentric Painters of Yangzhou, did say "难得糊涂 (literally, The rare quality is confusion)", but it has been misinterpreted by many.

What Zheng Banqiao really meant can be taken as not to be over-calculating on personal gains or losses. Instead of encouraging people to be over-calculating, he encouraged them to compromise and tolerate if necessary to lead a still and harmonious life. It can be said that implicitness, compromise, and tolerance are sources of Chinese peace and stability, which helps ancient Chinese civilization to continue.

Regarding the continuity of Chinese civilization, it is essential to mention traditional Chinese medicine established on thousands of years' accumulation of *jing yan* (literally, experience) which is hard to be explicitly explained. When consulting a practitioner of traditional Chinese medicine, people are inclined to believe that the more *jing yan* he has, the more resourceful he will be. Partly owing to *jing yan*-based medicine, Chinese civilization continues.

b. Mr. Cha Buduo

The greatest ugliness of implicitness is reducing all human activities to the level of immaturity, producing lazybones. Great scholars like Hu Shih and Lu Xun severely criticized the practice of implicitness. The essay "Mr. Cha Buduo" written by Hu Shih explicitly unmasks the ugliness of ambiguity. Excerpts of the article are as follows:

Do you know who is the most well-known person in China?

The name of this person is a household word all over the country. His surname is Cha and his given name, Buduo, which altogether mean "About the Same". He is a native of every province, every county and every village in this country. You must have seen or heard about this person. His name is always on the lips of everybody because he is representative of the whole Chinese nation.

...

When Mr. Cha Buduo was about to breathe his last, he uttered intermittently in one breath, "Live or die, it's about...about...the same....Whatever we do...it's OK...to be...just...just about right....Why ...why...take it...so seriously?" As soon as he finished this pet phrase of his, he stopped breathing.

After Mr. Cha Buduo's death, people all praised him for his way of seeing through things and his philosophical approach to life. They say that he refused to take things seriously all his life and that he was never calculating or particular about personal gains or losses. So they called him a virtuous man and honored him with the posthumous reverent title Master of Easy-going.

His name has spread far and wide and become more and more celebrated with the passing of time. Innumerable people have come to follow his example, so that everybody has become a Mr. Cha Buduo. But lo, China will hence be a nation of lazybones!

Unfortunately, the Mr. Cha Buduo Hu Shih severely criticized many years ago survives Hu and is converting more people. Despite this disappointing fact, some people arc doing their best to remove the bad influence of Mr. Cha Buduo. For instance, to overcome the ugly aspects of implicitness, Beijing volunteers launched many specific and explicit campaigns such as 规范语言环境迎奥运 (literally, Use explicit and standardized language to welcome the Olympics) and 微笑活动 (literally, the smile campaign) before the 2008 Beijing Olympic Games, setting up a good example for us to follow.

IV   Explicit Westerners

There are two newly-established disciplines in the West. One is known as Fuzziology (模糊学), and the other, Chaos Theory (混沌学) which is fuzzier or more ambiguous. Despite the fact, Western languages like English are known for their emphasis on explicitness. Western culture highly values logical and analytical thinking, which inevitably further boosts explicitness.

1. Westerners in the Eyes of Non-Westerners

To the Western marketing people in China, their Chinese counterparts are ambiguous and even unprincipled. But from the marketing perspective of many non-Westerners, Westerners seem so accurate that they appear insensitive and rigidly boorish. Some say, "The Westerner is very explicit. He wants a 'yes' or 'no'. If someone tries to speak figuratively, he is confused."

An Iranian said in his blog, "The first time my British professor told me 'I don't know, I will have to look it up,' I was shocked. I asked myself 'Why is he teaching me?'"

In my communication with Western scholars, I find I have to give further information when mentioning very Chinese stuff. When I discuss a Chinese celebrity, e.g. *Bai Juyi*, I have to add *the famous poet of the 8th century*; when I mention *Qin Shihuang*, I have to add *the first emperor of the Qin Dynasty, who united China for the first time in Chinese history in 221 BC*; when I talk about *Xinhai Revolution,* I need to add *the 1911 Revolution which overthrew the last Dynasty before establishing China's Republic*; when I explain *the Great Leap-forward*, I should add *a movement which attempted to have a high-speed development in the late 1950s*; when I come across *the ten year havoc*, I should add *a cultural revolution that caused a national turmoil from 1966 to 1976*. According to my experience, if not provided with explicit background information, they would be confused.

2. Western Preference for Explicitness

I came across an interesting English story the other day. It goes:

There was a man who planned to rob a convenience store. His plan was to give the clerk a ten-dollar bill. When the clerk opened the cash drawer to make change, the would-be thief would grab all the money. The man's plan worked perfectly. The clerk set the $10 bill on the top of the cash register and opened the drawer. The thief pushed the clerk back and grabbed all the money in the cash drawer—a grand total of $4.34. Since he had left his $10, he lost $5.66 on the transaction.

Interesting, isn't it? What interests me is not the story itself, but the accuracy of the amount mentioned over and over in the story.

Western love of accuracy and explicitness involves a scientific spirit. When we translate from Chinese to English we sometimes have to take this fact into consideration. For instance, the Chinese saying 解铃还需系铃人 (literally, Whoever ties the bell should untie the bell because he knows how to do it) is usually rendered into an explicit expression: *Whoever causes the problem should solve the problem*. In like manner, when we translate from English to Chinese, special attention should be paid to this fact as well. Take for instance the translation of the following passage from *Tess of the d' Urbervilles*:

It was a typical summer evening in June, the atmosphere being in such delicate equilibrium and so transmissive that inanimate objects seemed endowed with two or three senses, if not five. There was no distinction between the near and the far, and an auditor felt close to everything within the horizon. The soundlessness impressed her as a positive entity rather than as the mere negation of noise. It was broken by the strumming of strings.

Version 1:那是一个典型的六月黄昏。大气的平衡如此精微,传导力如此敏锐,就连冥顽的无生物也有了知觉——如果不是五种知觉的话,也有两三种。远和近已失去了差异,地平线以内的声音都仿佛近在咫尺。这一片寂静在她耳里并非是消极的默无声息,而仿佛是一种积极的实际存在。而这寂静却被拨弄琴弦的声音打破了。

Version 2:这是六月里特有的夏日黄昏。暮色格外柔和静美且极富感染力,连那些冥顽之物都仿佛平添了几分灵性,有了各种知觉。远近一切,难分彼此;天际间任何一丝声息,好像就在耳边,那是一种实实在在的感受,不想这静寂却被瑟瑟的琴声打破了。

Version 1 is a word-for-word translation. It seems faithful to the original, but sounds awkward to Chinese readers for it runs counter to our aesthetic concepts and expressing habits. The original passage is a beautifully written description, in which the wording of accuracy is very striking. For example, scientific and thus explicit expressions like *equilibrium, transmissive, inanimate objects* and *two or three senses, if not five* are used by the author to convey the beauty of explicitness. However, Chinese emphasis on the beauty of implicitness makes the word-for-word translation of Version 1 sound absurd and funny. So different ideas about what is beautiful and what is not should be considered in the translation process. That' s to say, it is necessary to freely translate the explicit English expressions into implicit Chinese ones sometimes, turning the charm of explicitness into the beauty of implicitness just as the translator of Version 2 does.

V   High Context vs. Low Context

Implicitness in everyday communication is usually resolved by their context. Therefore, the dimension of implicitness and explicitness is context-dependent: The same linguistic item (be it a word, phrase, or sentence) may be ambiguous in one context and less ambiguous in another. The preference for ambiguity or implicitness can cause high context communication, whereas the love of explicitness may lead to low context communication.

1. High and Low Context Communication

A high-context communication is one in which most of the information is either in the context or internalized, and little is in the coded, explicit, transmitted part of the message. Sources of high-context communication are neighbors, personal relationships, best friends, family members, etc. because they share context. Chinese people are disposed to be high-context communicators as compared to Westerners.

When people do not share context, they depend more on low context sources of information. A low-context communication is one in which most of the information is in the explicit codes in order to make up for what is missing in the context. People in most Western countries communicate primarily through language codes. They look for and receive information from low context sources like newspaper, textbooks, lectures, roadmaps, announcements, instruction sheets, and public signs.

2. "All Are High-context Communicators Sometimes"

High context communication is economical, fast, and efficient. It works very well when people communicating understand the meanings in the context. Everyone, the Chinese or the Westerner, communicates in this way on some occasions. The most common example is communication between roommates on the campus. They are so familiar with one another that a glance or a turn of the head carries more meanings than many words possibly could. In the intimacy of these relationships, people "discount" what the other person is saying if what is said is not consistent with the context, as can be seen in the article below entitled "Verbal Shorthand" from the widely read magazine *Smithsonian*:

I don't know why it is, but people who have been married for a long time tend to cut corners when it comes to spoken language. In fact, if it weren't for pronouns, I don't think many of us could communicate at all. A single word may convey several meanings, thoughts or requests, but somehow each partner knows exactly what the other is saying at any given time.

My wife and I are guilty of using such verbal shorthand. For example, the other evening I asked her if she would please hand me the thing. She knew immediately that I wanted the TV remote.

If she asks me to turn it down, I know she means the TV, if it's on. Otherwise, she's talking about the thermostat. See what I mean? "It" covers many bases. My wife may say, "Please put it back together when you are through." I understand she is referring to the newspaper.

"It's about time for it to come," I might proclaim. This could mean the mail, the paper, the bus, or the cab we called, depending upon the time and context. While in the laundry room, she might remark, "We've got to get a new one before long." "Yes," I reply. "It's given us many years of service." We both mean the washing machine. If she calls from the laundry room and inquires, "Is it on yet?" she means, are the commercials over and is the program starting?

She may say: "You would think he would be cold out there without a coat." If she is looking out our north window, I know she means Harry next door. If the south window, it's neighbor Bob. But when she asks, "Has he been out yet?" she means Earl, our dog.

When I exclaim, "I've had it for now!" my wife knows that I'm frustrated with whatever project I've been working on and am ready for a map. When she says, "You'd better do something for that," I know that she has heard me sneeze. When she's in another room and admonishes, "That will spoil your appetite," she's heard the rustle of my candy-bar wrapper.

If I head toward the garage, she may say, "Don't forget to fill it up." She means the car. But if I'm in the backyard and she says the same thing. I know she means the birdbath. When she says, "I think you can do better than that," I have either just finished mowing the lawn, trimming the hedge or (in winter) shoveling the sidewalk and driveway.

When my wife proffered a box of assorted chocolates the other evening and asked which I preferred, I said, "The one in the corner." I got the one I wanted. I didn't have to say, "the chocolate, nougat and caramel-covered macadamia nut cluster." She knew.

And so it goes. Somehow we manage to subsist on this sparse diet of words. Tonight, after the dinner dishes had been washed, dried and put back in the cabinets, she asked sweetly if I would carry out the garbage. I was a bit taken aback. The first noun today, and it's garbage.

(From "Verbal Shorthand," August 2001, Smithsonian)

The article above is about a high context communication between a husband and his wife. From the article, we can conclude that all are high context communicators sometimes. However, while high-context communication is fast and efficient, it takes a long time to learn. That's why high-context communication can bring people together. Naturally, we feel close to those with whom we can communicate in this way.

3. Differences Between Low-context and High-context Communicators

Low-context communicators pay less attention to messages sent non-verbally. They think communication is the exchange of verbal messages, though aware of some non-verbal behavior such as facial expressions and voice tone. So when they respond, they respond to what people say, paying little attention to the situation, the roles of participants and other factors that make up the context of the communication. For this reason, they often fail to notice things such as the status of the people they are communicating with, what the other person is not stating, and social rituals not expressed in words, expecting what other people say to be informative. On the contrary, high-context communicators pay less attention to messages sent verbally. They seldom fail to notice such things as the status of the listener or speaker, what is implied, and implicit social rituals. Therefore, people from different cultures often misinterpret each other. For instance, when a host from the high-context culture says, "We welcome you to come again," the low-context guest may interpret this as an actual invitation rather than identifying it as a polite parting.

Low-context communicators assume that the speakers and writers are responsible for the success of communication, and expect them to make meanings explicit, whereas listeners and readers are supposed to ask for clarification or further information. That is a reason why it is a custom in the West for a lecturer to spare some time to answer questions at the end of his lecture. In more informal situations a speaker will specifically encourage listeners to interrupt to ask questions. However, people from high context cultures don't say things clearly or specifically, but instead derive meanings from the context—what we might call "reading between the lines." High-context communicators expect listeners or readers to take more responsibility for interpreting the meaning of messages. They assume that speakers or writers do not always express their meaning fully or precisely in words. It is up to the listeners or readers to interpret the meaning of words by paying attention to the context in which they are produced, which can explain why there are one thousand versions of Lin Daiyu(the heroine of *The Story of the Stone*) among one thousand readers. To sum up, Chinese culture is like this: I tell you everything around the center. So you must know what I mean. From all the information I give you, you should know; you cannot miss it.

VI　"Chicken and Duck Talk"

"鸡同鸭讲(chicken and duck talk)", a neutral Cantonese expression, is often used to refer to the communicators who don't understand each other. To describe the intercultural communication relationship between native Chinese speakers and native English speakers, there is no expression more appropriate than this one.

1. In the Advertising Industry

Cultural differences have been attached great importance to by many people, especially those in the advertising industry.

Owing to its successful promotion campaign, Nesta Coffee is selling well in China, and its consumers like the way the commercial slogan "味道好极了(The taste is great)" is pronounced and presented. For Chinese, to know a celerity enjoys drinking Nesta Coffee is enough because many of us habitually take the communication between us and the celebrities on the TV screen as a fact-to-face talk, a source of high-context information exchange. As for how great it tastes, that is not our concern since different people have different taste buds. What we shall do is to buy and drink it and see what it is like.

However, Nesta Coffee's advertising campaign did not enjoy the same success in Germany. When Germans heard "It tastes great" their first response was: "How great?" They won't buy it unless they are given an explicit answer.

2. At the Workplace

When a Chinese answers "We must give it more thought" to a request at the workplace, he is turning down a request that cannot be met. He is implicit because he does not want to disrupt the relationship with the person making the request and expects the other person to interpret his answer for a polite refusal. But his Western coworker may keep asking him why he must give it more thought. In a similar situation, many Westerners would not hesitate to say, "Sorry, it can't be done." For this reason, when low-context Western communicators encounter Chinese implicitness at the workplace, they feel they are being deliberately lied to.

3. At the Dinner Table

Different ideas about what is beautiful and what is ugly have left some Chinese hungry at a Western dinner table, for Chinese politeness calls for three refusals before one accepts an offer, but the Western host takes "no" to mean "no " whether it is the first, second or third time. Likewise, some Westerners have left the Chinese table with a bursting stomach, for Western politeness requires them to praise their Chinese hostess' cooking skills and the hostess may take the praise as the sign of a big appetite and thus offers more for fear that her guest should leave her dinner table hungry or thirsty.

Differences between the two cultures are sources of misunderstandings. A low-context hostess, if complimented for her cooking skill, is likely to say, "Oh, I am so glad you like it. I cook it especially for you." But a high-context hostess will instead apologize for "Nothing to eat" out of politeness with an apologetic smile on her face. She will say, "随便做几个菜, 不好吃(literally, I just cooked some dishes casually and they are not very tasty)." Upon that, the low-context guest will probably feel confused and a little bit upset: Why do you invite me to your family and have the untasty food, then?

4. A Painful Communication Breakdown

Maybe you are good at English, but due to different cultures, you may find yourself failing to communicate well. Let us look at the following dialogue:

Mr. Jefferson: It looks like we were going to have to keep working on the project on Saturday.

Mr. Zhang: I think so.

Mr. Jefferson: Can you come in on Saturday, Mr. Zhang?

Mr. Zhang: Yes. I think so.

Mr. Jefferson: That'll be a great help.

Mr. Zhang: Yes. Saturday's a special day, you know.

Mr. Jefferson: What do you mean?

Mr. Zhang: It's my wife's birthday. We will have a birthday party.

Mr. Jefferson: How nice. I hope you all enjoy it very much.

Mr. Zhang: Thank you. I appreciate your understanding.

Mr. Jefferson: See you Saturday.

The conversation taking place between a Western boss and his Chinese employee indicates that Mr. Zhang, though good at English, experienced a painful failure in intercultural communication. From the very beginning, he wanted to tell the boss that he didn't want to work on Saturday. However, direct refusal is impolite for good-mannered Chinese like him, so he chose to refuse implicitly by saying "I think so".

Unfortunately, the boss didn't understand him and went on to ask him a question which could be answered only by "Yes" or "No". In order to save the boss' face, he had to answer, "Yes, I think so." The answer in Chinese just means "I heard what you say, but I didn't want to come." If he was willing to come, he would say "Sure" or "Of course, I will." But the boss misunderstood him once more. Even after he told the boss that Saturday was his wife's birthday, the boss didn't know what he really meant. Here Mr. Zhang violated the principle of explicitness or straightforwardness in Western culture while the boss needed some knowledge about Chinese rules of etiquette. In Western culture, "explicitness" is regarded as a polite manner in communication, whereas indirectness or implicitness is more appreciated in Chinese culture, especially when requests are made.

Further Reading

1. Davis, L. (2001). *Doing Culture*. 北京：外语教学与研究出版社.

2. Beiswinger, G. (August 2001). "Verbal Shorthand," *Smithsonian*. Washington DC.

3. Hardy, T. (2005). *Tess of the d'Urbervilles: A Pure Woman Faithfully Presented*. 北京：中国对外经济贸易出版社。

4. Blackman, C. (1997). *Negotiating China: Case Studies & Strategies*. Sydney: Allen and Unwin.

5. 牟宗三(1983)：《中国文化的省察》,台北：台湾联合报社。

6. 包惠南等(2004)：《中国文化与汉英翻译》,北京：外文出版社。

7. 郭志族、郭京龙(2005)：《谎言研究》,北京：中国社会出版社。

8. 赵晓军(2007)：《会听是金会说是银》,北京：地震出版社。

9. 冯友兰(2013)：《中国哲学简史》,北京：北京大学出版社。

Part V

Different Cultural Standards

We are familiar with concepts like gold standard and silver standard, but many of us have little idea about cultural standard(文化本位).

Cultural standard is a combination of all forms of perception, thought, evaluation and action which are regarded by the majority of the members of a particular culture as normal, typical and obligatory. According to the central cultural standards that regulate wide areas of thought, evaluation and action, personal behavior and the behavior of others are judged and regulated. The individual and group-specific manner of handling central cultural standards for behavior regulation can vary within a certain range of tolerance. Manners of conduct outside the given limits are rejected and discredited. Those who behave in a different way are seen as outsiders.

In one word, cultural standards give orientation, influence the perception of one's material and social environment as well as the evaluation of things and persons, and thus guide one's actions and behavior. The table below shows previous research findings on cultural standards in China, Germany and US:

Chinese Cultural Standards	German Cultural Standards	US Cultural Standards
Peace	Conflicts/War	Conflicts/War
Egalitarianism	Inegalitarianism	Inegalitarianism
Good human nature	Evil human nature	Evil human nature
Rule of individuals	Rule of law	Rule of law
Harmony	Focus on practical issues	Individualism
The concept of face	Importance of rules & regulations	Goal orientation
Etiquette	Directness	Directness
Relationship	Differentiation of interpersonal distance	Equality of chances
Groups	Importance of hierarchy and authority	Interpersonal openness

In this part, we are to explore into the first four dimensions.

Unit 17　Peace vs. Conflict

He that makes a good war makes a good peace.

—An English aphorism

What does a good war mean to you and your international teachers of English?

Great things can be reduced into small things, and small things can be reduced into nothing.

—A Chinese aphorism

Chinese recognize the necessity of human efforts but also admit the futility of it. This general attitude has a tendency to develop passive defense tactics. On this general principle, all Chinese disputes are patched up in the same way as the aphorism advocates. For discussion: Cite some examples to illustrate its use in your life.

I　Great Names and Different Cultural Standards

The 2008 Beijing Olympic Games won American swimmer Michael Phelps many fans from every part of the world. His fans in China cordially call him "Flying Fish" and his American fans hail him "the Baltimore Bullet". Different nicknames for Phelps revealed one of the fundamental differences between Chinese and Western Cultures: peace vs. conflict. It should be noted that "peace" in this unit is identical with *passiveness, harmony, stillness, stability, serenity*, etc. while "conflict" here is synonymous with *aggression, war, confrontation, discord, debate, fight*, and *strife*.

1. Chinese Philosophers and Peace

Chinese cultural standard of peace largely originates from the three philosophies:

Confucianism, Taoism and, later, Buddhism.

a. Confucian Doctrine of Harmony as the Most Valuable Principle

Confucianism has been the dominant ideology of Chinese society since the Han time practiced "rejecting other schools of thought, respecting Confucianism only (罢黜百家, 独尊儒术)". Many of its doctrines encourage peaceful efforts. For instance, the doctrine of rites or ritual which includes everything from funeral ceremonies to offerings of food and wine to ancestral spirits declares, "In observing the rites, seeking peace is the most valuable principle (礼之用, 和为贵)."

The Confucian idea of peace or harmony has greatly influenced many departments of Chinese society, such as city construction. Emperor Cheng (1360—1424) of the Ming Dynasty had his new capital city built around the Forbidden City which radiated symmetrically from a central axis. This symmetrical requirement is an extension of the harmony concept of Confucianism. Under the influence of Confucianism, Beijing was built with an axis line that ran north to south and through the center of the Forbidden City.

The harmony concept of Confucianism is also present in relations with ethnic minorities, one of the top concerns of the ruling class. To cement relations with ethnic minorities, Liu Bang(257BC—195 BC), the first emperor of the Han Dynasty, though at the pinnacle of Han society, sent daughters of the Liu family to their rulers as their wives, which started a tradition of marriage-for-peace policy. The story of Zhao Jun's matrimonial journey to what is now Mongolia of the Eastern Han Dynasty is a continuation of this policy. But the marriage of the Tang Princess Wen Cheng and Tibetan King Songtsän Gampo can be regarded as a perfect example of Chinese peace-loving by nature, given the fact that the Tang Dynasty China was very powerful. There were altogether 20 princesses of this kind during the 280 years of the Tang Dynasty. From historical records, except six of these "princesses", all the others were not the daughters of the emperors but the girls in the royal clans, most of them were emperors' nieces or the daughters of officials with outstanding service to the royal family. Though most of these princesses were "fake ones", their families all had close relationships with the royal family Li, and their status had no marked difference from those of the "genuine ones".

b. Lao Zi's Harmony Theory

Lao Zi encouraged harmony, discouraging argument. To him, "a good man does not prove things by argument; he who proves things by argument is not good (善者不辩,辩者不善)." For the sake of harmony, a man is required to swallow up humiliation without making any complaint. "He who bears the humiliation of the whole state can be the lord of the country (受国之垢,是谓社稷王)." To maintain peace and harmony, Lao Zi stressed the importance of taking precautions and said, "Deal with things before they happen, and get things in order before the onset of their disorder (为之于未有,治之于未乱)."

c. Buddhist Peace and Compassion

The Buddhist doctrine of peace teaches that whether we have global peace or global war is up to us at every moment. The situation is not hopeless and out of our hands. If we don't do anything, who will? Peace or war is our decision. The fundamental goal of Buddhism is peace, not only peace in this world but peace in all the worlds. According to the Buddha the first step on the path to peace is to understand the causality of peace. When we understand what causes peace, we know where to direct our efforts. No matter how vigorously we stir a boiling pot of soup on a fire, the soup will not cool. When we remove the pot from the fire, it will cool on its own, and our stirring will hasten the process. Stirring causes the soup to cool, but only if we first remove the soup from the fire. In other words, we can take many actions in our quest for peace that may be helpful. But if we do not first address the fundamental issues, all other actions will come to naught. Buddhism stresses peaceful minds that can lead to peaceful speech and peaceful actions. If the minds of living beings are at peace, the world will be at peace. Meditation in Buddhism can help people to find the inner peace. But it is up to us to master this technique since it is hard and requires a lot of patience.

Meanwhile the Buddhist doctrine of nonviolence expresses belief in the sacredness of all living creatures. Buddhist philosophers show compassion, mercy, leniency, generosity, and indulgence, calling on the multitude never to kill or injure any living creatures.

2. Western Elites and Conflict

The formation of Western cultural standard of conflict owes a lot to the elites of its society like great philosophers, economists, and politicians.

a. Philosophers and Their Doctrines of War

Heraclitus, probably the most significant philosopher of ancient Greece until Socrates and Plato, is the first one to come up with the doctrine of war. To him, "Strife is the origin of everything and war is the father of all things." So he deemed it necessary to understand that war is common, strife is customary, and all things happen because of strife and necessity. He said: "We must know that war is common to all and strife is justice, and that all things come into being through strife necessarily." Meanwhile he held that strife is absolute while harmony is relative. Heraclitus disliked Homer, declaring that Homer should be driven out of the races and whipped because Homer prayed for peace, not knowing when the strife is gone everything will die.

For Socrates who was once an army man, philosophy as critical inquiry is itself a kind of war. Given the stakes involved, nothing could be more critical than bringing philosophy as war to bear on the topic of war.

Likewise, many of the ancient Greek philosophers saw that harmony and discord depend upon one another. One way of naturalizing and thus justifying war is to claim that conflict and strife constitute the very order of things. Greek thinking has greatly influenced the entire Western world so that many public festivals throughout ancient Europe had to do with preparing boys to be warriors, girls to be mothers.

Like Heraclitus, Hegel held that two forces, love and strife, peace and war, interact together. His *Philosophy of Right* is one of the great works in political philosophy and its importance to contemporary philosophy has been ongoing. In the book he points out, "War is the state of affairs which deals in earnest with the vanity of temporal goods and concerns—a vanity at other times a common theme of edifying sermonizing." Hegel is notorious for "rationalizing" war to the point of glorifying it. He advocated war as a good thing and held that the rationality of war reveals itself in the way sovereign states relate to each other. Hegel realized that there are many ways for states to recognize one another: treaties, border agreements, and alliances. But the one paradoxical way is in the case of war: "It follows that if states disagree and their particular wills cannot be harmonized, the matter can only be settled by war." In one word, Hegel regarded war as a healthy system, necessary to ensure the domestic health of a nation.

Friedrich Wilhelm Nietzsche (1844—1900), although different from Hegel, also agreed about the central role played by conflict and war.

b. Social Darwinists and Their Doctrines of Conflict

By the last quarter of the 19th century, the English naturalist Charles R. Darwin (1809—1882) promulgated his theory of natural selection, of "survival of the fittest", which was being applied to human societies known as social Darwinism. Social Darwinism is a belief, popular in the late Victorian era in England, America, and elsewhere, which states that the strongest or fittest should survive and flourish in society while the weak and unfit should be allowed to die. The theory was chiefly expounded by Herbert Spencer, whose ethical philosophies always held an elitist view and received a boost from the application of Darwinian ideas such as adaptation and natural selection. Thus, in the evolution of mankind, those civilizations which failed to respond to the challenges of external forces would lose the struggle for survival. The process was relentless and through it the species evolved.

Social Darwinism gave support to Western colonization (outward expansion). Western imperialist nations felt they needed colonies in order to maintain their status as great powers. Meanwhile, they could justify their colonial activities by considering them altruistic attempts to provide the natives with the secrets necessary to succeed in the brutal struggle for survival. In this way, Darwinism gave Westerners a great excuse to adopt conflict as one of their cultural standards.

c. Politicians and Economists and Their Doctrines of Conflict

The Western society has been promoting conflict as the main arbiter. Its politicians such as the founding fathers of the U.S. used narrow conflict in their political system so as to avoid dictators. All the Western countries base their politics on political partisanship, allowing different parties to compete against each other for people's support in order to reduce government corruption and supervise one another.

Meanwhile, economists brought up with the concept of "the invisible hand of the market" to explain the function of the market on the demand and supply of commodities. To avoid uncertainties, people are encouraged to use contracts to establish transactional relationships. At the same time, "the visible hand of management" is expected to take action.

II External Factors and Cultural Standards

Although great names mentioned above are extremely wise, their success depends much on external factors such as their upbringing and education. It can be said with certainty that the formation of cultural standards owes a lot to the external factors. Here factors such as ecology, social practice, and traditions are to be discussed.

1. Natural Environment

a. Natural Environment of Ancient China

Natural environment of the Central Plains Region—the cradle of Chinese civilization, primarily consisting as it does of relatively fertile plains, low mountains and navigable rivers, favored agriculture and made centralized control of society relatively easy. Generally, agricultural people need to get along with one another—not necessarily to like one another—but to live together in a reasonably harmonious fashion. This is true wherever irrigation is required, as in the Yellow River Valley of northern China, particularly true for rice farming, characteristic of southern China, which requires people to cultivate the land in concert with one another.

b. Natural Environment of Ancient Greece

Natural environment of ancient Greece—the cradle of Western civilization, on the other hand, consisting as it does mostly of mountains descending to the sea, favored hunting, herding, fishing, and trade. These occupations require relatively little cooperation with others. According to Hegel, the inhabitants living along coastlines are brave and adventurous, daring to open up new sea routes and make more progress.

In fact, with the exception of trade, the economic activities ancient Greeks took part in did not strictly require living in the same stable community with other people. Settled agriculture came to Greece almost two thousand years later than to China, and it quickly became commercial. The soil and climate of Greece were congenial to wine and olive oil production and, by the sixth century BC, many farmers were more nearly businessmen than peasants. The Greeks were therefore able to act on their own to a greater extent than were the Chinese. Not feeling it necessary to maintain harmony with other fellows at any cost, the Greeks were in the habit of arguing with one another in the marketplace, debating with one another in the political assembly, and resorting to war to solve their conflicts. As legend has it, when Socrates was in his forties or so, he began to go around Athens asking people he met these questions: "What is wisdom?" "What is piety?" Sometimes people would try to answer him. Then Socrates would try to teach them to think better by asking them more questions which showed them the problems in their logic. Often this made people angry. Sometimes they even tried to beat him up.

2. Special Occasions

Cultural standards also stem from social customs while creating them.

a. Special Occasions for Greeks

In ancient times, attending to the Olympics or debate was a special occasion for Greeks. During the Olympic Games the entire Greek nation laid down its tools and many even went on a long journey for the sole purpose of participating in the Olympics as athletes or audience. Hence many Greek vases and wine goblets exhibit pictures of battles, athletic contests, and bacchanalian parties.

b. Special Occasions for Chinese

When Greeks had fun at the Olympic Games, theatres, or markets, the Chinese of the same period were visiting with friends and family. Visits meant to show respect for the old or friends were especially important during the major holidays. Hence in paintings on Chinese screen, embroidery work, porcelain, woodcarving, etc., families having fun together or visiting each other is a popular theme.

3. Tradition of Debates

Within the Chinese social group, any form of confrontation, even debate, was disfavored. Although there was a time called the period of the "contending hundred schools of thought" of 600 BC to 200 BC, during which polite debates occurred, mainly among philosophers, anything resembling public disagreement was discouraged. Even as late as today, the concept of a "heated discussion" hardly exists in China—because of the risk to the harmonious relationship. But the whole rhetoric of argument or debate is regarded as a second nature to Westerners. North Americans begin to express opinions and justify them as early as the show-and-tell sessions of kindergarten.

III   Cultural Standards and Their Unique Products

1. Old Rogues, Fatalism, Harmony, and Pacifism

Old rogues, fatalism, harmony, and pacifism are unique products of a culture with peace as one of its cultural standards.

a. Old Rogues

Old rogues (老成持重之人) are popular in China, according to Lin Yutang. Some of the young men like being referred to as "an old rogue", because that means in others' eyes they appear mellow and good-tempered and many girls' mothers prefer them for their future sons-in-law. An old rogue usually has a rich knowledge of the vicissitudes of life, thus has formed his peculiar shrewd philosophy, working against action. They can not only recite but also put to practice proverbs like *By losing that pawn, one wins the whole game* (丢卒保车), *A true hero never incurs present risk* (好汉不吃眼前亏), *Taking a step backwards in your thought* (退一步, 海阔天空), and *Of all the thirty-six alternatives, running away is the best* (三十六计, 走为上策). Life is then for them full of second-thoughts and of the "thirty-sixth alternatives". You can predict how they will respond because they tend to act in their own best interest.

This roguery, traditionally a peaceful force in China, has permeated the whole fiber of Chinese thought and can be found in our blood. It has been helping to establish a stable, still and harmonious environment.

b. Fatalism

Fatalism (宿命论) is a great source of peace and contentment in China. A talented young man may ambitiously try hard to climb up the upper social ladder despite all kinds of hardship, torture and "eating bitter". The expression "eating bitter" describes putting up with difficulties. But with time passing by, when he becomes old but remains poor, he may convince himself that it is Heaven who has decreed such a result, he can at once, through an act of understanding, become a happy husband, contented father, and proud grandpa. For himself his youthful struggle or "eating bitter" has become a "predestined fate", and he has to do as the proverb says, "You can fight against Heaven, earth and man, but you have to be obedient to your predestined fate." With that understanding, he values his remaining years, knowing all the time that Heaven is looking on.

c. Harmony

It is known to many that it was the ancient Chinese who invented dynamite. Then, how did they use it? They used it to make firecrackers which were exploded on major holidays to create a festive atmosphere instead of employing it in the process of making weapons and warships as the Westerner did. Why so? Because our ancestors went out of their way to avoid wars and conflicts since harmony is the greatest source of peace and contentment in China. The Confucian emphasis on harmony as the ideal of life is usually written on red paper and pasted on all house-doors on the Eve of Spring Festival: "家和万事兴 (freely, Harmony brings good luck)." When visitors come during the Spring Festival, a nice treat is necessary. The *Zuozhuan*, a classic Confucian text, makes the distinction in a metaphor about cooking. According to it, when a good cook blends the flavors, he usually makes sure no flavor is completely submerged, and creates something harmonious and thus delicious, which owes a lot to the blended but distinctive contributions of each flavor.

d. Pacifism

Pacifism is regarded as a virtue of Chinese people. The proverb *It's better to be a dog in a peaceful time than be a man in a chaotic period* (宁为太平犬,不做乱世人)

reveals our love of peace. On many occasions when a man is wronged, offended, bullied, humiliated or enraged, if he can hold his tongue or keep his temper, he is expected to rise higher or do something great in the future, as the saying warns, "A man who cannot tolerate small ills can never accomplish great things (小不忍，则乱大谋)."

In fact, pacifism can also become a vice of cowardice. When a nation is at peace with itself, it is for a calm and passive strength rather than for progress. When a man is at peace with himself, he cannot understand the youthful enthusiasm for progress and reform. As a people, we hate war, believing good people never fight, for "good iron is not made into nails, and good men are not made soldiers (好铁不做钉，好男不当兵)".

The responsibility for our family we are born with makes us sober and ready to compromise. Before adventures, most of us have a wife and little babies to think about, and aged parents to remember. When wronged or humiliated, we comfort ourselves, "A real man can bend and stretch (大丈夫能屈能伸)." In such a society, pacifism has no reason not to exist; people seem ready to tolerate unfairness and bitterness as long as their standard of living improves.

2. Heroic Code, Chivalry, Competition and Cold War Mentality

A culture with war or conflicts as one of its cultural standards has its peculiar products such as heroic code, chivalry, competition, and Cold War mentality.

a. Heroic Code

Heroic code has something to do with the Homeric heroes who have been respected and honored since the Homeric epic. The heroic code which governs the conduct of the Homeric heroes is a simple one: The aim of every hero is to achieve honor, that is, the esteem received from one's peers. Honor is essential to the Homeric heroes so much so that life would be meaningless without it. As you will notice in reading the *Iliad*, when a hero is advised to be careful to avoid a life-threatening situation in battle, his only choice is to ignore this warning. A hero's honor is determined primarily by his courage and physical abilities and to a lesser degree by his eloquence. The highest honor can only be won in battle. The competition is fiercest and the stakes are the greatest. Two other heroic activities, hunting and athletics, could only win the hero an inferior honor. An even lesser honor is won by the sole non-physical heroic activity—debating.

b. Chivalry

Chivalry is the generic term for the knightly system of the Medieval Times (the 5th to the 15th century) and for virtues and qualities it inspired in its followers. It first appeared with military activities against non-Christian states. During the Medieval Period, Western Europe aggressively sought to expand its area of control. The first orders of chivalry were very similar to the monastic orders of the era. Both sought the sanctification of their members through combat against "infidels" and protection of religious pilgrims, and both had commitments that involved the taking of vows and submitting to a regulation of activities.

The thirteenth century conventions of chivalry directed that knights honor, serve, and do nothing to displease ladies and maidens as members of the noble class, socially as bearers of arms, economically as owners of horse armor, and officially through religious-oriented ceremony. While some were knighted on the battlefield, most spent years as a squire, practicing the art of war while serving his master.

After the Crusades, knights continued to show their prowess and skills in medieval tournaments.

Today chivalry is reflected in rules of etiquette and specific things like opening and holding doors for women or running errands for women.

c. Competition

Westerners believe that competition occurs naturally whenever two or more parties strive for one goal which cannot be shared. For example, Humans, like animals, compete over water supplies, food, and mates. When these needs are met deep rivalries often arise over the pursuit of wealth, prestige, and fame. In the West, election campaign is often associated with competition as most candidates are in competition with at least one over the same group of voters.

Many people in the West hold that competition originates internally and is biologically motivated. It exists to further the survival of an individual or species.

Social Darwinists state that competition is moral and necessary for the survival of the species. Moreover, competition is believed to be able to give incentives for self-improvement. For example, if two shoemakers are competing for business, they will hopefully lower their prices and improve their products to increase sales.

Over the years, competition has greatly released Westerners' potentiality and energy, and helped to develop Western economic and political civilization. Meanwhile, it is also because of competition that the two world wars erupted in the first half of the 20th century.

d. Cold War Mentality

The cultural standard of conflict or war explains why there exists the Cold War mentality, even in the 21st century when the real Cold War has already ended.

The Cold War that arose from the intense competition influenced nearly all aspects of Western political and cultural life from 1946—when the former British Prime Minister Winston Churchill announced the descent of an Iron Curtain separating the Soviet Union and her Eastern European satellite states from the non-communist West—to the disintegration of the Soviet Union in 1991. Throughout this period, rivalry between the two superpowers was expressed through military coalitions, propaganda, espionage, weapon development, industrial advances, and competitive technological development, e.g. *the space race*. Both superpowers were engaged in costly defensive spending, a massive conventional and nuclear arms race, and numerous proxy wars so that the Cold War influence on the Western political life was deep and long-lasting.

Today some politicians in some Western countries are still using the Cold War thinking. The US Defense Department in 2015 issued an annual report on China's military power, continuing to peddle the so-called "China threat". It said that China was developing weapons that could disable its enemies' space technology, such as satellites. It added that "numerous" intrusions into computer networks around the world, including some owned by the US government, in the past year seemed to have originated in China. The China threat theory is not in accordance with the facts and seriously interferes in China's internal affairs.

Under the influence of the Cold War mentality some scholars in some Western countries are selling their theory of conflicts, refusing to shed the Cold War mentality. The influential political scientist and former Harvard professor Samuel Phillips Huntington (1927—2008) is best known for his views on the so-called clash of civilizations. Huntington argued that conflicts in our post-Cold War world would be rooted in cultural and religious differences among major civilizations, rather than ideological rifts between nations.

The Cold War mentality is a reflection of Western concern that some civilization is to replace it. This over-alertness explains a reason why there is among some Westerners a phenomenon of "seeking the enemy". It seems that they have to find an opponent. Otherwise, they are not sure of their trend and direction.

IV   Better Ways to Know Each Other

The Military Power of the People's Republic of China 2015 released by the US Department of Defense says: "China has a long-term ambition to extend its military clout to whole continental Asia. In the future, China's leaders may be tempted to resort to force or coercion more quickly to press diplomatic advantage, advance security interests, or resolve disputes." Is that really so? Let's try answering this question through the Golden Rule (金科玉律) in both Chinese and Western cultures.

1. Golden Rule

The Golden Rule, often stated by Westerners as "Do unto others as you would have others do unto you, (己所欲,施于人)" has long been used and referenced in the business literature. But it is not equivalent to the Chinese Golden Rule "己所不欲,勿施于人" which means "Refrain from doing to others what you don't want to be done by others" or "Do not impose on others what you do not wish for yourself." This rule was one of the guiding principles of life that Confucius taught his followers more than two thousand years ago before Jesus taught the Golden Rule with similar words "Whatsoever ye would that men should do to you, do ye even so to them."(Matt. 7: 12) "As you wish that others would do to you, do so to them" (Luke 6:17-46)which has been used as "Do unto others as you would have them do unto you." The two forms of Golden Rule cannot be interchanged since they betray the fundamental difference between Chinese and Western Cultures we are exploring into in this unit—peace vs. conflict.

The rule "Do unto others as you would have them do unto you", in fact, reflects the aggression and expansion which characterize the Western civilization. How do you know what you wish for is what is wanted and that you wish for to give what you want to others? It is equal to imposing your will on the others. For example, the Crusades to restore Christian control of the Holy Land were fought over a period of nearly 200 years between 1095 and 1291. Other campaigns in Spain and Eastern Europe continued into the 15th century. The Crusades were fought mainly against Muslims, although campaigns were also waged against pagan Slavs, pagan Balts, Jews, Russian and Greek Orthodox Christians, Mongols, Cathars, Hussites, Waldensians, Old Prussians, and political enemies of the popes. To spread what they wanted, the so-called "civilization" to the uncivilized lands, some European powers dominated American and Australian continents. Today, to safeguard the world peace, some Western countries export their values to other areas, interfering in their internal affairs. It can be said that "Do unto others as you would have them do unto you" has something to do with what is Western culture today.

"Refrain from doing to others what you don't want to be done by others" is quite the opposite. Its negative side is passiveness and its positive one is treating peace and harmony as the most valuable.

The combination of the two forms may be perfect: "Do to others as you would have them do to you; and refrain from doing to others what you don't want to be done by others." If we merge them and practice them together, we can better understand each other, and there will be less misunderstandings and conflicts.

2. Peace with Differences Reserved

The cultural standard of harmony has been pushing Chinese to go on with the policy of peace. When asked how to treat people who are not so kind, many Chinese scholars will cite this dialogue between two Tang Buddhist monks:

A monk asked, "If one slanders me, insults me, sneers at me, despises me, injures me, hates me, and deceives me, what should I do?"

"Only bear with him, yield to him, let him, avoid him, endure him, respect him, and ignore him. And after a few years, you just look at him," replied the abbot.

The peace made through this kind of pacifism has been regarded as the highest product of Chinese intelligence. But as a Chinese proverb goes, "The tree may prefer to be calm, but the wind refuses to subdue (树欲静而风不止)." Despite China's persistent stand for dialogue and cooperation, some countries have time and again provoked confrontation and antagonism in the South China Sea between China and its neighbors, taking China as the main target for their attack. In spite of that, we believe that the policy of "peace with differences reserved" will be carried forward by the Chinese government and its influence as a force for peace and harmony in the world will grow.

Further Reading

1. Hegel G.W.F. (1991). *Philosophy of Right*. Cambridge, UK: Cambridge University Press.
2. Tannen, D. (1998). *The Argument Culture: Moving from Dialogue to Debate*. New York: Harper, Collins.
3. 冯友兰(2013):《中国哲学简史》,北京:北京大学出版社。
4. 林语堂(1998):《生活的艺术》,北京:外语教学与研究出版社。
5. 饶尚宽译注 (2006):《老子》,北京:中华书局。
6. 杨伯峻译注 (2006):《论语》,北京:中华书局。
7. 冯波 (2002):《中西哲学文化比较研究》,北京:中国传媒大学出版社。
8. 程志敏 (2008):《荷马史诗导读》,上海:华东师范大学出版社。

Unit 18   Egalitarian and Inegalitarian Distribution

The law cannot make all men equal, but they are all equal before the law.

—Frederick Pollock

How shall we understand the remark made by the noted British jurist?

From shirtsleeves to shirtsleeves is only three generations.

—Andrew Carnegie

This saying has been attributed to Andrew Carnegie (1835—1919), a manufacturer and philanthropist. Shirtsleeves denote the need to work hard for one's living. Does the Chinese proverb "It takes three generations to make a gentleman" express the same idea?

I   Hate-the-rich Mentality

"Hating the rich" is an abnormal psyche, which encourages the thinking that if you have more, then I must have less. Misconducts of some affluent people as well as the illicit channels they are using to accumulate their wealth will undoubtedly add a further irritant to the discontent of the less fortunate. Such terms as *corrupt rich, stinking rich* and other much harsher things are often used by ordinary Chinese to describe those "wealthy but bad guys" in their eyes. Actually, the mainstream public is not hostile towards wealthy people. If one can get rich quickly through hard work, the general public response will be admiration, not hatred. But in real life some people get rich overnight in illegal ways. In such cases, the public will naturally question their behavior and despise them. Therefore, the hate-the-rich mentality is not targeted at all wealthy people, but only at those who have acquired their wealth through illegal means such as tax evasion, taking bribery, and injuring the consumers' right.

However, an undeniable fact is that a handful of people do have a blind prejudice against the rich. They openly declare, "The rich are not humane (为富不仁)." The root cause of this prejudice may be that the age-old system of egalitarian distribution has been broken and their psychological balance is thus destroyed. Some of them even go so far as to want the system of egalitarian distribution to return. Will egalitarianism come back, then? To answer this question, it's better to know what egalitarianism really means in the first place.

Egalitarianism is a trend of thought in political and social philosophy. An egalitarian favors equality of some sort: People should get the same, be treated the same, or be treated as equals, in some respect. Egalitarian doctrines tend to express the idea that all human persons are equal in fundamental worth or moral status. Because in both China and the Western societies the term "egalitarian" is often used to mean equality in the distribution of income, wealth, and resources, "egalitarianism" used in this unit is referred to only as a concept in economical thought.

II   Chinese-style Egalitarianism

The egalitarian concept is characterized by a passion for equality at least in distribution and a strong sense of solidarity with other people. It figured prominently in traditional Chinese culture.

1. Philosophers and the Pursuit of Plenty

Egalitarian distribution was regarded as an economic issue by pre-Qin period Legalists, Confucianists, and Taoists, who agreed that people in all communities should have the same standard of living and be equal in the distribution of resources, although, in practice, many of the philosophers were more in favor of the concept "pursuing plenty(求足)" and worked hard to systematically elaborate on its necessity and significance.

a. Guan Zhong

In the book named after Guan Zhong (723 BC—645 BC), the Legalist minister of the powerful state of Qi during the Spring and Autumn period (770 BC—476 BC), illustrated the importance of "pursuing plenty" this way:

"One cannot tell the difference between what is honorable and what is shameful until he has plenty of food to eat and plenty of clothes to keep warm; one cannot know ritual until he has plenty of food and clothes for future use(衣食足而后知荣辱,仓廪实而后知礼仪)." Obviously great priority was given to plenty.

b. Confucianists

The *Analects* makes it clear that it is necessary to enrich people before educating them: "If the ordinary people have plenty of food and clothes, the king will surely find himself in possession of plenty of belongings (百姓足,君孰与不足)."

In ***Xunzi***, the last great Confucian scholar of the pre-Qin period Xun Kuang (325 BC—235 BC) promulgated his theory of "pursuing plenty" by informing the rulers, "People's desire should be satisfied and their demands should be met (养人之欲,给人以求)." Clearly, plenty rather than egalitarianism was his main concern.

c. Why Not Accept "Pursuing Plenty" as the Orthodox?

The pursuit of plenty has always been in existence in China. But why was the theory of "pursuing plenty" out and egalitarian distribution in?

First, the schools of the pre-Qin period philosophy differed in value systems, but unanimously wanted people to be happy with what they had and live harmoniously with one another, however poor and simple their life might be. This expectation was in conflict with the concept of "pursuing plenty", but in agreement with the idea of pursuing egalitarian distribution.

Second, in an agrarian economy where sources of income were few, the concept of "The more sons, the more blessings" and the need for more human resources boosted population growth. In a populous country, it was impossible to attain plenty. On the contrary, the goal of egalitarian distribution could be more easily achieved.

Third, Buddhist and Taoist literature propounded an egalitarian view, which, to some extent, encouraged people to favor the egalitarian ideal and disfavor the theory of pursuing plenty, although the two religions did not uphold the equal status of women. For instance, Buddhist doctrine of five obstacles(五障) maintained that women were incapable of becoming a Buddha.

2. Egalitarian Practice in China

a. Misinterpretation of One of Confucius' Doctrines

In a populous poor agrarian economy, it was impossible to pursue plenty, and hence pursuing egalitarian distribution (求均) as an economic ideal became the only alternative available to people. For a long time, the doctrine "Don't worry about being scanty, but do worry about being unequal (不患寡而患不均)" has been misinterpreted because it provided no context. Confucius didn't mean he advocated egalitarian distribution. Instead, he was talking about an ideal. For him production was more important than distribution and the pursuit of plenty more significant than pursuing egalitarian distribution. Because of the misinterpretation, equalitarian distribution was passionately pursued. As a consequence, if not equally rich, being equally poor merely made people poorer and poorer.

b. Wang Mang's Practice of the Egalitarian Ideal

Egalitarian distribution had been so beautiful a dream that Wang Mang (45 BC — 23 BC) tried hard to make it come true.

In 22 BC Wang Mang managed to usurp power, declaring himself the emperor of the Han. With great passion he began a series of radical reforms. The most radical one was his effort to set up an equal land-holding system. This project included the nationalization of all land, abolition of private land-holding system, prohibition of trade of land, etc. But people in power were not ready for such a reform that suggested egalitarianism. Soon Wang Mang's brief reign became unpopular with all social classes of the nation and in the end he even lost the backing of the Confucian bureaucracy which had earlier supported him because of his impractical attempts. Without the support of the people, his measures, however lofty and effective theoretically, were doomed to failure, but his egalitarian land reform inspired the later reformers.

c. Egalitarian Practice before China's Opening-up and Reform

Egalitarianism greatly impeded Chinese economic development before 1979. Take the practice of "Iron Rice Bowl" for instance. The "Iron Rice Bowl" was the name of the Chinese social security system that guaranteed food, housing and social benefits for everybody. The benefits were especially good for people who worked for the state. The cradle-to-grave social security system of the state offered everyone free education and low-rent housing, guaranteed lifetime jobs, pensions, and workers' holiday camps, subsidized theaters and concerts, and free medical and dental care, organized tours and trips, provided workers with kindergartens, sports stadiums, holiday centers, summer camps for children, cultural centers, sports facilities, and rest and rehabilitation spas. Women were given a year's paid maternity leave, access to free day-care centers and free abortion on demand. Once you held the iron-rice bowl, you would feel safe because the iron bowl was not easy to break, regardless of how much you did or what poor performance and bad work habits you had. This egalitarian policy in the distribution of incomes created a nation of sluggish, unenterprising and lazy people dressed in grey, blue, and green. It was unnecessary to close the door at night and there was a great social stability, but the cost was so high that Chinese economy almost stopped its development and the country became more isolated while the other countries were developing at a fantastic speed.

III　Western-style Inegalitarianism

In the Western societies, "inegalitarianism" is an economic concept often used to refer to a position that favors, for any of a wide array of reasons, a greater degree of inequality in income and wealth across persons.

1. Aristotle's Inegalitarian Distribution Theory

It is agreed that inegalitarianism originates from Aristotle, who established the idea by analyzing justice.

a. Aristotle's Concept of Justice

For Aristotle, justice is a virtue obtained from the law and its administrators. In the legal sense, whatever laws lay down is assumed to be just. Law covers the whole field of virtuous action so that in this general sense justice is an inclusive term equivalent to righteousness.

b. Aristotle's Thoughts on Distributive Justice and Corrective Justice

For Aristotle, one can be wicked without being greedy and greedy without being otherwise wicked. He divided justice into two types. One type of justice, distributive justice(分配正义), is concerned with the distribution of money or honor or other resources that are divided among all who have a share in some public organization. In cases of distributive justice, things must be distributed equally. Equal distribution must be determined carefully. Things should be distributed so that individuals get their share based on merit. Thus, if things are to be divided based on some property, each individual should receive a portion proportional to their possession of that property. The other type of justice is corrective justice(修正正义). This justice governs personal transactions between individuals, whether mutually agreeable (voluntary) or forced upon a particular party(involuntary).

In the Western cultural tradition, egalitarianism is not so popular a concept partly because of Aristotle's emphasis on distributive justice.

2. Three Great Principles of Western Civil Law

In 1804, the three great civil law principles were established in French Civil Code (1804): unlimited ownership of private possessions, free contract, and neglect of duty (私有财产神圣不可侵犯、契约自由、过错责任原则). The three principles lay solid and stable foundation for French civil law, so the Code can survive after about two centuries and is being used in France until now. According to the three principles, no man should benefit from his injustice, pacts must be respected, and private possessions should not be violated. To improve efficiency and realize fairness, most Western countries follow the three great principles in the distribution of resources and wealth— a manifestation of the inegalitarian qualities of Western culture.

IV   Egalitarianism and Inegalitarianism in China and the West

1. "Birth Can't Make a Great Person"

As the saying goes that birth can't make a great person while his endeavor do (将相本无种,男儿当自强), we believe that no man is born successful or great, so any man can become a great asset to his country as long as he studies and works hard. The imperial examination system (科举制度) exemplified this belief by effecting a qualitative selection and enabling talent to reproduce and propagate itself. With the imperial examination system in the Sui Dynasty put into effect the door had been opened down to 1905 for all men to rise from poverty to power, fame, and hence wealth as long as they studied hard.

As far as the Western European and Anglo-American philosophical tradition is concerned, there is one significant source of egalitarianism—the Christian notion that God loves all human souls equally and gives love to all humans equally. In spite of this, the Bible says, "Jesus looked up and saw some rich people tossing their gifts into the offering box. He also saw a poor widow putting in two pennies. And he said, 'I tell you that this poor woman has put in more than all the others. Everyone else gave what they didn't need. But she is very poor and gave everything she had.'" It seems to me that Jesus, although equally loving every Christian, is not against the inegalitarian distribution in wealth.

2. An Ancient Curse for the Rich Family

It is believed by many Chinese, poor or rich, that a family cannot prosper for more than three generations (富不过三代). To the poor it is a positive sign, for their children are most likely to become rich in the future through efforts although they themselves are still in poverty; to the rich it is a kind reminder that they should provide their children with good moral education so that they will do well and will not end up in bankruptcy. Unfortunately, it is rumored that however hard rich people tried, the proverb used to turn out to be true. Therefore, many rich people did not regard the proverb as a reminder, but a curse. Actually it was hard for rich people not to become poor. In ancient China, the throne was available to the first-born son of the queen, which was exceptional. As for ordinary families, wealth was evenly distributed among sons when they grew up, which would decrease the family wealth which would be further evenly distributed among the following generations. If the wealth were not evenly distributed, there would be troubles. In this way, two generations later, the family members might become poorer and poorer if they sat, ate and did nothing. However, in some Western countries the rich would be probably richer, because the family wealth inheritance right was available only to the eldest son and the younger sons had to start from the beginning when they grew up.

Apart from the egalitarian practice mentioned above that made Chinese rich families become poor, for famous Qing general Zeng Guofan(1811—1872) , "the official families whose children learn expensive habits of living, prosper only for a generation or two, the merchant families who are industrious and frugal may prosper for three or four generations, the families who till the ground and study books and have simple and careful habits prosper for five or six generations, while the families who have the virtues of filial piety and friendliness prosper for eight or ten generations." Judging from recent reports about the so-called "rich second generation" who have learned expensive living habits it seems that Zeng was right. Most of today's "rich second generation" belong to the generation born after the 1980s, and 52 percent of them have study abroad experience. Their dreams of becoming rich and successful were realized long ago, while others of the same age are still fighting for a comfortable life. Many of the rich kids have committed crimes, like causing traffic trouble to pursue feelings of excitement. For them, committing a crime is probably just a game. Negative news about the rich kids could always be seen in all the mass media, and the impressions they leave to the public are usually "flaunting wealth", "overbearing" and "extravagant". As the "first rich generation" become old, the question arises, "how should the 'rich second generation' keep prospering? And what could keep the 'poor second generation' from becoming rich?"

3. "Fame Portends Trouble for Men Just as Fattening Does for Pigs"

It is hard for one to give enough in a work unit or ***dan wei*** where egalitarianism seems to prevail. Every year the teaching faculty is called upon to donate money to people in the disaster-stricken areas. Every time I will check up the average amount of donation to make sure that I will not unknowingly become the biggest or the smallest donor before I reach into my pocket. Somehow I just want to follow the crowd.

When explaining why they are slow in giving and try all means to evade tax, in support of their opinion some new moneyed Chinese quote the old egalitarian sayings like *Wind damages the flourishing tree in the forest* (木秀于林,风必摧之), *Fame portends trouble for men just as fattening does for pig* (人怕出名,猪怕壮), and *Birds that come forward will be shot first* (枪打出头鸟).

Speaking of office politics, an American colleague of mine said, "In my firm they shoot you down before you even stand up." But many Westerners are not afraid to let others know they are wealthy. Some of them like showing off their wealth, a manifestation of their own personal success, and they are ready to pay taxes. The tax rate is much higher than in China, but overall people appear more willing to pay tax, because their country provides a lot of benefits in return for the tax they pay. Also those who earn more are generally willing to pay progressive tax to help those less fortunate in the society. They know this will stabilize the society. I still remember my shock when I read about Berkshire Hathaway's annual meeting a few years ago. During the Q &A period, Warren Buffett answered one question by saying that the company was more than willing to pay tax and they paid more than US$ 1 billion in tax that year. At that, the whole audience stood up and applauded. Different from their Western counterparts, many rich Chinese people don't want to give a large sum of money away, afraid that might reveal that they are rich and have the tax department go after them or draw attention from others.

4. Efforts to Break with Egalitarianism in China

Before China's reform and opening-up, workers received nearly the same amount of wages regardless of their contributions. In spite of a frugal living they led, people seemed happy. But a society without producing wealthy people is never progressing on the healthy track. Indeed, even the Bible says, "Money is the root of all evils." In this light, a highly commercialized society is not a noble one, either. It is noteworthy here that wealth in itself has nothing to do with guilt or innocence, and what matters is how to manage it. In 1979 the egalitarian practice of "eating from the same big pot" was officially stopped and there arose a gap between the poor and the rich and uneven distribution. About this, Deng Xiaoping (1904—1997) stated that the problem of the poor-rich gap and unfair distribution "shall be particularly brought up and resolved at the end of this century when China will have reached a moderately prosperous level." He aimed at an egalitarian welfare in the end, i.e. establishing a system requiring the "strata and regions which got rich first" to feed the "late wealth-winning" strata and regions. For this end, Deng Xiaoping urged Chinese people during his 1992 tour of South China to be "more emancipated in our thoughts, more courageous in reform and opening-up to the outside world, and quicker in our development steps and on no account to allow our opportunities to slip through our fingers."

In order to improve efficiency and increase aggregate wealth as quickly as possible, the three groups of Chinese leaders after Deng Xiaoping further efforts to "smash egalitarianism, widen the income gap to a reasonable degree and to persist in encouraging some areas and some people to get rich sooner than others by honest labor and by lawful means." This line captures perfectly the spirit of "giving priority to efficiency while taking justice into account", which was put forward at the Third Plenary Session of the 14th Party Central Committee in the light of the nation's actual conditions and development needs.

Now, egalitarianism seems have been smashed. However, remnants of egalitarianism from the era of the central planning system remains a major factor in restricting the increase of efficiency and productivity growth.

Further Reading

1. Aristotle, trans. by J.A.K. Thomson (1976). *Ethics*. London: Penguin Books.

2. (1997).《圣经/Holy Bible》. Nanjing: 中国基督教三自爱国运动委员会 &中国基督教协会.

3. Davies, N. (1997). *Europe: A History*. New York: Harper Perennial.

4. Bond, M. H, ed. (1986). *Handbook of Chinese Psychology*. Hong Kong: Oxford University Press.

5. (1992):《邓小平南巡讲话》。

6. 冯友兰(2013):《中国哲学简史》,北京:北京大学出版社。

7. 牟宗三(1983):《中国文化的省察》,台北:台湾联合报社。

8. 赵焕祯校注(2007):《曾国藩家书》,武汉:湖北辞书出版社。

Unit 19   Good vs. Evil Human Nature

If tyranny and oppression come to this land, it will be in the guise of fighting a foreign enemy.

—James Madison

James Madison made this remark while he was a United States Congressman. How do you understand his remark?

There is no difference, they are altogether sinners; there is none that doeth good (according to the spirit of the law), no, not one.

—the Bible

What do you think of the remark made by the apostle mentioned in the Bible? Might what the apostle says be true of men universally?

Men are born to be good. It is education and practice that set them apart (人之初,性本善。性相近,习相远).

—Wang Yinglin

*The Three-Character Classic (or **San Zi Jing**) was attributed to Wang Yinglin (王应麟). It is not one of the traditional five Confucian classics. It is rather the distillation of the essential Confucian thought, expressed in a way that is suitable for teaching young children. It is written in couplets of three syllables for easy memorization. Do you agree with the beginning lines of the book on human nature? Why or why not?*

I Key Concepts

1. Human Nature

What is human nature? A passage from the National College English Test Band IV of January 2004 puts it this way, "For most thinkers since the Greek philosophers, it was self-evident that there is something called human nature, something that constitutes the essence of man. There were various views about what constitutes it, but there was agreement that such an essence exists—that is to say, that there is something by virtue of which man is man. Thus man was defined as a rational being, as a social animal, an animal that can make tools, or a symbol-making animal." In other words, human nature is the concept that there is a set of inherent distinguishing characteristics, including ways of thinking, feeling and acting that humans tend to have.

The concept "human nature" has often been used as a shield behind which the most inhuman acts are committed. In the name of human nature, for instance, Aristotle and many European thinkers up to the eighteenth century defended slavery. In order to prove the rationality and necessity of capitalism, scholars have tried to make a case for acquisitiveness, competitiveness, and selfishness as innate human qualities. Often, one refers cynically to "human nature" in accepting the inevitability of such undesirable human behavior as greed, cheating, lying, and even murder.

2. Good and Evil

In religion and ethics, the phrase "good and evil" refers to the location of objects, desires, and behaviors on a two-way spectrum, with one direction being morally positive or good, and the other morally negative or evil. "Good" is a broad concept and is difficult to define, but typically it deals with an association with life, continuity, happiness, desirability, or human flourishing. "Evil" is often defined as the opposite of good. Depending on the context, good and evil may represent personal judgments, societal norms, or claims of absolute value related to human nature or to transcendent religious standards.

There is no consensus over whether either good or evil is intrinsic to human nature.

1. Different Ideas About Human Nature

In China where Confucianism is widely accepted, people are believed to be basically good in nature, hence young children are believed to be pure and innocent but may become mean and bad as they grow older and have more contact with society where there might be bad influences. Because of this possibility, it is the obligation of those in authority, such as parents, caregivers, educators, public figures, and civil servants to protect the morality of those under their care and to be role models of virtue themselves, and hence we are apt to idealize our parents, professors and honored historic figures and regard them as models.

In the West where the belief that "we have all sinned and fall short of the glory of God" is a widely accepted truth, many people believe man is basically evil in nature, and even the greatest figures are believed to have flaws but may become good as they grow older and receive moral education. Former American President Bill Clinton's sex scandal conforms to the Western expectation that noble men can be ruined by something bad inherent in nature. On the other hand, some Westerners assume that good and bad exist side by side. For them the categories of good and bad appear everywhere in the society. The point is the good should be praised and the bad eliminated to the minimum possible. However, Western people agree unanimously that it is necessary to confess the bad you do. You should admit to your mistakes and shortcomings. This is the first step to become good. Even Clinton was forgiven for his lying desperately about his extra-marital affairs with a White House intern after he publicly admitted to having had an "improper relationship" and promised not to do it again.

2. Common Expectations for Education

Although the direction of moral changes is likely to be from good to bad in China, and from bad to good in the West, China and the West share common expectations for education.

a. School Education

Chinese and Westerners agree that education should be a good moral influence on children. Confucius said he educated without any care about the students' social classes, thus bringing moral education to all young men, poor or rich. The ancient Greek philosopher Aristotle also emphasized education and stated, "The roots of education are bitter, but the fruit is sweet." In fact Chinese expect schools and universities to be places of virtue. That can explain why a news report about an immoral educator or a scandal relevant to a university professor can become very sensational in China. However, Westerners do not expect particular institutions to be more virtuous than other institutions, believing that good and bad are found everywhere, within each person, and therefore within each organization. In their thought, it is as possible to be a virtuous businessman as it is to be a virtuous professor if proper education is provided to improve human nature, increase the good and reduce the bad.

b. Older People as Educators

Both Chinese culture and Western culture stress the role of older people in education. The Chinese saying 有其父必有其子 (literally, what kind of a father has what kind of a son) means the same as the English proverb *Like father, like son*. The idiom 身教言传 (literally, what the parent says and does is a silent influence) is synonymous with *Children are what the mothers are*, and the idiom 严师出高徒 (literally, what kind of a teacher has what kind of a student) is identical with *Like teacher, like pupil*. The equivalence of these proverbs or idioms shows that both cultures emphasize the role of older people in educating the younger generation.

c. Friends as Educators

It is widely believed in China that one will unconsciously become good if he hangs out with good people. As Confucius put it, "To live with good people is like staying in a room of orchids where, after a long time, one would naturally be sweet-scented; to associate with bad people is like living in a dried-fish shop, where one would unavoidably become imbued with the odor(与善人居,如入芝兰之室,久而不闻其香,即与之化矣; 与不善人居,如入鲍鱼之肆)." Therefore, it is important to choose friends for Chinese.

In like manner, Westerners are careful in choosing their friends, which finds expressions in English proverbs like *A man is known by his friends, Birds of a feather flock together* and *If you live with a lame person you will learn to limp*.

III   Theorization of Assumptions About Human Nature

I. Chinese Philosophers in the Theorization of the Assumption Concerning Human Nature

Ancient Chinese philosophers emphasized the innately good by nature and managed to theorize this assumption.

a. Confucius

Confucius held that men are pretty much alike by nature, but it is learning and practice that set them apart(性相近也，习相远也). His theory of human nature abolished the status distinctions of a feudal society, and replaced them with a new classification by educational level because education was assumed to raise man to a higher moral status. Meanwhile by prescribing rules of behavior for the educated people—the gentleman or *Junzi*, Confucius declared that man, good by nature, needed education to bring out his moral qualities, and the *Junzi*, both by example and teaching, would lead society and state to moral harmony, because he firmly believed, "The gentleman understands what is right; the inferior man understands what is profitable (君子喻于义，小人喻于利)." For Confucius, "the gentleman makes demands on himself; the inferior man makes demands on others (君子求诸己，小人求诸人)." And he declared, "The resolute scholar and humane person will under no circumstances seek life at the expense of their humanity; on occasion they will sacrifice their lives to preserve their humanity (志士仁人，无以求生以害仁，惟以杀生以求仁)."

b. Mencius

Confucius' view was later developed by Mencius who theorized issues untouched by Confucius. As the first philosopher to systematically elaborate on the good human nature assumption, Mencius advocated that man, as a rational being, is endowed with four dispositions **Ren**, **Yi**, **Li** and **Zhi** (humanity, righteousness, propriety and wisdom), a reflection of being good by nature. He went on to illustrate his theory that man is endowed with the good human nature from birth by using the example of a child falling into a well and the rescuer's psychological reaction: "When I say that all men have a mind which cannot bear to see the suffering of others, my meaning may be illustrated thus: Even nowadays, if men suddenly see a child about to fall into a well, they will without exception experience a feeling of alarm and distress. They will feel so: not as a ground on which they may gain the favor of the child's parents, nor as a ground on which they may seek the praise of their neighbors and friends, nor from a dislike of the reputation of having been unmoved by such a thing (所以谓人皆有不忍之心者,今人乍见孺子将入于井,皆有怵惕恻隐之心,非所以内交于孺子之父母也,非所以要誉于乡党朋友也,非恶其声而然也)." Mencius observed that the rescuer's reaction was spontaneous and had no other motive. He went on to say that good human nature is innate and should be developed:

"From this case we may perceive that the feeling of commiseration is inherent in man, that the feeling of shame and dislike is inherent in man, that the feeling of modesty and complaisance is inherent in man, and that the feeling of approving and disapproving is inherent in man (由是观之,无恻隐之心,非人也;无羞恶之心,非人也;无辞让之心,非人也;无是非之心,非人也)."

For Mencius the four dispositions are undoubtedly innate. In his words, "We are born to be endowed with **Ren**, **Yi**, **Li**, and **Zhi**, which are not imposed on us from the outside (仁义礼智非由外铄我也,我固有之也)." While Mencius placed emphasis on the four innate dispositions of man, he also knew fully well one's character depended much on his upbringing and education, that is, on external factors. He said, "In good years most children are good, while in bad years most of them abandon themselves to evil. It is not owing to their natural powers conferred by Heaven that they are thus different. The abandonment is owing to the circumstances by which they allow their mind to be snared and drowned in evil (富岁,子弟多赖;凶岁,子弟多暴。非天之降才尔殊也,其所以陷溺其心者然也). "

c. Importance of the Innately Good Human Nature Theory

The theory of good human nature took up a predominant position in traditional Chinese culture, and it greatly influenced the ancient concepts of traditional Chinese politics and law and became the theoretical starting point of humane government which ushered in the rule of individuals.

2. Western Scholars in the Theorization of the Assumption Concerning Human Nature

The theory of innately evil human nature is a denial of good human nature theory. The traditional Western assumption about human nature is that humans are basically evil. Those who have contributed to this theory are many. The most influential are authors of the Bible, Thomas Hobbes, Georg Wilhelm Friedrich Hegel, and some Western jurists.

a. Christian Scholars

According to Christian scholars God created Adam and Eve, the human ancestors, and allowed them to live in the Paradise, but told them never to have the fruit in the Tree of Knowledge. But driven by their greed, they ate the forbidden fruit. Then in anger God drove them out of the Garden of Eden. Because they sinned all their offspring have been born with original sin and should atone for their crime as soon as they are born. This Biblical story means humans do evil as part of their nature, hence laying the foundation for the establishment of the theory on innately evil human nature.

St. Augustine (354—430), who was born 905 years after Confucius, defended the doctrines of original sin and the fall of man in systematizing Christian thought and thus reaffirmed the necessity of God's grace for man's salvation and further formulated the Church's authority as the sole guarantor of Christian faith.

b. Hobbs' View of Evil Human Nature

In *The Leviathan* (利维坦), great British philosopher Thomas Hobbes(1588—1679) illustrates his views of human nature. Hobbes believed that humans are born to be selfish and in the face of limited wealth, human relationship would become that of one wolf and another wolf.

According to him, human beings naturally desire the power to live well and they will never be satisfied with the power they have. He also believed that all people are created to be equal, and that everyone is equally capable of killing each other because although one man may be stronger than another, the weaker may be compensated for by his intellect or some other individual aspect. Hobbes held that the nature of humanity leads people to seek power. When two or more people want the same thing, they become enemies and attempt to destroy each other, starting war. There are three basic causes for war—competition, distrust and glory. In each of these cases, men use violence to invade their enemies' territory either for their personal gain, safety or glory. Without a common power to unite the people, they would be in a war of every man against every man as long as the will to fight is known. He believed that this state of war is the natural state of human beings and that harmony among human beings is artificial because it is based on an agreement. If a group of people has something in common such as a common interest or a common goal, they would not be at war and united. One thing he noted that is consistent in all men is their interest in self-preservation. Therefore, he concluded that humans are selfish, thus bad and evil by nature.

c. Hegel's Theory of Evil Human Nature

German philosopher Georg Wilhelm Friedrich Hegel (1770—1831) came up with a theory on evil human nature, too. According to him, the theory of evil human nature is greater than that of good human nature, explicitly stating that evil nature has played an important part in the development of history.

Hegel influenced writers of widely varying positions, including both his admirers (e.g. Bauer, Marx, Bradley and Sartre) and his detractors (e.g. Schopenhauer, Nietzsche and Russell).

d. Russell's Theory of Evil Human Nature

According to Bertrand Arthur William Russell (1872—1970), the most influential philosopher of the 20th century, moral evil or sin is derived from the instincts that are transmitted to humans from human ancestry of beasts. This ancestry originates when certain animals became omnivorous and employed predation in order periodically to ingurgitate the flesh as well as the fruit and produce of other once-living things to support metabolism in competition with other animals for scarce food-animal and food-plant sources in the predatory environment. Therefore, the simple fact that humans must eat other life or else starve, die and rot is the probable primordial origin of contemporary and historical moral evil, i.e. the bad things humans do to each other by lying, cheating, slandering, thieving and slaughtering.

e. Jurists and the Rule of Law

Western jurists have established the rule of law on the theory of evil human nature, believing humans are born to be selfish and discriminatory and therefore conflict and fight against each other, and hence it is essential to set up a series of regulations and laws to solve human conflicts and disagreement in order to ensure the stability of society.

f. Sigmund Freud's Theory of Human Nature

The traditional Western view of human nature showed up in modern theories that seem to have nothing to do with religious beliefs. In his psychological theories, Austrian psychiatrist Sigmund Freud (1856—1939) include the idea that infants are controlled by primitive desires and learn to control them as the personality develops. This contrasts sharply with the Chinese view that children are pure and good and learn to do bad things as a result of contact with bad influences in the society. Typically Westerners stress the ability of people to change for the better. Now they are more likely to assume that education and other good influences will save them.

To sum up, human nature is believed to be basically good in China, and therefore education is valued to protect and keep people's virtue inherent in nature, some systems are established to reward good behavior, and virtuous rulers are expected to find the most virtuous people to help them run the state. For Westerners, human nature is basically evil, and therefore education is valued to help get rid of the evil, some watch dogs are used to find evil and fight against it, bad behavior is punished, and also people should believe God so that they can be saved from their evil nature.

IV　Human Nature Theories and the Rule of Ethics vs. Law

1. Rule of Ethics

The concept "The rule of ethics", a cultural heritage handed down by Confucianism, is built on the idealistic assumption that human nature is innately good. The theory of good human nature emphasizes the rationality and necessity of moral government, but it is short of forewarning mechanism. Moreover, the rule of rites and ethics is very likely to be turned into the rule of individuals who are apt to take law as an art.

2. Rule of Law

The Western concept of law is built on the hypothesis that human nature is basically bad. The theory of evil human nature emphasizes the possibility of evil, so it is not short of forewarning mechanism.

The American founding fathers believed that people are selfish, coveting more and more property and that leaders lust after more and more power, and they assumed such human nature is unchangeable. In the fourth US President James Madison's words, "If men were angels, no government would be necessary." Therefore, the founders fragmented American government's power, which is reflected in the three concepts they built into the structure of government—federalism, separation of powers, and checks and balances. With the three concepts, the founders expected conflict and invited the parts of government to struggle against each other in order to limit each other's ability to dominate all. Meanwhile they hoped for "balanced government". The national and state governments would represent different interests. The House would represent the common people and the large states; the Senate, the wealthy people and the small states; the President, all the people; and the Supreme Court, the Constitution. Although each part would struggle for more power, it could not accumulate enough to have absolute control over the others. Eventually, its leaders would have to compromise and adopt policies in the best interests of all the parties. In this way, the founders expected narrow conflict to produce broader harmony. To them, the legislative branch of government and media journalists should keep an eye on the President, state governors and other government officials to make sure they do not do anything evil. If some wrongdoing were discovered, the person should be punished or removed from office.

Further Reading

1. Benedict, R. (1946). *The Chrysanthemum and the Sword: Patterns of Japanese Culture*. Rutland, VT and Tokyo, Japan: Charles F. Tuttle Co.

2. Russell, B. (1945). *History of Western Philosophy*. New York: Pocket Books.

3. Twitchett, D. & Fairbank, J. K. (1978). *The Cambridge History of China*. NY: Cambridge University.

4. 张忠利、宗文举(2002):《中西文化概论》,天津:天津大学出版社。

5. 杨伯峻译注(2006):《论语》,北京:中华书局。

6. 万丽华、蓝旭(2006):《孟子》,北京:中华书局。

7. 冯友兰(2013):《中国哲学简史》,北京:北京大学出版社。

8. 梅仁毅(2002):《美国研究读本》,北京:外语教学与研究出版社。

Unit 20 Rule of Individuals vs. Rule of Law

The rule of law is better than the rule of any individual.

—Aristotle

Do you agree with Aristotle? Why or why not?

"Remember the law my servant Moses gave you. Remember the rules and laws I gave him at Mount Horeb. They were for the whole nation of Israel," says the **Lord.**

—the Bible

For further exploration: Imagine for yourself how ancient Hebrew rulers ran their state.

I An Unexpected Complaint

Interracial marriage can encounter many problems within the family. How to solve domestic disputes is one of them. Just the other day Li Juan happened to get in an English chat room and read the following complaint from a guy named David:

Since my parents-in-law have retired they come to visit us very often and stay in our house for several weeks in a row. My father-in-law became very irritable after retirement, he constantly fights with me, yells at his wife and does different things in the house and the yard that I do not want him to do. Last time he had the ugliest expression of his anger toward me because he thinks that I am not the right husband for his daughter. I feel like uninvited guest in my own home all the time when he is there. My wife does not want to interfere. Is there any legal way of preventing my father-in-law from visiting and staying in our house?

"Oh my gosh, it is David, my husband!" Li Juan got shocked, "Is he serious? Legal way he is talking about? He can't be serious! My father is not doing anything illegal! My home is his home. Sheesh!" Li Juan never tried to discuss her family problems with outsiders because she believes "even an impartial judge will find himself worthless in hearing a case of domestic disputes". For her, time and love can solve everything: Someday her father will come to terms with his retirement and her husband will get along well with his father-in-law as long as she tries harder to mediate between them. She never expected that her American husband is thinking of using a legal way to solve their family problem. Li Juan felt quite angered and humiliated.

Indeed Li Juan has read about Western rule of law, and knows the Western economic growth, political modernization, protection of human rights and other worthy objectives are all believed to hinge, at least in part, on the rule of law. She admits that Chinese people need to get more legal education, but the rule of law in China is believed to has accelerated progress towards a healthy and sustainable future since 1979, although remnants of the traditional rule of individuals are not easy to be eliminated, given that the rule of individuals has existed in traditional Chinese thought for so long. However, solving family problems in any legal way is absolutely unacceptable for many Chinese, no matter what happens.

II　Rule of Individuals in Traditional Chinese Thought

Chinese advocates of the rule of law differ on many things, but at least agree on this historical fact: In governing the state traditional China practiced "the rule of ethics and rites (以德治国，以礼治国)". Based on the principle of "promoting ethical standards without resorting to punishment (明德慎罚)" and a theory of rule by self-restraint, Confucianism advocates "the rule of rites" and "the rule of ethics", which unavoidably ushered in the rule of individuals with Chinese characteristics.

1. Confucian Advocacy of the Rule of Rites and Ethics

a. Rule of Rites

The rule of rites is largely marked by protecting the hierarchical system, in which the higher position one is in, the more virtuous and thus more powerful he should be. For instance, the patriarchal hereditary system of the Zhou time provided noblemen of all levels with rights to enjoy independent administrative, legal, and judicial privileges in their own fiefs, which emphasized the role of the ruler with extraordinary abilities as an individual as well as a role model of morality.

Among the five Confucian classics there is a special book on rites—the *Book of Rites* expected to be the controlling document on civilized behavior. In the Confucian world view, the rule of law is applied only to those who have fallen beyond the bounds of civilized behavior. Civilized people are expected to observe proper rites. Only social outcasts are expected to have their actions controlled by law. Thus the rule of law is considered a state of barbaric primitiveness, prior to achieving the civilized state of voluntary observation of proper rites. What is legal is not necessarily moral or just. In identifying the importance of the rule of rites, Confucius pointed out, "Respectfulness, without the rules of rites, becomes laborious bustle; carefulness becomes timidity; boldness becomes insubordination; straightforwardness becomes rudeness (恭而无礼则劳,慎而无礼则葸,勇而无礼则乱,直而无礼则绞)." Accordingly, a superior ruler should cultivate qualities of a virtuous man. Only then would his morality influence his ministers around him. The ministers in turn would be examples for others of the lower ranks, until all men in the state were permeated with noble, moral aptitude. The same principle of trickle-down morality would apply to every aspect of life. So Confucius further pointed out, "If a man lacks the human virtues, what has he to do with ritual? If a man lacks the human virtues, what has he to do with music(人而不仁,如礼何? 人而不仁,如乐何)?"

But how should the rites be observed? The answer is by observing rites of Five Relationships or *wu lun*. Each individual shall clearly understand his social role, and each shall voluntarily behave according to proper observance of rites that meticulously define such relationships. No reasonable man shall challenge the rites of the Five

Relationships. It is the most immutable fixation of cultural correctness in Chinese consciousness. The Five Relationships governed by Confucian rites are those of: sovereign to subject, parent to child, elder to younger brother, husband to wife and friend to friend (君臣、父子、兄弟、夫妇、朋友). These relationships formed the basic social structure of Chinese society. Each component in the relationships assumed ritual obligations and responsibility to the others while he enjoyed privileges and due consideration accorded by the other components (i.e. 忠、孝、悌、忍、善).

b. Rule of Ethics

The rule of individuals in ancient China was ethics-centered and could only be founded on ethics just as Confucius said, "The government of King Wen and King Wu is displayed in the records. Let there be the right men and the government will flourish. But, without the right men, the government will decay and cease (文武之政, 布在方策, 其人存, 则其政举; 其人亡, 则其政息)."

As time went by, the rule of rites and ethics gave impetus to the formation of the rule of individuals which was applied to traditional Chinese politics bit by bit.

2. Confucian Doctrines of Governance

a. Rule of Individuals

What Confucianism held conflicted with the Legalist school which advocated the rule of law and stressed the dominant role of laws in governing people. Their debates which focused on individuals and laws played a decisive role in governance. In debating with Legalists, Confucianists stuck to the rule of rites and ethics, putting forward such basic doctrines as follows:

First, "Governance or administration depends on individuals (为 政 在 人)." Confucius said, "If one promotes the straight and sets them on top of the crooked, they will be submissive; if one promotes the crooked and sets them on top of the straight, they will not be submissive (举直错诸枉, 则民服; 举枉错诸直, 则民不服)." He proposed using virtuous people to rule the country and enforce the law. For Confucianists, good or bad governance was decided by the ruler, particularly the top leader. They hoped that rulers could be as virtuous and wise as sage-kings Yao, Shun, King Wen,

King Wu and Duke of the Zhou, the Dao of Yao and Shun should be followed, and the system of King Wen and King Wu should be imitated (祖述尧舜, 宪章文武). In other words, they valued the politics of wise men, believing prosperity or chaos of a state was brought about by virtuous or evil rulers, just as Confucius declared, "Administration depends on individuals." If the ruler is in his position his policy might be practiced, but once out of his position, his policy might go unnoticed (人亡政息). Mencius echoed Confucius' theory on the rule of individuals by pointing out, "It's good to put only those who are humane in high positions (惟仁者宜在高位)." He said, "Kindness is not enough to govern a state, and law is not enough to restrain oneself (徒善不足以为政, 徒法不足以自行)." These sayings show that Mencius paid great attention to the virtuous quality of the ruler, and that he advocated equal importance of virtue and law in administering the state.

Second, "Only rulers can bring stability to the state, but no laws can make the state stable (有治人, 无治法)." This view was illustrated by Xun Zi, who valued law and its significance more than any other pre-Qin Confucian thinkers, since he maintained that human nature is innately bad. But when comparing "individuals" and "law" in governing the state, he regarded the individuals (rulers) to be more important, promulgating the famous doctrine, "There are only rulers who bring stability to the state, but no laws that can make the state stable." To prove this theory, Xun Zi gave three reasons: First, law is important to running a state (法者, 治之端也), but law is made by gentlemen, and therefore decided by them (君子者, 法之原也); Second, even if there is a good law, it is gentlemen who enforce it, otherwise law is nothing (得其人则存, 失其人则亡); Third, state affairs are so complicated and changeable that laws cannot cover all or flexibly adapt to changing situation, and hence it depends on the flexible handling of man (故法不能独立, 类不能自行). Inspired by his research, Xun Zi concluded, "There have been chaos even with good laws; but since ancient times there have been no chaos under the leadership of gentlemen (故有良法而乱者, 有之矣; 有君子而乱者, 自古及今未尝闻也)." Hence from the perspective of jurisprudence, Xun Zi provided interlinear explanations for "the rule of individuals" and "the rule of law".

The third is the Confucian concept "true rulership responding to people's need (政在得民)." Mencius believed that it is humanity and a sense of obligation that characterize the true ruler. According to him, the reason why the ruler exists is that he brings the ruled peace and prosperity, educates them, and leads them by exemplifying virtue; if the ruler neglects his duty, or worse, oppresses his people, he is not a true ruler, and the people have right to overthrow him. The belief that people are of the first importance while the ruler is of the least importance (君轻民贵) caused the *Mencius*, one of the Confucian Four Books, to be regarded by some rulers as a "dangerous" book.

b. Rule of Law

The Confucian doctrines of the rule of individuals were bequeathed to later dynastic rulers and became the core of orthodox ideology. The assumption that individuals of virtue are able to play a more significant role in running the state does not mean that Confucianists belittled the role of law, or negated law and the significance of "the rule of law". As a matter of fact, not only Xun Zi gave great priority to law and rites (礼法并重), Confucius and Mencius also called on people not to violate laws and rites. Confucius even came up with the doctrine of "rectification of names (正名)", an undertaking that was essential to ensure social stability and rule by law. Mencius was against "those who are high above ordinary people do not follow righteousness and Dao, and those who are low in their social position do not follow the law (上无道揆，下无法守)." They put forward the important legal principle "Do not give privileges to relatives when governing a country or enforcing the law (执法不避亲)", which indicates that they strictly abided by the principle that everybody is equal before the law. However, Confucius also mentioned concealment between father and son, although it is not concerned with law enforcement, but about giving witness. He pointed out the testimony given by relatives is not reliable. This is not contradictory to the principle that everybody is equal before the law; it is simply human nature. The Confucian legal idea is also reflected in its requirement of fair punishment. Confucius was strongly against using the law for purposes of revenge, and Mencius proposed severely punishing the tyrant. To ensure everybody was equal before the law,

Confucianism advocated that punishment should fit the crime, nobody should be above the law, and equal punishment for all guilty of the same offence (法度严谨,执法不避亲,不避贵). These are ancient Chinese expressing forms of equal legal rights and fair justice, and they have great influence on modern legal and human right concepts in China.

III   Rule of Law in Western Thought

Law is believed to be one of the pillars of Western civilization and able to ensure sound government, commercial confidence, and orderly society.

1. Solon and the Rule of Law

It is said that the concept of the rule of law originated from the reforms of Solon of ancient Greece. In 594 BC, Solon (c. 638 BC-558 BC) divided Athenian society into four classes based on wealth. The two wealthiest classes were allowed to serve on the Areopagus (the council of elders). The third class was allowed to serve on an elected council of four hundred people. This council was organized according to the four tribes making up the Athenian people; each tribe was allowed to elect one hundred representatives from this third class. This council of four hundred served as a kind of balance or check to the power of the Areopagus. The fourth class, the poorest one, was allowed to participate in an assembly; this assembly voted on affairs brought to it by the council of four hundred, and even elected local magistrates. This class also participated in a new judicial court that gradually drew civil and military cases out of the hands of the wealthiest people, the Areopagus.

Solon's new state perished soon, but invented the concept of the rule of law. Later he was considered by the Athenians the great hero of their state and his reforms were pointed to as the basis of their state.

2. Theorization of the Rule of Law

The thought of the rule of law was not theorized until Aristotle whose rule of law theory is based on negating Plato's rule of individuals and later developed by Roman jurists.

a. Plato's Rule of Supremely Virtuous Individuals

Plato, the most renowned thinker in the Western history, enjoyed the same position in the West as Confucius in ancient China and East Asia. He advocated "the politics of wise man", and belittled the role of law. Nevertheless in his later works, he began to believe that law was the second best choice, only inferior to "the politics of wise man" or "the rule of a supremely virtuous individual", moreover he was inclined to admit that law was omnipotent.

b. Aristotle and the Rule of Law

Among all the Greek thinkers, Aristotle has advanced the richest and most profound thoughts of law. For example, he deems that law restricts both the common people and the men in power. His thoughts include that the rule of law is better than the rule of individuals; the rule of law means people generally obey the law which should be well enacted; the law reflects the justice, which means a kind of equality. For Aristotle, "a central function of the law is to compensate for the imperfect and random judgment of men," since he believed that law is order and good law is good order.

c. Early Greek Vision of Law

The early Greek philosophers had a vision of law as a system of rules whose source lied outside of the ruler himself. For them, law was inherent in the natural order or arose from the timeless customs of the people, although for the Christian philosophers law came from God. Accordingly, if a king were to rule according to law, he would be constrained and his powers would be limited.

d. Ancient Roman Jurists

Jurists in ancient Rome strongly advocated the rule of law. Besides developing well-legislated law, especially the private law reflecting advanced simple commodity production relationship, they had done a good job in theorizing the rule of law. By using concepts like *natural law, reason*, and *justice*, they managed to illustrate the nature of law and stressed the authority and significance of law. For instance, Marcus Tullius Cicero (106 BC—43 BC), the famous Roman philosopher, statesman, and constitutionalist, developed Plato's idea that law as a divine order in the sky is articulated by the philosopher-king, but borrowed from Aristotle the belief that everybody has an innate knowledge of the divine law. He argued that all laws that differ from this universally known divine law are not real laws, but only the instruments of men in rebellion against the divine law. Cicero wrote, "According to the law of nature it is only fair that no one should become richer through damages and injuries suffered by another." He insisted that laws should be interpreted in a liberal sense so that their intention may be preserved and he said explicitly, "The magistrates are the ministers for the laws, the judges their interpreters, the rest of us are servants of the laws, that we all may be free." Many people accept implicitly and without questioning the truth of Cicero's aphorisms just as *When men are pure, laws are useless; when men are corrupt, laws are broken. The laws of each are convertible into the laws of any other. If there were no bad people, there would be no good lawyers. We are in bondage to the law in order that we may be free, and Liberty consists in the power of doing that which is permitted by the law.*

There also existed the concept of the rule of law in Medieval Europe. Peter Lombard (1100—1160), a scholastic theologian, held that one is not to be punished as a sinner unless there are written rules to refer to, which had been developed into the principle of "the rule under written law."

The ancient Greek and Roman theory on the rule of law has a far-reaching influence on the Western law culture.

3. Institutionalization of the Rule of Law

Out of their reflection on the Western social history, the Enlightenment thinkers held the banner of "reason, democracy and the rule of law" and worked on theoretical issues such as what is the rule of law, why there is a need for the rule of law, and how to practice the rule of law. Their efforts ushered in the institutionalization of the law theory.

a. British Jurists

In Britain jurists like John Lock (1632—1704) and A.V. Dicey (1835—1922), with great passion, put forward and proved the necessity of institutionalizing the rule of law.

John Locke is the first to talk about the division of power, especially between the legislative power of the parliament and the administrative power of the king. He did not claim the need of the separation of judicial power, but realized its importance in setting up a system of mutually limiting and balancing powers and authorities. From the outset, Locke openly declared the remarkable theme of his political theory: In order to preserve the public good, the central function of government must be the protection of private property. According to him, the actions of every human agent—even in the unreconstructed state of nature—should be bound by the self-evident laws of nature. Understood in this way, the state of nature vests each reasonable individual with an independent right and responsibility to enforce the natural law by punishing those few who irrationally choose to violate it. Because all are equal in the state of nature, the proportional punishment of criminals is a task anyone may undertake.

Dicey is believed by some to be the first one in history to explicitly elaborate on "the rule of law". He declared obliterating dictatorship, the superiority of law, equality of all classes and all people before law, etc. as the basic principles of institutionalizing the rule of law.

b. French Jurists

As the center of the Enlightenment, France produced influential figures like Jean-Jacques Rousseau and Baron de Montesquieu, who helped to institutionalize the rule of law.

In *On Spirit of Laws* and other writings, Montesquieu (1689—1755) proposed theories as follows:

1) The theory of natural origins of society. According to him, human society and its laws are not invented at will, but are formed naturally, based on human nature and natural laws. He agreed neither with the theory of social contract nor Hobbes' theory of mutual conquest.

2) Geographical and environmental theory. He held that laws and other social systems contributed to national character and the material environment.

3) Division of power. To him dividing political authority into the legislative, executive, and judicial powers means the most effective way of ensuring liberty. He argued that these three powers must be assigned to different individuals or bodies, acting independently; otherwise, they would give rise to misuse of power and corruption. The core of his political theory is to argue for the separation of political power into three parts, according to who holds power and the attitudes towards the law of those holding the power. The three political systems are: republican, monarchical and the totalitarian.

Montesquieu's most important contribution is the concept of the division of power. Both the 1789 *Declaration of Human Rights* and the later constitution of France acknowledged his theory. Its application became a weapon in the struggle against feudalism and autocracy, making a major contribution to the historical development of the Western world.

c. American Jurists

Thomas Paine (1737—1809) and Thomas Jefferson (1743—1826) totally accepted French and British theories on democracy and the rule of law and actively put them into practice in America. The American founders established the idea of a written constitution, first in the Articles of Confederation and then more prominently in the Constitution itself. They felt that a constitution should be a fundamental law above all other laws—not a mixture of customs and laws.

IV   Rule of Law in China

The rule of law has been regarded by Western scholars as a central aspect of modernity. Since the rule of law was the basis of the first unification of China in 221 BC, modernity occurred about 2,300 years ago in China.

1. Rites, Ethics, and Law in Traditional China

The rule of law does not have a precise definition, and its meaning can vary between different nations and legal cultures. Generally, however, it can be understood as a legal-political regime under which the law restrains the government by promoting certain liberties and creating order and predictability regarding how a country functions. In the most basic sense, the rule of law is a system that attempts to protect the rights of citizens from arbitrary and abusive use of government power. But why were rites and ethics regarded as more important than law in traditional Chinese culture?

a. Confucian Answer

Confucius stated, "If the people are led by law, and uniformity is sought by punishments, they will try to avoid the punishments, but have no sense of shame. If they are led by morality, and uniformity is sought by rules of ritual, they will have a sense of shame and, moreover, will become good (道之以政，齐之以刑，民免而无耻；道之以德，齐之以礼，有耻且格)." This remark can be understood as follows:

Although both will accomplish the goal of governing the people, the rule of ethics and the rule of rites are superior to the rule of law because the former creates in people an understanding of right from wrong so that people will voluntarily follow the rules and do the right things. On the other hand, the rule of ethics and rites may win over the hearts of people, while the rule of law would achieve superficial obedience by the people. The effect of ethics and rites is achieved through teaching and persuasion, and is therefore adopted by rational governments. However, the effect of law is through oppression by forces and is therefore adopted by authoritarian governments. The root of ethics and rites is the innate nature of the sages and the natural order of the world. And the root of law is the power men use to secure their political positions. All of the above mean that law does not have the legitimacy of ethics and rites.

The Confucian *Book of Rites* is expected to be the controlling document on civilized behavior, not law. In the Confucian world view, the rule of law is applied only to those who have fallen beyond the bounds of civilized behavior. Civilized people are expected to observe proper rites. Only social outcasts are expected to have their actions controlled by law. Thus the rule of law is considered a state of barbaric primitiveness, prior to achieving the civilized state of voluntary observation of proper rites. What is legal is not necessarily moral or just.

b. Semantic Answer

A powerful Confucian argument for rejecting rule by law has its root in Semantics. In Chinese vocabulary, law has always been equated with punishment. According to Confucianism, everybody must be punished according to the law if found guilty, whether the felon was from the royal family, a high-ranking government official or an ordinary person. If the emperor's father was found guilty, he could not enjoy the privilege of going unpunished. Confucius strictly practiced this legal principle when he served the State of Lu and was highly praised by the people. If law simply means punishment, naturally it is inferior to ethics and morality. No wonder ancient Chinese people viewed law with hostility: They believed that law would not only betray human ethics and morality, but also destroy the order of the world.

2. Benefits of the Rule of Law

Building a rule-of-law state is becoming an irreversible trend in all democracies throughout the modern world. What are the benefits of the rule of law?

The benefits of the rule of law depend on how the rule of law is defined. For the Christian philosophers, the rule of law is identified with the triumph of the substantive commandments of God; to Chinese people, it is valuable because it is equivalent to good government. More generally, the advantages of the rule of law are the advantages of whatever rules are to be implemented, for example, the guarantee of basic human rights such as the right to life, the freedom of thought, the right to get education, privacy and personal liberty. The narrower procedural definition of the rule of law has virtues as well. Take for instance American Constitution Article II, Section 1, which provides that before the President-elect enters on the Execution of his Office, he shall take the following Oath or Affirmation: "I do solemnly swear (or affirm) that I will faithfully execute the Office of President of the United States, and will to the best of my ability, preserve, protect and defend the Constitution of the United States." On January 21, 2009 Chief Justice John Roberts came to the White House and administered a second oath of office to President Obama at 7:35 p.m. ET in the Map Room. Regarding this unusual procedure, White House counsel Greg Craig said in a statement, "We believe that the oath of office was administered effectively and that the president was sworn in appropriately yesterday. But the oath appears in the Constitution itself. And out of an abundance of caution, because there was one word out of sequence, Chief Justice Roberts administered the oath a second time." It appears that Obama was doing what is required by the American constitution. In reality, he expects to make government actions predictable. This predictability is supposed to encourage investment and allow people to plan their lives meaningfully.

3. Future Trends of the Chinese-style Rule of Law

The Chinese-style rule of law, which is moving towards a healthy future, is of its own particular trends.

a. Inclination to the Rule of Ethics

Conceptually our society today is still inclined to the rule of ethics, and the core of the construction of spiritual civilization remains to be the construction of morality. If we go through materials on spiritual civilization, we would find many expressions of the same viewpoint. In practice we also witness the spirit of ethics permeate all aspects of our society.

b. Gradual Shift from the Rule of Individuals to the Rule of Law

The rule of law in China is co-existing with the rule of individuals, which is most obviously revealed in **Guanxi**. The existence of **Guanxi** is unavoidable, since for the moment China is gradually changing from an agrarian civilization based on the rule of ethics to the market economy based on the rule of law. To promote the rule of ethics could only mean one of two things: to bring the tradition of an agrarian civilization and the rule of individuals into an industrial civilization ruled by law, or to continue the emphasis on ethics in an industrial civilization ruled by law. The former is obviously impractical.

c. Rule of Law with Chinese Characteristics

Today's Chinese government, composed of talented and virtuous people, advocates the rule of law. Deng Xiaoping, the architect of socialism with Chinese characteristics, pointed out, "We are now building two civilizations: one materialistic and the other spiritual... We shall use the methods of law and education to handle this issue." Resolution on the issue of spiritual civilization passed at the Sixth Plenary Session of the Twelfth CPC Central Committee also stressed, "The formation, strengthening and development of socialistic morality depend on education, and also on the rule of law." Now under the leadership of the CPC Central Committee, China is marching to the future. The quintessence of this future society can be simply summarized as the socialist rule of law with Chinese characteristics. Because only under the conditions of the socialist rule of law can we transcend the traditional rule of ethics, overcome the shortcomings of the Western-style rule of law, and truly realize the harmonious society.

Further Reading

1. Raz, J. (1979). *The Authority of Law—Essays on Law and Morality.* Oxford: Clarendon Press.
2. Russell, B. (1945). *History of Western Philosophy.* New York: Pocket Books.
3. Davies, N. (1997). *Europe: A History.* New York: Harper Perennial.
4. 冯友兰(2013):《中国哲学简史》,北京:北京大学出版社。
5. 庞万里(2005):《中国古典哲学通论》,北京:北京航空航天大学出版社。
6. 冯波(2002):《中西哲学文化比较研究》,北京:中国传媒大学出版社。
7. 郭齐勇(2005):《中国古典哲学名著选读》,北京:人民出版社。
8. 祝吉芳 (2010):《中国文化经典英语导读》,南京:河海大学出版社。

Bibliography

Anderson, W. T. (1990). *Reality Isn't What it Used to Be.* San Francisco: Harper & Row.

Benediot, R. (1974). *The Chrysanthemum and the Sword: Patterns of Japanese Culture.* Rutland, VT and Tokyo, Japan: Charles E. Tuttle Co.

Bhabha, H. K. (1994). *The Location of Culture.* London, New York: Routledge.

Biersack, A. & Hunt, L. A. (1989). *The New Cultural History: Essays.* Berkeley, CA: University of California Press.

Blackman, C. (1997). *Negotiating China: Case Studies and Strategies.* Sydney: Allen and Unwin.

Clyne, M. (1994). *Intercultural Communication at Work: Cultural Values in Discourses.* Cambridge, UK: Cambridge University Press.

Edwards, J. (1994). *Multilingualism.* London: Routledge.

Gudykunst, W. & Young Yun Kim (1997). *Communicating with Strangers: an Approach to Intercultural Communication.* New York: McGraw-Hill.

Wierzbicka, A. (1999). *Emotions Across Languages and Cultures: Diversity and Universals.* Cambridge, UK: Cambridge University Press.

Young, D. E. & Goulet, J.G. (1994). *Being Changed by Cross-Cultural Encounters.* New York: Broadview Press.

Bond, M. H. (1996). *Handbook of Chinese Psychology.* Hongkong: Oxford University Press.

Brick, J. (2004). *China: A Handbook in Intercultural Communication.* Sydney: NCELTR Publications.

Brislin, R. W. (1990). *Applied Cross-Cultural Psychology.* Newbury Park, CA: Sage Publications.

Bull, P. (1983). *Body Movement and Interpersonal Communication.* New York: Wiley.

Carr, D. & Zhang, C. (2004). *Space, Time, Culture.* Dordrecht; Boston: Kluwer Academic Publishers.

Clinton, H. (Saturday, June 7th 2008). "Hillary Clinton's exit speech".

Davies, N. (1997). *Europe: A History.* New York: Harper Perennial.

Davis, L. (2001). *Doing Culture.* 北京：外语教学与研究出版社.

Duiker, W. J. (1978). *Cultures in Collision: The Boxer Rebellion.* San Rafael, CA: Presidio Press.

Frank, M. O. (1990). *How to Get Your Point Across in 30 Seconds or Less.* New York: Simon & Schuster.

Friedman, T. L. (2005). *The World Is Flat: A Brief History of the Twenty-First Century.* New York: Farrar, Straus and Giroux.

Goatly, A. (1997). *The Language of Metaphors.* London: Rutledge.

Hall, D. L. & Ames, R. T. (1995). *Anticipating China: Thinking Through the Narratives of Chinese and Western Culture.* Albany, NY: State University of New York Press.

Hall, E. T. (1959). *The Silent Language.* New York: Doubleday & Company.

Hall, E. T. (1966). *The Hidden Dimension.* New York: Doubleday& Company.

Hall, E. T. (1976). *Beyond Culture.* New York: Doubleday & Company.

Hall, E. T. (1983). *The Dance of Life: The Other Dimension of Time.* New York: Doubleday.

Hall, E. T. (1990). *Understanding Cultural Differences.* Yarmouth, ME: Intercultural Press.

Hall, E. T. and M. R. Hall (1987). *Hidden Differences: Doing Business with the Japanese.* Garden City, NY: Anchor Press/Doubleday.

Harvard Business school (2004). *Face-to-face Communications for Clarity and Impact.* Boston, MA: Harvard Business school Press.

Hegel, G.W. F. (1991). *Philosophy of Right.* Cambridge: Cambridge University Press.

Hofstede, G. (1980). *Culture's Consequences, International Differences in Work-related Values.* Beverly Hills, CA: Sage Publications.

Hofstede, G. (1998). *Masculinity and Femininity: The Taboo Dimension of National Cultures.* Thousand Oaks, CA: Sage Publications.

Hofstede, G. (2001). *Culture's Consequences, Comparing Values, Behaviors, Institutions, and Organizations Across Nations.* Thousand Oaks, CA: Sage Publications.

Hofstede, G. (2004). *Cultures and Organizations: Software of the Mind.* New York: McGraw-Hill.

Holland, D. & Quinn, N. (1987). *Cultural Models in Language and Thought.* London: Cambridge University.

Kluckholn, F. & Strodtbeck, F. (1961). *Variations in Value Orientations.* Evanston, OH: Row &Peterson.

Lakoff, G. & Johnson, M. (1980). *Metaphors We Live By.* Chicago, IL: University of Chicago Press.

Lerner, G. (1997). *Why History Matters: Life and Thought.* New York & Oxford, UK: Oxford University Press.

Levathes, L. E. (1994). *When China Ruled the Sea: The Treasure Fleet of the Dragon Throne.* New York: Simon & Schuster.

Medearis, M. & Medearis, A. S. (1983). *Daisy and the Doll.* Middlebury, VT: Vermont Folklife Center Book.

Menzis, G. (2002). *1421: The Year China Discovered America.* US: HarperCollins.

Myers, Isabel B. & Myers P. B. (1980). *Gifts Differing: Understanding Personality Type.* Palo Alto, CA: Consulting Psychologists Press.

Nisbett, R. E. (2003). *The Geography of Thought: How Asians and Westerners Think Differently and Why.* New York: The Free Press.

Pattberg, T. (2009). *The East-West Dichotomy.* New York: LoD Press.

Pearl, J. (1966). *Experiments in Induction.* San Francisco, CA: Morgan Kaufmann Publishers.

Russell, B. (1945). *History of Western Philosophy.* New York: Simon and Schuster.

Samovar, L. & Porter R. (1997). *Intercultural Communication: A Reader.* Belmont, CA: Wadsworth Publishing Company.

Schumacher, E. F. (1973). *Small Is Beautiful: Economics As If People Mattered.* London: Blond & Briggs.

Schwartz, S. H. (1994). *Beyond Individualism/Collectivism: New Dimensions of Values.* Newbury Park, CA: Sage.

Smithsonian. Smithsonian Institution, Washington, DC.

Stewart, Edward C. & Milton J. Bennett (1991). *American Cultural Patterns: A Cross-Cultural Perspective.* Yarmouth, ME: Intercultural Press.

Tannen, D. (1998). *The Argument Culture: Moving from Dialogue to Debate.* New York: Harper, Collins.

Thomson, L. (1998). *Personality Type.* Boston, MA: Shambhala.

Toffler, A. (1980). *The Third Wave.* New York: William Morrow and Company.

Trompenaars, F. and C. Hampden-Turner (1997). *Riding the Waves of Culture: Understanding Cultural Diversity in Business.* London: Nicholas Brealey Publishing.

Wechsler, H. J. (1974). *Mirror to the Son of Heaven: Wei Zheng at the Court of Tang T'ai-tsung.* New Haven and London: Yale University Press.

Wu, J. (1990). *Encountering the Chinese.* Yarmouth, ME: Intercultural Press.

Zhang, L. (2007). *Unexpected Affinities: Reading Across Cultures.* Toronto: University of Toronto Press.

Zhang, Y. (1998). *China in a Polycentric World: Essays in Chinese Comparative Literature.* Standford, CA: Stanford University Press.

包惠南等(2004):《中国文化与汉英翻译》,北京:外文出版社。

陈鼓应(2001):《庄子译注》,北京:中华书局。

陈立夫(2008):《陈立夫解读〈大学〉》,北京:中国友谊出版公司。

董德福(2003):《梁启超与胡适》,长春:吉林人民出版社。

冯　波(2002):《中西哲学文化比较研究》,北京:中国传媒大学出版社。

冯友兰(2013):《中国哲学简史》,北京:北京大学出版社。

顾雪梁(2006):《中西文化比较》,北京:国防工业出版社。

郭齐勇(2005):《中国古典哲学名著选读》,北京:人民出版社。

胡文仲(2000):《跨文化交际面面观》,北京:外语教学与研究出版社。

胡文仲(2000):《跨文化交际学概论》,北京:外语教学与研究出版社。

季羡林(2007):《季羡林谈翻译》,北京:当代中国出版社。

梁启超(1999):《梁启超全集》,北京:北京出版社。

梁漱溟(1987):《中国文化要义》,北京:学林出版社。

梁漱溟(1999):《东西文化及其哲学》,北京:商务印书馆。

林语堂（1998）:《生活的艺术》,北京:外语教学与研究出版社。

林语堂（2000）:《吾国吾民》,北京:外语教学与研究出版社。

刘彦生（2007）:《西方创新思维方式论》,天津:天津大学出版社。

刘　毅（2001）:《英文谚语辞典》,北京:中国青年出版社。

罗素著,马元德译（1976）:《西方哲学史》,北京:商务印书馆。

马玉珂（1985）:《西方逻辑史》,北京:中国人民大学出版社。

梅仁毅（2002）:《美国研究读本》,北京:外语教学与研究出版社。

牟宗三（1983）:《中国文化的省察》,台北:台湾联合报社。

庞万里（2005）:《中国古典哲学通论》,北京:北京航空航天大学出版社。

饶尚宽（2006）:《老子译注》,北京:中华书局。

商务印书馆辞书研究中心编（2005）:《新华谚语辞典》,北京:商务印书馆。

宋开之（1999）:《中外文化概论》,南京:河海大学出版社。

万丽华、蓝旭（2006）:《孟子译注》,北京:中华书局。

萧立明（2002）:《英汉比较研究与翻译》,上海:上海外语教育出版社。

徐行言（2004）:《中西文化比较》,北京:北京大学出版社。

许力生（2004）:《跨文化交流跨文化交际英语教程》,上海:上海外语教育出版社。

许渊冲译(2003):《中国古诗精品三百首》,北京:北京大学出版社。

杨伯峻（2006）:《论语译注》,北京:中华书局。

易中天（2006）:《闲话中国人》,上海:上海文艺出版社。

张隆溪（2014）:《阐释学与跨文化研究》,上海:复旦大学出版社。

张培基（2006）:《英译中国现代散文选》,上海:上海外语教育出版社。

张忠利、宗文举（2002）:《中西文化概论》,天津:天津大学出版社。

赵焕祯注(2007):《曾国藩家书》,武汉:湖北辞书出版社。

周　宁（2010）:《世界的中国形象》,北京:人民出版社。

周　宁（2011）:《跨文化研究:以中国形象为方法》,北京:商务印书馆。

祝吉芳（2009）:《翻译方法与试笔》,北京:北京大学出版社。

祝吉芳译(2008):《刚性排名》,北京:商务印书馆。

祝吉芳译(2008):《教出领导者》,北京:商务印书馆。

祝吉芳译(2005):《面谈:清晰互动的交流》,北京:商务印书馆。

周云之编（2004）:《中国逻辑史》,太原:山西教育出版社。